Political Brokers in Chile

POLITICAL BROKERS IN CHILE: Local Government in a Centralized Polity

Arturo Valenzuela

Duke University Press   Durham, N.C.   1977

To

Raimundo Valenzuela

Dorothy Bowie Valenzuela

Contents

Preface

Chile, the long narrow country which stood at the periphery of the Spanish colonial empire, has always fascinated observers because it did not conform to the general pattern of Latin American politics. As far back as 1815, Simón Bolivar, disillusioned by the failure of representative institutions in the southern hemisphere of the new world, remarked that "if any American republic is to have a long life, I am inclined to believe it will be Chile. . . . Chile will not alter her laws, ways, and practices. She will preserve her uniform political and religious views. In a word, it is possible for Chile to be free."[1] Only a few years after independence, Chilean elites were able to structure viable representative institutions. Though restricting participation to the few, these institutions managed to provide the country with strong civilian leadership in a continent where rule by armed forces was the norm. By the turn of the century a dominant legislature encouraged the development of strong party networks that would serve to channel and control increasing participation in the nation's political affairs. The brief Socialist Republic of 1932 and the Popular Front of 1938 were early precursors of the more basic reforms which were attempted by the governments of Eduardo Frei and Salvador Allende in the 1960s and 1970s.

But Allende's Popular Unity government failed in its attempt to bring about fundamental change within the framework of traditional Chilean institutions. The reaction to his experiment ushered in military rule and marked the most severe political breakdown in the nation's history. It is too early to tell whether Chile's institutional system will emerge once again, as it did after the difficult period of the Great Depression. Whether it does or not, the Allende years, as well as the unique Chilean system will be the subject of scholarly interest for years to come.[2]

This study, based on field research conducted in Chile in 1969, focuses on a neglected aspect of Chilean politics — local politics. A good deal is known about national politics, but no significant work has attempted to describe local government and the place local politics held in the overall political system. Thus we know little of the extent

1. Vicente Lacuna and Harold Bierck, Jr. (eds.), *Selected Writings of Simon Bolivar*, Vol. 1 (New York: Colonial Press, Inc.), p. 117.
2. For a review essay of 31 studies of the Allende government see, Arturo Valenzuela and J. Samuel Valenzuela, "Visions of Chile," *Latin American Research Review*, 10, No. 3, pp. 155–75.

to which Chile's strong national parties penetrated peripheral areas and structured the issues and conflicts of local communities. And we know little about the role of local government, the government closest to the people, in responding to the needs of the community in a rapidly changing society.

Because of the lack of any previous analytical study on the local dimension of Chilean politics, and the uncertainties involved in following predetermined research strategies, from the very outset this study proceeded in an inductive fashion. The goal was to provide a careful and thorough description of the subject matter. In accomplishing that task an effort was made to analyze as systematically as possible a few preliminary but basic questions and then use the tentative answers as clues for structuring the next questions. This methodology explains the basic structure of the book.[3]

Part I attempts to answer general questions on the role of political parties and the jurisdiction of local government using data for all of the country's municipalities. The first chapter concludes that local politics were highly competitive and that parties had indeed penetrated the local arena. However, the second chapter points to the scarcity of municipal resources and the limitations of municipal jurisdictions. Chapter three attempts to answer, in part, the puzzle provided by the first two. Why was it that local politics were so competitive, when resources and stakes appeared to be so limited?

The findings of Part I, while useful in falsifying some hypotheses and providing a broad overview of local politics, left too many questions unanswered. Part II is consequently based on a more in-depth study of local government based on field research in a sample of 14 communities in southern Chile. The first two chapters of this section argue that the scarcity of financial resources did not prevent local officials from leading an extremely busy existence. And yet their actions had little to do with the formal operation of the municipal government per se. Local officials engaged in the important tasks of processing particularistic demands for followers and, even more significantly as far as the community as a whole was concerned, extracting resources from the center. The mayor was a key official in this political process, and competition to achieve the mayoralty was a vital feature of local politics. Since resources were obtained from

3. Thus the historical section was deliberately placed at the end. It was designed to describe the evolution of a system which was discovered through an inductive study at one point in time. Though dealing with only one case, the author has sought to follow a "disciplined configurative approach" in Sidney Verba's terms. See his "Some Dilemmas in Comparative Research," *World Politics*, XX, No. 1 (October, 1967), pp. 111–127.

the center through individualistic transactions, there was little incentive for collective action at the local level.

The vital importance of ties to the center in obtaining resources for local progress led to a detailed examination of the brokerage networks structured to channel those resources. While the mayor or municipal councilor was the key broker at the local level, the congressmen played the dominant brokerage role in the capital city, intervening before the bureaucracy to help their local "clients." The network defining these center-local linkages was the political party, and ultimately votes and political support were the *leit motif* of the system.

The existence of the brokerage networks from the locality to the center and the predominance of individual transactions did not mean that the Chilean party system was diffuse or unideological. Chapter seven summarizes the major findings of the study noting the place of the system described within the general political system. This theoretical chapter also suggests the place of the work within the general literature on patron-client politics, evaluates the utility of cultural explanations for the phenomenon described, and provides a framework for understanding the difference between brokerage politics of the Chilean variety and other similar types of political patterns. It concludes that factionalism and competitiveness at the local level were not the product of peculiar cultural norms, but the logical result of the structural characteristics of the system. Field research conducted in Chile in the summer of 1972 was very valuable in completing this chapter and updating the work.

Part III of the study is an historical analysis of center-local relations over time. The goal of the chapter is to explain the origins of the most important feature of the system described earlier in the book: the networks of brokerage relations which continued to make local government viable in Chile in the 1960s. In the process it provides a broad interpretation of the evolution of democratic politics in Chile and the role which legislators and local councils played in the maintenance of a representative regime.

However, the book could not end there. One of the first acts of the military junta which overthrew Salvador Allende was the dissolution of the municipal councils. This move was followed shortly by the closing of the Congress and the suspension of all political parties. The Postscript, based on field research in Chile during a seven month period in 1974 in which the author returned to eight of the municipalities studied earlier, describes the impact which these decisions have had on the country's lowest governmental units. It suggests that the removal of local councils and the Congress not only undermined democracy, but severely undermined the ability of local communities to obtain the necessary services for basic survival.[4]

In preparing this study I have benefited greatly from the assistance of several individuals. Douglas Chalmers extended encouragement and help far beyond his formal duties. I am very indebted to him for his intellectual guidance both as an excellent teacher and a conscientous dissertation supervisor. I am also grateful to Mark Kesselman, whose fascinating book on local government in France provided me with the initial impetus to explore local politics in another, not too dissimilar society. Juan Linz probably does not realize what a profound impact he had on a whole generation of Columbia students who eagerly sat through his fascinating lectures savoring every moment of his often lengthy tangents. His concern for history, his skepticism of passing social science fads, and his profound knowledge of politics and society could not help but rub off, even if superficially, on most of us. I am appreciative of the fact that years later he took time out of his busy schedule to read this book and give me his insightful suggestions. The rewriting of the manuscript also benefited from the generous and helpful comments of Robert Kaufman and the continued intellectual stimulation I have received from my good friend Alexander Wilde.

Interviews with local officials in small towns in rural Chile would not have been as meaningful and as enjoyable without the assistance of Julio Samuel Valenzuela. His thorough knowledge of the country and his deep sensitivity to its people and problems were invaluable assets in the early stages of field research. Appropriately the often tiring traveling through rural Chile was interrupted in March of 1969 so that we could both attend his wedding to the daughter of a municipal councilor from a small rural town in the southern province of Bío-Bío. Later I was again the lucky recipient of his trenchant comments and suggestions on an earlier draft of this book. My father, Raimundo Valenzuela, shared with me his profound understanding of Chilean history, helping me to clarify many aspects of the study.

Many colleagues in Chile, especially, Jorge Tapia, Jose Daie, Francisco Zalazar and Miguel Maldonado at the Institute of Administratión (INSORA) of the University of Chile, provided me with guidelines and advice that were helpful in the early stages of research. I want to thank the Instituto for providing me with excellent office

4. It must be stressed that this study will not analyze the breakdown of the Chilean regime in 1973. The subject has been treated elsewhere. See Arturo Valenzuela, *The Breakdown of Democracy in Chile* (Baltimore: The Johns Hopkins University Press, 1977). This study forms part of a larger series on the "Crisis and Breakdowns of Democratic Regimes" under the general editorship of Juan Linz and Alfred Stepan. For a condensed version see Arturo Valenzuela, "Il Crollo di la Democracia en Chile," *Revista Italiana di Scienza Politica*, v. 5, No. 1 (April 1975), 83–129.

facilities and access to their library and computer facilities during my research year in 1969. Rafael López and Steven Sinding, both in Chile at the time, cheerfully listened to the latest finding and problem. I also want to thank the Instituto de Ciencias Políticas of the Catholic University for their hospitality during my stay in Chile in 1974.

Subsequently, three colleagues, Taylor Cole, Federico Gil, and Allan Kornberg provided much needed encouragement during the long process of converting a manuscript into a book.

My greatest debt is to my wife, Marilyn Stoner Valenzuela, without whose help in coding names and numbers and tabulating data much of this project would never have been completed. Only she knows how difficult and time consuming it was to come up with the simplest and most basic facts.

Finally, I wish to acknowledge the financial support from several sources which made my graduate education and this book possible. The Department of Political Science at Columbia University provided me with a three year fellowship for course work and independent study leading to the doctoral examinations. A Fulbright-Hays Graduate Fellowship and a Columbia University Traveling Fellowship enabled me to conduct the field research in Chile. The Danforth Foundation, through its Danforth Graduate Fellowship supplemented with research money and provided funds for writing in residence at Columbia after the research year. Subsequently, grants from the Duke Research Council and from the American Philosophical Society have enabled me to compile a data bank on Chilean politics which has been helpful in some of the revisions of the first draft.

I cannot conclude without drawing attention to the fact that many local elected officials in Chile died and suffered imprisonment and pain in the aftermath of the brutal military coup which deprived the country of representative institutions going back to colonial times. Without the cooperation of hardworking, generous, and idealistic local leaders this study would not have been possible. With them, I look forward to a better day.

Durham, N.C.
December, 1975

Part I

1. Local Government and Chile's Competitive Party System

On September 19, 1973, eight days after it deposed President Salvador Allende's government, proclaiming the objective of "restoring broken institutions" to preserve "national tradition," Chile's Junta Militar dismissed all of the country's elected municipal councils. Within the next ten days the military government had closed Latin America's strongest legislative body and disbanded or severely curtailed all political party organizations. By force of arms the self proclaimed saviors of the nation abolished representative institutions fashioned by several generations of Chileans.[1]

These dramatic events in Chile marked the breakdown of one of the most stable and democratic regimes in the world. In Russell Fitzgibbon's periodic surveys of the state of democracy in Latin America, Chile was consistently placed among the two or three "most democratic" polities.[2] A study of seventy-seven different countries placed Chile among the top five in democratic political development.[3] Indeed, from 1830 to 1973 most of the country's presidents were constitutionally elected and served their terms of office without being forced to resign. The only exceptions to this pattern occurred in 1891, when President Balmaceda resigned a few days before the end of his term after his forces were defeated in a bloody civil war, and in the turbulent period between 1924 and 1932 when military officers intervened directly in the formation of governments.[4]

1. See the Acta de Constitución de la Junta de Gobierno and Decree Laws no. 25, 27, 77, and 78 published in *100 Primeros Decretos leyes Dictados por la Junta de Gobierno de la República de Chile* (Santiago: Editorial Jurídica de Chile, 1973). Portions of this chapter were published as "The Scope of the Chilean Party System," *Comparative Politics*, 4, no. 2 (January, 1972), 179–99.

2. For the latest version, see Russell Fitzgibbon, "Measuring Democratic Change in Latin America," *Journal of Politics*, 29 (February, 1967), 129–66.

3. See Phillips Cutright, "National Political Development: Measurement and Analysis," *American Sociological Review*, 28 (April, 1963), 258. Other rankings include: Martin Needler, *Political Development in Latin America* (New York: Random House, 1968), p. 87; Peter Ranis, "Modernity and Political Development in Latin America," *Studies in Comparative International Development*, 4, no. 2 (1968–69), 37; Peter G. Snow, "A Scalogram Analysis of Political Development," *The American Behavioral Scientist*, 9 (March, 1966), 35.

4. For general treatments in English of Chilean politics, see Fredrick Pike, *Chile and the United States* (South Bend: Notre Dame University Press, 1963), and Federico Gil, *The Political System of Chile* (Boston: Houghton Mifflin Co., 1966). For a discussion of these two crises in light of center-local linkages, see Chapter viii of this book. It must be stressed that Chile's political democracy has not been accompanied by social democracy. Sharp social inequities and a stagnating economy are also important fea-

Studies of Chilean politics proliferated in the last few years as scholars attempted to analyze the intriguing features of this Latin American deviant case. Most attention was focused on Chile's highly developed party system.[5] This is not surprising, for as K. H. Silvert noted, Chile stood "alone in Latin America with respect to the number of political parties ... their national scope, their high degree of impersonalism, and the way which they fit into three major ideological groups."[6] Thanks to several studies we know a great deal about the ideology, history, organization and national leadership of Chilean parties.[7] Other works have focused on the electoral dimension of political parties or on the role of parties in the Congress or the labor movement.[8] However, there is one aspect of the party system, mentioned by Silvert, which has not been examined systematically: the scope of the Chilean party system. Did the Chilean party system extend nationwide? The difficulty in answering that question is that, despite the large number of recent studies focusing on Chilean institutions, one important area of Chilean politics has been completely neglected. That area is Chilean local government, the first institution to be proscribed by the military government.[9] The absence of systematic examinations of local politics means that we know little of the

tures. On this theme see Fredrick Pike, "Aspects of Class Relations in Chile," *The Hispanic American Historical Review*, 43 (February, 1963), 14–33; Osvaldo Sunkel, "Change and Frustration in Chile," in *Obstacles to Change in Latin America*, ed. by Claudio Veliz (New York: Oxford University Press, 1965), pp. 116–44; José Cademártori, *La economía chilena* (Santiago: Editorial Universitaria, 1968).

5. See Peter Ranis, "Trends in Research on Latin American Politics: 1961–67," *Latin American Research Review*, 3 (Summer, 1968), 77.

6. K[alman] H. Silvert, *Chile: Yesterday and Today* (New York: Holt, Rinehart and Winston, 1965), p. 99.

7. General studies of Chilean parties include the following: Alberto Edwards and Eduardo Frei, *Historia de los partidos políticos chilenos* (Santiago: Editorial del Pacífico, 1949); Sergio Guilisati, *Partidos políticos chilenos* (Santiago: Editorial Nascimento, 1964); Germán Urzúa, *Los partidos políticos chilenos* (Santiago: Editorial Jurídica, 1968); James Petras, *Politics and Social Forces in Chilean Development* (Berkeley and Los Angeles: University of California Press, 1969), chs. 3–6; Gil, *Political System of Chile*, chs. 2, 6.

8. See footnote 10 for electoral studies. A useful work on the Congress is Weston Agor, *The Chilean Senate* (Austin, Texas: The University of Texas Press, 1972). James Protho and Patricio Chaparro's "Public Opinion and The Movement of the Chilean Government to the Left 1952–1970" is a very perceptive analysis of the "parties in the electorate." Julio Samuel Valenzuela deals with the parties in the labor movement in "The Chilean Labor Movement: The Institutionalization of Conflict." Both articles are from Arturo Valenzuela and J. Samuel Valenzuela, *Chile: Politics and Society* (New Brunswick: Transaction, Inc., 1976).

9. Only a small monograph has appeared in English on the subject. See Peter Cleaves, *Developmental Processes in Chilean Local Government*, Politics of Modernization Series, no. 8 (Berkeley: Institute of International Studies, University of California, 1969). Chilean works are listed in n. 1, p. 19.

extent to which institutions such as political parties were able to penetrate into the local level.

This chapter will provide a preliminary picture of local politics in Chile by examining the degree of penetration of the competitive party system into Chilean society. This task will be accomplished by focusing on a key party system variable, party competition, and answering two basic questions. First, was the intense party competition over national issues and candidates transposed vertically into the arena of local politics? Secondly, did this high level of electoral competition extend horizontally across the nation, reaching small, backward communities as well as their large socioeconomically developed counterparts? Both of these dimensions of the scope of the competitive party system can be systematically examined by turning to the wealth of electoral and socioeconomic statistics available in Chile.[10]

Hans Daalder has noted that the study of the "center-local axis" can contribute to an understanding of the "permeation of the party system."[11] Chilean municipalities provided the only stage for electoral politics below the national stage of congressional and presidential races, and yet we know very little about the nature of local politics and the competitiveness of local elections.[12] Were the cleavages in a

10. Philippe Schmitter has argued for the greater utilization of aggregate data in the study of Latin American politics. While Schmitter is primarily concerned with the utility of testing propositions in a cross-national perspective with aggregate statistics, he also notes their importance in "specifying structural and sub-systemic relationships within the political system: party types and degree of competitiveness, interest group strategies and strengths, civic-military relations, electoral arrangements, etc." See his "New Strategies for the Comparative Analysis of Latin American Politics," *Latin American Research Review*, 4 (Summer, 1969), 91. Aggregate statistics have not been employed much in the analysis of Chilean politics. The few exceptions include: Glaucio Soares and Robert L. Hamblin, "Socio-economic Variables and Voting for the Radical Left: Chile, 1952," *American Political Science Review*, 61 (December, 1967), 1053–65; James Petras and Maurice Zeitlin, "Miners and Agrarian Radicalism," *American Sociological Review*, 32 (August, 1967), 578–86; Rafael López, *Algunos aspectos de la participación política en Chile* (Santiago: INSORA, 1969); Ronald H. McDonald, "Apportionment and Party Politics in Santiago, Chile," *Midwest Journal of Political Science*, 13 (August, 1969), 455–70; Sandra Powell, "Social Structure and Electoral Choice in Chile, 1952–1964" (Ph.D. dissertation, Northwestern University, 1966); Robert Ayres, "Unidad Popular and The Chilean Electoral Process," in Arturo Valenzuela and J. Samuel Valenzuela, *Chile: Politics and Society*. An earlier study in the French tradition of "political geography" is Ricardo Cruz-Coke, *Geografía electoral de Chile* (Santiago: Editorial del Pacífico, 1952).

11. See Hans Daalder, "Parties, Elites and Political Development in Western Europe," in *Political Parties and Political Development*, ed. Joseph LaPalombara and Myron Weiner (Princeton: Princeton University Press, 1966), p. 64.

12. Municipalities in Chile were formed by *regidores* or councilors elected under a proportional representation system for four-year terms. The regidores in turn elected the *alcalde* or mayor from their midst. (In the municipalities of Santiago, Valparaiso and Viña del Mar, the alcalde was appointed by the president of the republic.) Provin-

given community's local voting behavior as salient as in the same community's national voting behavior? Or did the local arena exhibit a substantially different style of politics, with little resemblance to the sharp contrast over issues and candidates which characterized the national arena?

One can hypothesize that the latter alternative is more likely. Scholars specializing in Latin American studies have emphasized the importance of personalism and strong leadership (*caudillos* and *caciques*) particularly in community-level politics.[13] If the local political system in Chile was still dominated by a political boss, then the competitive party system had not become a significant feature in local politics. Divisions in elections for municipal councilors would have been less pronounced than divisions in elections revolving around national issues and candidates.

This hypothesis will be tested by examining electoral competition in municipal elections in contrast to competition in congressional elections. Comparable competition rates in both contests would provide evidence to reject the hypothesis and conclude that the competitive Chilean party system has extended into the arena of local politics.[14] In order to provide a comparative referent, the Chilean results will be compared to results from a similar study of French politics.

This chapter will then turn to the second basic question and expand the analysis by seeking to determine whether the competitive party system had extended beyond the major urban centers of the country into peripheral areas. Was sharp electoral cleavage also a feature of Chile's backward and rural localities? Or was party competition

---

cial assemblies, prescribed in the Constitution of 1925, were never created. For a more complete discussion of the formal structure of Chilean local government, see Appendix I. For the statutory basis of municipal government, see the classic though dated work by Mario Bernaschina, *Derecho municipal chileno* (3 vols., Santiago: Editorial Jurídica, 1952–54); see also Lionel Bastías, *Responsabilidad en el régimen municipal* (Santiago: Editorial Jurídica, 1966). On the financial bases of municipalities, the best work is DESAL, *Antecedentes y criterios para una reforma del gobierno municipal*, 2 (Santiago: DESAL, 1967).

13. For example, see Frank Tannenbaum, *Ten Keys to Latin America* (New York: Random House, 1966), pp. 158–59.

14. It should be emphasized that this analysis does not deal with the extension of particular parties into the local arena, but with the extension of the competitive party system. It is conceivable that parties competing in local elections are different from those competing in national elections. However, in the analysis that follows, which makes use of two contemporary elections, the same parties presenting candidates for national office presented candidates for local office. As the discussion in chapter 6 will show, this does not necessarily mean that the local-level branches of parties deal with the same issues and perform the same political functions. The latter part of this chapter will focus on individual parties as opposed to the party system.

contingent upon the level of socioeconomic development of a particular community?

An influential body of literature in the social sciences suggests the hypothesis that underdeveloped communities divide less politically than developed communities.[15] This literature maintains that economic growth affects the social structure of society, contributing to greater social mobility and increasing differentiation in a country's (or region's) organizational life. In turn these developments may affect the pattern of cleavages in the political sphere and contribute to greater political heterogeneity, increasing participation and heightened political competition. Electoral divisions increase as the party system responds to demands exerted by a multiplicity of emerging interests.

The chapter will test this second hypothesis by examining the relationship between party competition as the dependent variable and selected socioeconomic indicators as independent variables. Party competition indices for both municipal and congressional elections will be used in order to explore whether the findings from the first part of the analysis are affected by controlling for the environmental characteristics of communities. Low or nonexistent correlations between party competition and socioeconomic variables would provide evidence to reject the hypothesis and conclude that the competitive Chilean party system had extended horizontally across the country.

Competitive Party Politics and Municipal Contests

Discussion of the permeation of the party system into local contests and peripheral areas is appropriate in the Chilean case, since, in Duverger's terms, Chilean parties were "internally created."[16] The first modern parties emerged from the legislative arena during the Parliamentary Republic (1891–1924), inaugurated after the collapse

15. See especially S. N. Eisenstadt, "Social Change, Differentiation and Evolution," *American Sociological Review*, 29 (June, 1964), 375–87, and Talcott Parsons, "Evolutionary Universals in Society," *American Sociological Review*, 29 (June, 1964), 339–57. Political consequences of social differentiation resulting from economic development are discussed by Karl Deutsch, "Social Mobilization and Political Development," *American Political Science Review*, 55 (September, 1961), 493–515; and Daniel Lerner, *The Passing of Traditional Society* (New York: Free Press, 1958). See also James R. Elliot, "A Comment on Inter-Party Competition, Economic Variables, and Welfare Policies in the American States," *Journal of Politics*, 27 (February, 1965), 185–91. For works directly relating socioeconomic development to party competition, see n. 32.

16. Maurice Duverger, *Political Parties* (New York: John Wiley & Sons, Inc., 1965), pp. xxiv–xxx.

of presidential authority. In this key period control over the electoral process passed from the hands of the executive and his officials into the hands of local notables. Parties crystallized when legislative cliques instituted alliances with local leaders in different regions of the country in order to maximize their own electoral fortunes. In return for votes delivered, local notables sought a share in the wealth generated by the booming nitrate industry by pressing their congressional cronies for local public-works projects and other favors.[17] Contemporary Chilean parties either date from the parliamentary period, or were splinters of parties dating from that epoch.[18] With only a few minor exceptions, regional or sectional parties have not developed in Chile.[19]

Before the breakdown in 1973, Chile's party system was composed of five major parties and several minor parties spanning the ideological spectrum. On the Right was the National party, formed in 1966 by a fusion of the traditional Conservatives and Liberals. These parties saw their electoral strength greatly diminished in the 1965 congressional election in favor of the Christian Democrats, whose presidential candidate they supported in 1964. In 1969, however, the united Right made a strong comeback, winning the second largest plurality and raising National hopes for a strong presidential bid under the leadership of aging former president Jorge Alessandri in 1970. Alessandri, however, surprised most observers by placing second in a very tight race won by Allende with a plurality of thirty-six percent of the vote.[20]

In the center was the Christian Democratic party and the traditional

17. For discussions of this period, see Manuel Rivas Vicuña, *Historia política y parlamentaria de Chile* (3 vols., Santiago: Editorial Nascimento, 1964), and Paul S. Reinsch, "Parliamentary Government in Chile," *American Political Science Review*, 3 (November, 1909), 507–38. See also chapter 8 below.

18. The Socialist party was an exception, having been formed in 1933 from the fusion of several Socialist groups which emerged in the period of the ill-fated Socialist Republic of June, 1932. All of these groups were centered in the capital city of Santiago. See Lía Cortés and Jordi Fuentes, *Diccionario político de Chile* (Santiago: Editorial Orbe, 1968), p. 469. This work is the only comprehensive reference including descriptions of most Chilean parties and factions.

19. The major example of a regional party in Chile is the Partido Agrario. Founded in Temuco in 1931, it represented southern agricultural interests and succeeded in electing several deputies and a senator before it joined several neo-Nazi groups in 1945 to become the Partido Agrario-Laborista, a national organization which supported Carlos Ibáñez in his successful presidential bid of 1952. See Cortés and Fuentes, *Diccionario*, pp. 10–11.

20. Studies of the Chilean Right include Marcial Sanfuentes, *El Partido Conservador* (Santiago: Editorial Universitaria, 1967); Robert Kaufman, *The Chilean Political Right and Agrarian Reform* (Washington, D.C.: ICOPS, 1967); Pike, *Chile and the United States*, ch. 8; Gil, *Political System of Chile*, pp. 245–56; Petras, *Politics and Social Forces*, ch. 3.

Radical party. The Christian Democrats swept Eduardo Frei to power in 1964. But six years in the government took their toll, and the 1970 presidential candidate, Radomiro Tomic, failed to retain the presidency for his party. The Radicals, adhering to their long tradition of frequently changing their ideological tendencies, sided with the Right in support of Alessandri in the early 1960s, then switched to the Left during the Frei administration. The Radicals supported Allende's Popular Unity coalition though this support led to two splits which virtually destroyed the party.[21]

The Left in Chile was dominated by the Communist and Socialist parties. The former was the largest Communist party in Latin America, outside of Cuba, and adhered closely to the Moscow line. The Socialist party, which has been racked by dissension since its creation, was more radical than the highly disciplined Communists, at times advocating a nonelectoral route to national power.[22]

Several minor parties split in recent years from the major ones. The MAPU (Movement of United Popular Action) was formed in 1969 by dissident elements in the Christian Democratic party who felt that there was not enough revolution in Chile's much-heralded "revolution in liberty." In the same year the Democratic Radicals split from the Radical party, fearing that the party, by shifting to the Left, was deemphasizing liberty. Earlier the Popular Socialists were created by dissidents from the Socialist party who objected to that party's less revolutionary stance (though personality differences among major leaders were a basic factor in the schism). During Allende's administration the Christian Democrats lost another faction which became the Izquierda Cristiana, and the Radicals lost the Partido de Izquierda Radical (PIR).

21. The Christian Democratic party, which originated in the youth wing of the Conservative party, has been the subject of several recent studies. Among these see George W. Grayson, *El Partido Demócrata Cristiano Chileno* (Buenos Aires: Editorial Jorge Alvarez, 1968); James Petras, *Chilean Christian Democracy: Politics and Social Forces* (Berkeley and Los Angeles: Institute of International Studies, University of California, 1967); Giles Wayland Smith, "The Christian Democratic Party in Chile: A Study of Political Organization with Primary Emphasis on the Local Level," (Ph.D. dissertation, Syracuse University, 1968); Gil, *Political System of Chile*, pp. 266–76. Studies on the Chilean Radical party include the following: Luis Palma, *Historia del Partido Radical* (Santiago: Andres Bello, 1967); Florencio Durán, *El Partido Radical* (Santiago: Editorial Nascimento, 1958); German Urzúa, *El Partido Radical: Su evolución política* (Santiago: Escuela de Ciencias Políticas y Administrativas, 1961); Gil, *Political System of Chile*, pp. 257–66.

22. A few works dealing with the origins and development of the Chilean Left are: Ernst Halperin, *Nationalism and Communism in Chile* (Cambridge, Mass.: MIT Press, 1965); Robert Alexander, *Communism in Latin America* (New Burnswick, N.J.: Rutgers University Press, 1958), ch. 10; Julio Cesar Jobet, *Luis Emilio Recabarren: Los orígenes del socialismo chileno* (Santiago: n.p., 1955); Gil, *Political System of Chile*, pp. 276–79.

A glance at electoral results in national elections shows that Chile has a long tradition of numerous competing parties. Thus, in the twelve congressional elections which have been held since the adoption of the Constitution of 1925, no single party has achieved a majority of the votes, and only twice has any party won more than thirty percent of the total ballots cast. The most recent case of a party's obtaining more than this figure occurred in 1965, when the Christian Democrats won 42.3 percent. In the congressional election of 1969 their percentage of the vote declined to 29.8 percent.[23]

Were elections at the municipal level characterized by similar levels of party competition? In other words, were there as many parties competing for seats in Chile's 276 municipal councils, and was their share of the vote roughly similar to that observed in congressional elections?

Contrary to expectation, an examination of nationwide totals in municipal elections from 1925 to the present reveals that competition between political parties in local contests was as significant as in national contests. Thus, until the Christian Democrats obtained 36.5 percent of the total vote in the 1967 municipal election, no party had ever obtained more than thirty percent of the vote.[24] Table 1.1 summarizes the percentage of the vote obtained by the major Chilean parties in recent municipal and congressional elections.

While these observations imply that there was a high rate of party competition in local as well as in national elections in Chile, they assume that political patterns in individual municipalities were consistent with the political patterns revealed by nationwide totals. Obviously this assumption is not warranted. Nationwide totals may mask important differences among contrasting types of municipalities and contrasting types of elections. It is possible that different parties monopolized the politics of particular localities, as a result, for example, of the influence of dominant local personalities. Nationwide

23. All electoral results in this chapter come from published, mimeographed, and unpublished sources found in the Dirección del Registro Electoral, Ministerio del Interior of the Republic of Chile.

24. In considering the competitiveness of elections it should be realized that not all of the competing lists represent political parties; some represent independent candidacies. In municipal elections independent candidates and lists have appeared more often than in national elections, suggesting that personality and other such factors have been more important in local contests. In global terms, however, independent candidacies were never predominant. In the period under consideration, independent candidacies never received more than fifteen percent of the total vote. After the 1953 municipal elections such candidacies declined steadily, so that in 1967 only eight out of a total of 1,714 municipal councilors were elected as independents. This trend was aided by a strengthening of national parties and by modifications in electoral laws. Information on 1967 regidores was taken from Dirección del Registro Electoral, "Nómina de Ciudadanos Elegidos Regidores," (n.p., 1967, mimeographed).

Table 1.1 Percentage of the vote received by the major Chilean parties in every other congressional and municipal election, 1935 through 1973.

Party	Municipal elections							Congressional elections					
	1935	1941	1947	1953	1960	1967	1971	1937	1945	1953	1961	1969	1973
Conservative	26.4	16.3	20.2	15.4	13.9	–	–	21.3	23.6	14.4[b]	14.3	–	–
Liberal	20.4	19.9	13.3	12.8	15.4	–	–	20.7	17.9	10.9	16.1	–	–
Nacional[a]	–	–	–	–	–	14.1	18.1	–	–	–	–	20.0	21.1
Radical	18.3	29.9	20.0	15.7	20.0	15.1	8.1	18.7	19.9	13.3	21.4	13.0	–
Falange-Christian Dem.	–	–	3.4	4.5	13.9	35.6	25.7	–	2.6	2.9	15.4	29.6	28.5
Agrario and Agrario Laborista	–	1.1	4.5	18.5	–	–	–	–	1.9	15.2	–	–	–
Socialist	0.1	14.4	8.7	11.1[c]	9.7	13.9	22.3	11.2	7.2	14.2[c]	10.7	12.2	18.4
Communist	–	–	16.5	–[d]	9.2	14.8	16.9	4.2	–	–[d]	11.4	15.9	16.2
Independent	17.1	12.6	3.6	14.6	1.6	0.7	0.9	4.1	.09	5.1	0.2	0.1	0.0
Abstention	12.6	30.5	16.0	31.4	30.5	23.7	25.2	13.3	29.9	29.2	25.5	25.8	18.4

[a] Conservatives and Liberals merged to form the Nationals in 1965.
[b] Includes Conservador Tradicionalista.
[c] Includes Socialista Popular.
[d] The Communists were outlawed from 1948 to 1958. (In 1973 parties faced each other in two coalitions. Party figures were calculated by using the vote for each candidate and identifying party affiliation.

Source: Compiled from mimeographed materials in the Dirección del Registro Electoral, Santiago, Chile.

totals would still convey the impression that electoral contests within each community were competitive.[25]

In order to ascertain the importance of the competitive party system in local communities, it is necessary to expand the analysis by examining the municipality as a unity and to compare systematically party competition for all municipalities in both national and local elections. Such an endeavor requires the calculation of an index of multiparty competition for each municipality in each election.

The index of multiparty competition selected for this study was developed by Duncan MacRae and used by Mark Kesselman in a similar study of French politics. According to Kesselman, the index "measures the degree to which votes in a commune are distributed among competing candidates or lists. It increases as the number of candidates or lists competing increases and as the proportions of the total vote received by candidates or lists converge. The value of the index lies in its ability to measure the closeness of the electoral outcome in multiparty systems."[26] The use of this particular index makes

Table 1.2. Party competition in Chilean and French communes: a comparison of a local and a national election.

Type of election	Party competition means	
	Chile	France
National	3.98	3.37
Local	3.84	1.64

Note: the formula for the index of multiparty competition is the following:

$$I = \underset{e}{\text{antilog}} \left\{ -\sum_i^k p_i \log_e p_i \right\}$$

where: k = number of candidates or lists; p_i = proportion of the vote for the ith list: $_i p_i = 1$. Lists or candidates receiving less than five percent of the vote were eliminated from the calculation of the index.

25. High rates of party competition may also be limited to larger cities and, since a large percentage of the Chilean population lives in larger cities, nationwide totals may simply reveal political patterns prevalent in these areas. For figures on urbanization in Chile, see Bruce H. Herrick, *Urban Migration and Economic Development in Chile* (Cambridge, Mass.: MIT Press, 1965).
26. Mark Kesselman, *The Ambiguous Consensus: A Study of Local Government in France* (New York: Alfred A. Knopf, Inc., 1967), p. 27. Kesselman further notes that "the index does not exactly measure conflict or competition but rather the convergence of votes among competing parties. Competition and conflict are dependent on electoral

it possible to compare the Chilean data with data which Kesselman derived from a large sample of French communes.[27]

Indices of multipartyism were calculated for the entire universe of Chilean communes in both the congressional election of 1965 and the municipal election of 1967.[28] The mean indices of multipartyism for both types of elections in Chile and France are presented in table 1.2.

This comparison of party competition rates in a national and a local election with commune-based data confirms the impressionistic evidence provided by nationwide totals and leads to a rejection of the hypothesis that electoral cleavages are less pronounced in local elections. In fact, electoral divisions in Chile were almost as sharp in the local arena as they were in the national arena. The mean party

laws and other factors, in addition to the distribution of votes among candidates. However, since the closeness of the election is a critical aspect of competition, the terms 'competition' and 'conflict' will be used below to refer to the index of multipartyism." In this chapter the same practice will be followed. The formula for the index of multipartyism is presented in the footnote to table 1.1. For a discussion of measures of party competition, see also David G. Pfeiffer, "The Measurement of Inter-Party Competition and Systemic Stability," *American Political Science Review*, 61 (June, 1967), 457–67.

27. Comparison with France is instructive as observers have often noted the "striking" similarity in the party systems of both countries. See, for example, Gil, *Political System of Chile*, p. 244. Kesselman's data are drawn from a sample of communes in three French departments, the Calvados, the Gironde, and the Nord, all in different regions. See *Consensus*, p. 22.

28. In Chile the commune was the lowest administrative unit, and it was administered by the municipality, as Appendix I discusses in more detail. Most Chilean communes had their own municipalities, though there were a few cases in which several communes shared one municipality. Since electoral and socioeconomic data are reported by commune, the commune is the actual unit of analysis. Data were available for 286 out of the 301 communes. A good discussion of the juridical basis of the commune and municipality within the framework of Chilean "interior government" can be found in Alejandro Silva Bascuñan, *Tratado de derecho constitucional* (3 vols., Santiago: Editorial Jurídica de Chile, 1963), vol. 3, 447–60. For the administrative subdivisions of the country, see Dirección de Estadísticas y Censos, *División político-administrativa* (Santiago: Dirección de Estadísticas y Censos, 1966). It might be objected that the two elections chosen are not representative because of the unusual success of the Christian Democrats. However, it is virtually impossible to talk of "representative" elections: the surge and subsequent decline of one party or group of parties was in Chile a commonplace phenomenon. Furthermore, the Christian Democrats did well in both elections. While this may have the effect of reducing overall party competition rates, there is no evidence that it would affect the comparison of both elections. The two elections were chosen because they were the most recent consecutive elections within the same presidential period for which data were available when field work was conducted. Elections from the Allende period could have been chosen for later analysis. However, they were conducted, by and large, as polarized contests between two camps. For a very good study of the 1965 congressional election, see Raul Morodó, *Política y partidos en Chile: Las elecciones de 1965* (Madrid: Taurus Ediciones, S.A., 1968). For a discussion of the 1967 municipal election, consult Michael Francis and Eldon Lanning, "Chile's 1967 Municipal Elections," *Inter-American Economic Affairs*, 21 (Autumn, 1967), 23–26. Francis and Lanning fail to give enough emphasis to the fact that local elections involve different issues and personalities than national elections.

competition index in the election for the Chamber of Deputies is 3.98, whereas the mean party competition index for the municipal election is a very close 3.84. Furthermore, in forty-four percent (125) of all communes in Chile, electoral cleavages were higher in the local election than in the national election.[29]

The index of party competition can be illustrated by presenting the electoral divisions of the small rural commune of Nacimiento in the southern province of Bío-Bío. In the 1965 congressional election the voters of Nacimiento split their vote between five different party lists. In that election the Conservatives obtained seven percent of the vote, while the Liberals obtained seventeen percent. The centrist Radical party received the largest plurality with thirty-two percent of the vote, followed by the Christian Democrats with nineteen percent. The Communist party was able to achieve a respectable seventeen percent of the ballots cast.

In the municipal election of 1967 Nacimiento's voters again divided among several competing political parties. This time the newly formed National party received twenty percent of the vote. The Radicals and the Christian Democrats increased their pluralities slightly, obtaining thirty-seven percent and twenty-one percent, respectively. On the Left, the Socialists presented a list and received nine percent of the vote, while the Communist total dropped proportionally to twelve percent.[30]

Since the distribution of the votes and the proportions received by the various party organizations were similar in both elections, the party competition rates in Nacimiento were virtually identical. In the congressional race the multipartyism index for the little commune was 4.35, whereas in the municipal election the index was 4.40.

The Chilean results contrast sharply with the results of the French study. As table 1.2 shows, party competition in French local contests was less than half of what it was in contests for the National Assembly. As Kesselman says, "a comparison of competition in national and local elections reveals that competition is much less widespread in local elections than it is in national. In virtually every commune there is

29. The standard deviation from the mean in the national election was .51, and in the local election it was .77. This means that in the national contest almost two-thirds of Chilean communes had party competition scores between 3.47 and 4.49. In the local election party competition was also uniformly high, but exhibited a wider range, with two-thirds of the communes scoring between 3.01 and 4.61. The high rate of party competition in both elections does not mean that these variables vary directly. In some regions, such as in the North, they do—and the correlation between them is .83. In the Valdivia Osorno region they are negatively related (−.10). The overall correlation coefficient between the two variables was .32.

30. Percentages don't add up to 100 percent because ballots and minor lists receiving a mere fraction of the vote were excluded from analysis.

far greater fractionalization of the vote for national elections than for local elections."[31] Comparing further the findings from both countries, one discovers that the overall party competition rates are substantially higher in Chile. Indeed, the average party competition index for Chilean municipal elections is higher than the average party competition index in the French national election.

Because Chile is a country that presents vast contrasts throughout its 2600 miles of narrow territory this same analysis was replicated for eight distinct historical regions. Ecological analysis requires maximum homogeneity within units, while maintaining maximum heterogeneity across units. By focusing on different regions it is possible to ascertain whether the similarity in competitiveness across elections is more a feature of some regions than others. Table 1.3 shows that with the possible exception of the region of Valdivia and Osorno the average party competition in local elections parallels the average party competition in national elections. In four of the eight regions local elections are slightly more competitive than national ones.

This comparative examination of party competition has revealed the wide scope of the competitive Chilean party system by showing the degree to which it penetrated the arena of local politics. Chilean

Table 1.3. Regional party competition indices for a national and a local election in Chile.

Region	National election	Local election
Region 1 Tarapacá to Coquimbo	3.86	3.89
Region 2 Aconcagua-Valparaiso	3.86	3.95
Region 3 Santiago	4.05	3.73
Region 4 O'Higgins to Ñuble	3.98	3.84
Region 5 Concepción-Arauco	4.12	3.79
Region 6 Bío-Bío to Cautín	3.92	4.10
Region 7 Valdivia to Chiloe	4.08	3.53
Region 8 Aysen-Magallanes	3.25	3.61
Nation	3.95	3.83

Note: the indices are the average of communal indices for each region. The elections are the 1965 congressional and 1967 municipal elections.

31. Kesselman, *Ambiguous Consensus*, p. 29.

voters were as divided in their choice of local municipal councilors as they were in their choice of national deputies. This evidence suggests that local politics were not monopolized by a dominant political *caudillo*. Instead the municipal arena was a highly competitive one where different party lists and personalities vied as strongly for the lowest elected office in the land as did the candidates for the most powerful congress in Latin America. Despite Chile's polymorphism, this competitiveness extended across the country's diverse regions.

The Penetration of the Party System into Peripheral Areas

The previous section dealt with one dimension of the scope of the Chilean party system by showing that competitive party politics have extended vertically into the local political arena. However, the analysis so far has left unclear the second dimension of the scope of the party system, namely, the horizontal extension of competitive politics into peripheral areas of the country. As noted in the introduction, one can hypothesize that party competition is lower in the smaller backward communes which lack the social heterogeneity that leads to increased electoral divisions. This hypothesis can be tested by examining whether party competition in both a local and a national election in Chile is significantly related in a positive direction to various socioeconomic indicators.

The association between socioeconomic variables and party competition has received much attention from political scientists studying politics at the state and local levels in the United States.[32] Most

32. See Austin Ranney and Willmore Kendall, "The American Party System," *American Political Science Review*, 48 (June, 1954), 477–85; Joseph A. Schlesinger, "A Two-Dimensional Scheme for Classifying the States According to Degree of Inter-Party Competition," *American Political Science Review*, 49 (December, 1955), 1120–28; Robert T. Golembiewski, "A Taxonomic Approach to State Political Party Strength," *Western Political Quarterly*, 11 (June, 1958), 494–513; Douglas S. Gatlin, "A Functionalist Theory of Political Parties: Inter-party Competition in North Carolina," in *Approaches to the Study of Party Organization*, ed. William J. Crotty (Boston: Allyn and Bacon, 1968), pp. 217–45. Other studies have related party competition to urbanization, following the assumption that urbanization reflects the major characteristics of socioeconomic development. Among these studies see Heinz Eulau, "The Ecological Basis of Party Systems: The Case of Ohio," *Midwest Journal of Political Science*, 1 (August, 1957), 125–35; David Gold and John M. Schmidhauser, "Urbanization and Party Competition: The Case of Iowa," *Midwest Journal of Political Science*, 4 (February, 1960), 62–75; Phillips Cutright, "Urbanization and Competitive Party Politics," *Journal of Politics*, 25 (August, 1963), 552–64. Other attempts have sought to relate party competition, socioeconomic development, and policy outcomes of state governments. See Richard E. Dawson and James Robinson, "Inter-party Competition, Economic Variables and Welfare Policies in the American States," *Journal of Politics*, 25

of these scholars have maintained that in the United States there is a positive relationship between indicators of socioeconomic development and party system variables such as party competition.[33]

The only study on a Latin American country based on similar premises was undertaken by Glaucio Soares and Amelia C. de Noronha in an analysis of Brazilian politics.[34] Using Duncan MacRae's index of party competition, these authors found that in Brazil party competition was affected by at least one kind of "modification of the social structure," namely, urbanization. In the more urban municipalities of fourteen Brazilian states multipartyism was found to be clearly higher than in the more rural municipalities.

Soares and de Noronha followed the assumption, made by some of the studies on United States state politics mentioned above, that urbanization embodies most of the important socioeconomic changes related to economic development. Several students of Latin America and other developing regions have cautioned against making this assumption. In a review article on urbanization in Latin America, Richard Morse makes this point by noting that one of the key components of economic development, industrialization, is not closely associated with urbanization in Latin America as it was in Europe and in the United States.[35] While it is true that industry tends to con-

(May, 1963), 265–89; Thomas R. Dye, "The Independent Effect of Party Competition on Policy Outcomes in the American States," in State Politics, ed. Robert Crew, Jr. (Belmont, Calif.: Wadsworth, 1968), pp. 249–69; Richard I. Hofferbert, "The Relationship Between Public Policy and Some Structural and Environmental Variables in the American States," American Political Science Review, 60 (March, 1966), 73–82; Charles F. Cnudde and Donald J. McCrone, "Party Competition and Welfare Policies in the American States," American Political Science Review, 63 (September, 1969), 856–66; Ira Sharkansky and Richard I. Hofferbert, "Dimensions of State Politics, Economics and Public Policy," American Political Science Review, 63 (September, 1969), 867–79; and Ira Sharkansky, "Economic Development, Regionalism and State Political Systems," Midwest Journal of Political Science, 12 (February, 1968), 41–61.

33. While Thomas Dye has stated that the relationship is "established" ("Independent Effect," p. 252), Ira Sharkansky has questioned this contention. Sharkansky notes that multiple regression analysis has shown that at best only forty percent of the variations in party competition are explained by socioeconomic factors in the United States. He further shows that region makes a statistically important contribution to the analysis and concludes that "the historical experience of regions may have greater impact upon current political traits than latter-day economic characteristics. . . . Once established, certain political traits seem capable of withstanding the influence of subsequent economic changes." See "Economic Development, Regionalism and State Political Systems," p. 61.

34. Glaucio Ary Dillon Soares and Amelia Maria Carbalho de Noronha, "Urbanização e dispersão eleitoral," Revista de Direito Publico e Ciencia Politica, 3 (July-December, 1960), 258–70.

35. Richard Morse, "Recent Research on Latin American Urbanization: A Selective Survey with Commentary," Latin American Research Review, 1 (Fall, 1966), 45. The concept of over-urbanization has been discussed many times. See also Phillip M. Hauser, ed., Urbanization in Latin America (Paris: UNESCO, 1961); K. Davis and

centrate in the cities, the percentage of urban dwellers engaged in modern industrial pursuits is much lower than in the developed nations of the West.

Francine Rabinowitz, after reviewing similar arguments, has suggested the utility of distinguishing, in Louis Wirth's terms, between "urbanization" and "urbanism." Urbanization can be defined as "urban development. . . . as a physical and spacial agglomeration process," while urbanism can be defined as the "host of social characteristics commonly associated with urbanization."[36] In Latin America's "overurbanized" or "preindustrial" cities these two distinct phenomena may not be strongly interrelated.

The inadequacy of urbanization as the principle or sole indicator makes it imperative in this study to select a series of indicators approximating "urbanism" as indicators of socioeconomic development. Fortunately, the Chilean census provides several such indicators at the commune level. Since Chile exhibits marked variations in different communities with respect to these indicators, it is possible to determine the effects of these variables on party competition. The selected variables fall into three general categories: standard of living, occupation, and education.

Many of the studies of the United States utilize per capita income figures as the main indicator of standard of living.[37] In the absence of such data at the local level in Chile, three important community services were selected as indicators of the standard of living of particular communes. These are the percentage of dwellings with potable water, the percentage of babies born with the assistance of a certified physician, and the percentage of children between the ages of seven and fifteen attending a fulltime schooling program.[38] Rabinowitz, using the first of these indicators in a cross-national study of Latin American urbanization, suggests on the basis of her findings that the level of urban services is a good indicator of "urbanism,"

H. Golden, "Urbanization and the Development of Pre-Industrial Areas," *Economic Development and Cultural Change*, 3 (October, 1954), 6–26; Alfred Stepan, "Political Development Theory: The Latin American Experience," *Journal of International Affairs*, 20 (2/1966).

36. Francine Rabinowitz, "Urban Development and Political Development in Latin America," *Comparative Urban Research*, ed. Robert T. Daland (Beverly Hills, Calif.: Sage Publications, Inc., 1967), p. 94.

37. For example, see Dawson, "Inter-party Competition, Economic Variables," and Dye, "Independent Effect."

38. The dwelling indicator was taken from the compilation of census material in Armand Mattelart, *Atlas social de las comunas de Chile* (Santiago: Editorial del Pacífico, 1965). The medical assistance indicator and the school attendance indicator were both calculated from census data by Jorge López, Francisco Salazar, and Diógenes Ramirez of the Instituto de Administración (INSORA) of the University of Chile.

correlating highly with the changing life styles resulting from economic development.[39]

The second category includes three occupational indicators. The first is the percentage of the active population engaged in industry.[40] It will be used, as in the studies of the United States, as an indicator of industrialization, though one must caution that the Chilean industrial sector includes individuals working in smaller craft industries as well as in modern factories. The second indicator is the percentage of the population active in the tertiary sector, an indicator of the development of public bureaucracy and services.[41] Morse and others have noted that the ratio of the tertiary sector to the secondary or manufacturing sector is much greater in Latin America than it is in Western Europe. This means that the tertiary sector may be less related to economic development in Chile than it is in the more developed nations.[42] Nevertheless, this indicator is useful, as it represents increasing social differentiation, which may have some direct political consequences. A third occupational indicator, the percentage of the population engaged in mining, was also included in the analysis.[43] Mining is a key economic pursuit in Chile which may have contributed to political cleavages in communes with important mining operations. Miners constitute a relatively homogeneous occupational group which, in Chile as elsewhere, has been noted for its radical politics.[44]

The final category refers to education. Higher levels of education are associated with the increasing diversity of the organizational infrastructure of more economically developed and socially differentiated areas. Higher educational levels may also contribute to greater awareness of group interests and higher levels of participation in political life.[45] In the absence of a better indicator of education for

39. Rabinowitz, "Urban Development."
40. Mattelart, *Atlas social*, p. 15.
41. Ibid., p. 18.
42. See Morse, "Recent Research," pp. 44–45. For a treatment of this question see also Denis Lambert, "L'Urbanisation accélérée de l'Amerique Latine et la formation d'un secteur tertiaire refuge," *Civilisations*, 15 (1965), 158–74, 309–25, 477–92. For a brief discussion of this question with reference to Chile, see Alieto Guadagni, *La estructura ocupacional y el desarrollo económico de Chile*, Documento de Trabajo (2nd ed.; Buenos Aires: Instituto Torcuato di Tella, 1967).
43. Jorge López et al.
44. For a discussion of miners in Chilean politics see Cruz-Coke, *Geografía electoral de Chile*, pp. 81–82, and Petras and Zeitlin, "Miners and Agrarian Radicalism." Multiple regression analysis conducted by the author shows that the percentage of the population in mining predicts the Communist vote more than any other occupational group. Furthermore, it is the highest predictor of the vote of any party with a coefficient of determination of .37 (calculations for the 1965 congressional election).
45. One of the best known statements of the role of education in political development is that of Daniel Lerner, *The Passing of Traditional Society*. For a more recent

Chilean communes, the average number of years of schooling of the adult population from the ages of twenty-five to thirty was utilized.[46]

Population size of communes, an additional variable indirectly related to the preceding ones, was also included in the analysis.[47] The existence of large population centers in Chile with greater political importance suggests the possibility that party competition may have been related to the size of a commune's population. Did elections divide small communes as much as they divided large ones? Or did the competitive party system penetrate less into smaller communities?

The relationship between party competition in the 1965 election for the Chamber of Deputies and the 1967 municipal election and the various socioeconomic indicators was analyzed with multiple regression statistical techniques.[48] The advantage of this technique is twofold. In the first place, it permits an assessment of the relationship between each of the independent variables and the dependent variable, while holding the other variables constant. Thus one is able to judge which of the independent variables is more strongly associated with party competition and in what direction. In the second place, multiple regression analysis provides a means for establishing how much of the variation in the dependent variable is accounted for by the joint action of the independent variables. In other words, it is possible to assess the percentage of party competition which is explained by all the socioeconomic variables employed in the analysis. Table 1.4 presents the results of multiple regression analysis as well as the simple correlations between party competition in a local and a national election and selected socioeconomic indicators.[49]

---

statement, see Donald J. McCrone and Charles F. Cnudde, "Toward a Communications Theory of Democratic Political Development: A Causal Model," *American Political Science Review*, 61 (March, 1967), 72–79.

46. Jorge López et al.

47. Calculated from projections of population size of communes in 1965 supplied by the Dirección de Estadísticas y Censos, Santiago.

48. For a discussion of this technique see Hubert M. Blalock, Jr., *Social Statistics* (New York: McGraw-Hill Book Co., 1960). The "ecological fallacy" is not a problem in this study since correlations of commune level data are not used to draw inferences about the behavior of individuals. Rather, the study seeks to analyze the characteristics of communities by focusing on community cleavages in relationship to the level of the community's socioeconomic development. For a recent discussion of this familiar problem, see W. Phillips Shively, "'Ecological' Inference: The Use of Aggregate Data to Study Individuals," *American Political Science Review*, 63 (December, 1969), 1183–96.

49. The reader will notice that the variable percentage of houses with potable water was not included in the regression equation. This is due to the problem of multicollinearity. When the simple correlations between two variables are very high, the partial regression coefficients may be affected, making it difficult to determine the

An examination of the simple correlations in the table reveals an interesting and unexpected finding. The correlations are uniformly different for the two types of election. In the local election, except for school attendance and mining, all of the socioeconomic variables as well as the population size of communes are significantly associated in a positive direction with party competition. On the other hand, in the election for the Chamber of Deputies, only school attendance is significantly associated with party competition. All of the other correlations are negligible.[50]

A similar pattern can be observed in correlating party competition with urbanization, the variable not included in the regression analysis.

Table 1.4. Simple correlations and multiple regression analysis with party competition as the dependent variable and selected socioeconomic indicators as independent variables in a Chilean national and local election.

Independent variables	Local election			National election		
	simple r	reg. coef.	sign. t	simple r	reg. coef.	sign t
School attendance	.03	−.003	− .75	.22[b]	.014	4.06[a]
Instruction	.26[b]	−.162	−1.70[c]	.07	−.003	−1.32
Medical assistance	.32[b]	.006	2.78[a]	.09	.001	.48
Population in services	.31[b]	.013	2.08[b]	.09	.004	1.63
Population in industry	.26[b]	.008	1.26	.02	−.006	−1.35
Population in mining	.03	.003	.74	−.03	−.003	− .99
Commune size	.28[b]	.004	1.19[c]	.04	.001	.62[d]
N: 286	R: .38	R^2: .14		R: .26	R^2: .07	
	F: 6.60			F: 2.98		

a. Significant at .01 level (two-tail test).
b. Significant at .05 level (two-tail test).
c. Significant at .10 level (two-tail test).
d. Significant at .001 level (two-tail test).
Note: technically significant tests are not necessary since the study deals with the entire universe of Chilean communes and not with a sample. However, significance tests can be of utility in identifying the strengths of the various associations.

---

relative contributions of each independent variable to the dependent variable. Leaving this variable out does not affect the multiple correlation coefficient. In other words, the potable water variable does not add to an explanation of the variation in party competition. For a discussion of this question see Hugh D. Forbes and Edward Tufte, "A Note of Caution in Causal Modelling," *American Political Science Review*, 62 (December, 1968), 1262–64, and Hubert M. Blalock, Jr., "Correlated Independent Variables: The Problem of Multicollinearity," *Social Forces*, 62 (December, 1963).

50. School attendance and mining are the two indicators least associated with urbanization.

In the local election the correlation between urbanization and party competition is .31, while in the contest for national office the same correlation is a mere .09.

These data suggest that in national elections party competition was uniformly high in all communes regardless of their level of socioeconomic development or their population size. Smaller and more backward communities are as divided in electoral contests for the Chamber of Deputies as their larger and more developed counterparts. By contrast, in elections of municipal councilors political division was more closely related to socioeconomic characteristics of particular localities. Larger and more developed communes divided slightly more in local elections than smaller and more backward ones.[51]

The regression coefficients generally support this picture. In the local election four of these coefficients are significant: size, population in services, and medical attendance are all related to party competition. Instruction, however, is negatively related to party competition, showing that the education variable is not as important when other variables are held constant. By contrast, in the national election only school attendance is significant.[52]

Nevertheless, the above discussion is far from conclusive in suggesting a real difference between the two types of election. The simple correlations make it quite clear that there is only a slight tendency for party competition to be associated with socioeconomic development in local elections. Indeed, the highest simple correlation between the dependent variable and one of the independent variables is the correlation with medical assistance, a correlation of only .32.

The weakness of the relationship between party competition and levels of socioeconomic development is confirmed by turning to the coefficients of determination (R^2). These coefficients, the square of the multiple correlation coefficients (R), specify the extent to which the variance in the dependent variable is occasioned by all of the dependent variables acting together. They show that in both types of elections only a very small part of the variation in party competi-

51. In analysing the same relationship by region for the local election, two out of eight regions fall below average, one is about average and the other five are above average. The highest coefficient is .54 for the region of O'Higgins to Ñuble. The lowest are .23 for the region of Antofagasta and .25 for the region of Bío-Bío, Malleco and Cautín.

52. It is interesting to note that education does not explain voting participation in Chile either. This is in agreement with the study done on cities in the United States. See Robert Alford and Eugene C. Lee, "Voting Turnout in American Cities," *American Political Science Review*, 62 (September, 1968), 805.

tion is explained by indicators of standard of living, occupation, education and size. In the local election only fourteen percent of the variance in party competition is accounted for by these variables, while in the national contest only seven percent is accounted for. Thus even in local elections eighty-six percent of the variation in party competition remains unexplained by all of the contextual variables.[53]

The foregoing analysis compels one to reject the hypothesis that the Chilean competitive party system was limited in scope and confined to large socioeconomically developed communities. Just as the competitive party system extended vertically into the arena of local politics, so it extended horizontally into diverse regions of the country. Especially in national elections, high rates of party competition were as much a feature of tiny underdeveloped communes as they were of large and developed ones. While in local elections the influence of socioeconomic characteristics of communities on the level of electoral division is higher than in national elections, this influence remains extremely weak.

The Extension of Party Structures

In order to complete this analysis of the penetration of the Chilean party system into the arena of local politics, this chapter will turn briefly to an examination of an additional question: do the findings presented above enable one to conclude that individual Chilean parties competed with other parties uniformly across the country regardless of the level of socioeconomic development of a particular region? Though the party competition evidence points in that direction, such a conclusion is unwarranted without an examination of the socioeconomic correlates of voting for individual parties, as distinct from an examination of the competitive party system. It is quite conceivable, for instance, that certain parties derived their strength from

53. The similarity of political behavior in local and national elections with respect to party competition is paralleled by similarities with respect to another political variable: political participation. Averaged based figures show that sixty-three percent of the eligible population voted in the national election, while fifty-nine percent voted in the local election. What is even more striking is that the relationship between voter turnout and the socioeconomic variables used in this chapter is the same for both elections. Thus in both the local and national contests thirty-one percent of the variation in voting turnout is explained by socioeconomic variables. Ecological factors are consequently more important in Chile in explaining voter turnout than party competition, but have a similar effect on local and national contests. This fact implies that the two political variables, turnout and party competition, are not strongly related to each other. This is the case, as the simple correlation between the two in the 1967 municipal election was .097.

social groups which emerged in more economically developed communities, while others received support in more traditional communities. If this should be the case, it is possible that high levels of party competition were merely a reflection of the fact that some parties competed in the more traditional areas of the country, while others competed in more modern ones. Though a final answer to this problem would entail a detailed analysis beyond the scope of this chapter, it is nevertheless possible to make some generalizations.

Multiple correlation analysis will once again be employed with a series of socioeconomic variables in order to determine the extent to which contextual characteristics of communities explained voting for the major Chilean parties, and to see whether there was any difference between a national and a local election.

Table 1.5 presents the relevant results of several multiple regression equations with the voting strength of the major Chilean parties in all communes in the 1969 election to the Chamber of Deputies and the 1967 election of municipal officials.

In the first place, it is clear that with the exception of the communists there is no great disparity between the two types of election. Socioeconomic variables explain individual party voting similarly in national and local elections. In the second place, the table shows that the percentage of the variance in the votes for the major Chilean parties and coalitions explained by socioeconomic factors is very low.

The Communist party is the only party whose vote is explained in

Table 1.5. Percentage of the variation[a] in the vote for each major Chilean party or alliance in a national and a local election explained by various socioeconomic indicators.[b]

Election	Nacionales	Radicales	Democracia Cristiana	Comunistas	Socialistas
Congressional election of 1969	28.3%	8.5%	18.5%	22.9%	9.8%
Municipal election of 1967	22.8%	13.5%	17.1%	40.0%	12.2%

[a] Coefficients of determination (R^2) expressed in percentage form. All multiple correlation coefficients (R) significant at .001 level.
[b] The independent variables are: medical assistance, homes with bathrooms, school attendance, population in industry, population in construction, population in services, population in mining, instruction, and population size. The dependent variables are the percentages of the vote which each party or alliance received in each election and in each commune.
Source: electoral data from the Dirección del Registro Electoral, Santiago, Chile.

any significant way by the socioeconomic characteristics of Chilean communes, with forty percent of the variance explained in the municipal election. Examination of the partial regression coefficients indicates that mining accounts for a substantial portion of the explained Communist vote. Nevertheless, even in the case of the Communist vote, about sixty percent of the variation for voting for that party is not explained by the socioeconomic characteristics of communes. In the case of the other parties eighty or ninety percent of their vote fails to be explained. All Chilean parties with the possible exception of the Communist party compete uniformly in different areas of the country regardless of socioeconomic characteristics.

A confirmation of this trend can also be obtained by examining the intercorrelation of party voting for the country as a whole. By correlating each party separately with every other party it is possible to ascertain whether some parties have a greater or lesser tendency to compete with each other. Table 1.6 presents the simple correlations between each party and every other party for the 1967 election.

The table confirms the notion that Chilean political parties tend to compete uniformly with other parties across the nation. Thus the data show no strong positive correlations, indicating that polarized party situations do not appear between any two parties in Chile. On the other hand, and more significantly for the purposes of this argument, there are no highly negative correlations. In other words, there are very few communes across the country where the presence of one party tends to exclude the presence of another political party. The strongest cases occur with the National party. Where the National party has strength there is a stronger likelihood that both the Radical

Table 1.6. Simple correlations between each party and every other party in the municipal elections of 1967 arranged from most congruent to least congruent.

Parties	Simple r's
Christian Democrats and Radicals	.05
Christian Democrats and Nationals	−.01
Christian Democrats and Socialists	−.03
Communists and Socialists	−.03
Radicals and Communists	−.15[a]
Radicals and Socialists	−.17
Christian Democrats and Communists	−.19
Nationals and Socialists	−.24
Nationals and Radicals	−.40
Nationals and Communists	−.42

[a] Data below this entry are significant at the .05 level (two-tail test).

and the Communist parties will not be present. The negative correlation between the strength of the National party and that of the Radical party is −.40, while the negative correlation between the strength of the National party and that of the Communist party is −.42.[54]

The brief examination of the socioeconomic correlates of individual parties, as well as the analysis of the intercorrelations of voting for each party with every other party, suggest that Chilean party structures, as distinct from the "competitive party system," have also extended broadly across the country. Consequently, this study supports the earlier findings that local politics in Chile is characterized by intense political activity regardless of the character of the locality. This research supports some recent studies which have shown that Chilean political parties do not sharply reflect class voting. Thus Sandra Powell, in a comparative study of voting behavior in several presidential elections noted earlier, observes that lower-class elements did not seem to support "change candidates" while upper class elements had a greater tendency to do so. Likewise, in a much more sophisticated study using data from survey research, Alejandro Portes notes that socioeconomic status was not directly related to voting preferences for the far Left. Portes suggested, in fact, that middle sectors may be the least inclined to radical voting behavior, while the upper and lower sectors are more inclined in that direction. Portes suggests the importance of examining the web of reference groups in determining Chilean radicalism and, by inference, voting behavior.[55]

Political party competition in Chile was not a mere dependent variable responding to environmental influences. Contrary to the implications derived from some of the structural-functional literature, competitive party politics resulted from the extension of party structures into local contests and peripheral areas with vastly different ecological characteristics. Though earlier in the century the penetration of parties may have been facilitated by certain characteristics of the social structure of communities, by midcentury the party system had become an independent variable structuring the political options

54. Preliminary analysis by the author of Chilean voting behavior indicates that the negative correlations between the National party and the Radical party mean that they do not compete in the same areas, but that they do appeal to similar constituencies. (The Radicals also appeal to other constituencies which are quite different.) On the other hand, the negative correlations between the National party and the Communist party indicate both that they compete in different areas and that they appeal to different constituencies. The table reveals clearly that the Christian Democrats made inroads into areas where all of the major Chilean parties had strength.

55. See Powell, "Social Structure and Electoral Choice," and Alejandro Portes, "Leftist Radicalism in Chile: A Test of Three Hypotheses," *Comparative Politics*, 2 (January, 1970), 254–57.

across the country. Local politics were not dominated by individual political caudillos nor was competition in local contests a feature only of larger more modern communities.

This chapter, by providing a general picture of local politics in Chile, has set the stage for more intensive analysis by raising more questions than it answers. Why was local politics so competitive? Were there important functions and stakes in local government enticing factions and individuals to compete for local office?

2. The Stakes in Local Politics: Jurisdiction and Finances of Chilean Municipalities

Every four years Chilean political parties mobilized their supporters from Arica to Punta Arenas in an effort to gain control of as many municipal governments as possible. Even in the most remote communities the suitability of this or that candidate became the primary topic of conversation. Local party committees, union organizations, employer associations and even sports clubs became more active as election time grew near. Invariably, community residents divided sharply in their choice of leaders to run the local government and manage its resources.

Paradoxically, the general scholarly opinion on local government in Chile suggests that once these leaders were elected to office they exercised little power and had few resources at their disposition. For example, in the most comprehensive work on Chilean politics, Federico Gil says that "legislation and political practice have more and more been buttressing the powers of the officials of the central government and restricting the activities and jurisdiction of municipalities to administrative matters of relatively minor importance."[1] The purpose of this chapter is to explore this assertion by examining the jurisdiction of local governments in Chile and the financial resources which they had at their disposition in the late 1960s.

The Nationalization of Municipal Functions

The Chilean Constitution of 1925 clearly specifies that the administration of local matters is the task of the municipality, although it is quite vague in specifying what this administration entails. Article cv of the Constitution notes that the municipalities are charged "especially" with the following: (1) Care to enforce standards of sanitation, comfort, beautification and recreation; (2) Promotion of education, agriculture, industry, and commerce; (3) Care for primary schools and other educational services to be financed with municipal funds; (4) Care for the construction and repair of roads, sidewalks, bridges and all other projects of necessity, utility and beautification financed with municipal funds; (5) Administration and investment of the *caudales de proprios y arbitrios*, in conformity

1. *The Political System of Chile* (Boston: Houghton Mifflin Co., 1966), p. 132.

with rules dictated by the law; (6) Creation of municipal ordinances with regard to these matters. . . .[2]

However, though the Constitution seemingly gave local governments a broad jurisdiction, it also made it clear that municipalities would "have the administrative attributions and income determined by law."[3]

Chilean scholars dealing with local government and administration concur with Federico Gil's view. They argue that a severe governmental crisis resulted from the national government's decision to deprive municipalities of precious attributions and financial support.[4] As table 2.1 reveals a sample of seventy-four mayors, municipal secretaries and municipal councilors interviewed by the author in 1969 also shared this view.[5]

All of the mayors and all of the municipal secretaries as well as the overwhelming majority of councilors questioned were very much in agreement with the proposition that agencies of the national government had left the municipal governments with little power. One discouraged mayor told the author: "National agencies are constantly encroaching on us, and all our funds go to national coffers. There is no justice in the fact that the municipality is no longer in charge of things within its own jurisdiction and that we get so little money back from the government."

The expansion of national governmental authority with its in-

Table 2.1. Reactions of a sample of local government officials to the statement: "Agencies of the national government have, according to some, left municipalities with little power" (pocas atribuciones).

Reaction	No. responses
Very much in agreement with this opinion	61
Somewhat in agreement with this opinion	2
In disagreement with this opinion	8
Don't know or Not applicable	3

2. Chile, *Constitución política de la República de Chile (Conforme a la Edición oficial)* (Santiago: Editorial Nascimento, 1969), p. 36.

3. Ibid.

4. For a good Collection of articles devoted to municipal problems by leading Chilean experts, see PLANDES (Sociedad Chilena de Planificación y Desarrollo), *Boletín informativo PLANDES*, 23 (September-October, 1967).

5. See Appendix II for methodological information dealing with these interviews, and Appendix III for the interview schedule.

creasing involvement in all aspects of national life meant that many formerly municipal functions had been taken over by government ministries and corporations. Examples of this phenomenon are numerous. For instance, the Ministerio de la Vivienda y Desarrollo Urbano (Ministry of Housing and Urbanism) was placed in charge of urban planning development. The Dirección General de Pavimentación (General Bureau of Paving) in the same ministry was charged with paving streets and sidewalks. Both of these functions were previously handled primarily by municipalities. In the area of education municipalities also saw their authority diminished. Thus the Ministerio de Educación (Ministry of Education) was charged with the establishment, maintenance and operation of all schools, while the semi-public Sociedad Constructora de Establecimientos Educacionales (Society for the Construction of Educational Facilities) was charged with planning and construction of educational buildings. Likewise, the Ministerio de Economía, Desarrollo y Reconstrucción (Ministry of Economics, Development and Reconstruction), and more particularly its Dirección de Industria y Comercio (Bureau of Industry and Commerce), took over much of the control which municipalities had over pricing of essential goods and articles, together with the supervision of local industry and commerce. Another agency of the same ministry, the Sub-Secretaría de Transportes (Under-Secretariat of Transportation), more recently took over control of taxis and the setting of prices for public transportation, for a long time regulated by the municipality. Finally, in the health field, the Servicio Nacional de Salud (National Health Service) gradually took over not only the supervision and administration of hospitals and medical care, but also the inspection and licensing of all commercial establishments which are potential health hazards.[6] The Código Sanitario states that it is up to the Servicio Nacional de Salud to "regulate measures tending to avoid public nuisances such as smoke, noise, bad odors, toxic gases, atmospheric dust, and emanations which might affect the well-being of the population, as well as establish sanitary conditions . . . which can be tolerated in any sector of the municipal territory."[7] While the municipality could deny a license to any establishment violating the SNS regulations,

6. This listing follows that in Diógenes Ramirez, Francisco Salazar and Hugo Zunino, *El sistema de gobierno local de Chile* (Santiago: INSORA, n.d., mimeographed), pp. 7–8.

7. Código Sanitario, art. xxvi, secs. 4, 13; Dictamen no. 49,530 of the Contraloría General de la República relating to Law 10,383, arts. i, lxiii, cited in Contraloría General de la República, *Boletín de la Contraloría General de la República*, 37 (January-December, 1964), 563–64.

these regulations were no longer within the jurisdiction of local government authorities.

This curtailment of municipal functions occurred gradually as a result of laws expanding governmental authority. Whenever a new regulatory policy was enacted, an agency of the central government was usually charged with carrying it out. For example, the provisions of the Chilean Constitution cited earlier make it clear that the municipality was charged with matters relating to recreation. Article lii of the Municipal Law concurs, holding that municipalities could "subsidize theaters and public diversions that are honest and free or inexpensive for the populace, and [are] authorized to cover the cost from [their] own funds or with economic aid provided the municipality by other laws."[8] And yet the municipality of Illapel had to turn to the departmental governor and ask for specific permission to set up a public address system aimed at entertaining people in the plaza. This was necessary because Article xxxi of Decree 3,375 of the Ministry of the Interior, which deals with the "stations of radio-communication," specifies that "the installation and operation of loudspeakers and amplifiers, wired to receivers of radiotelephone, . . . are subject to the authorization of Intendants or Governors. . . ." Should such equipment be set up without the proper permission, then the intendant or governor could report the case to the director of the Dirección General de Servicios Electricos y de Gas (General Bureau of Electrical and Gas Services), empowered to cut off electrical services.[9]

Another municipality found that it could not expropriate a piece of land next to the local hospital of the Servicio Nacional de Salud for the purpose of expanding hospital facilities. Article c of the General Law of Construction and Urbanization (Law 14, 171) specifically says that municipalities could expropriate land only to establish green areas (parks) or to construct buildings for the municipal government itself. In order to expropriate land for the hospital it would have been necessary to have the land declared of public utility for that specific end, and this could be done only through national legislation.[10]

The municipality of Limache discovered that it could no longer charge a license fee to a local chicken farm. Article i of Law 4,174

8. This law, 11,860, is the latest comprehensive municipal law and was published in the *Diario oficial*, September 14, 1955.

9. Dictamen no. 35,824, Contraloría General de la Republíca, *Boletín de la Contraloría General de la República*, 37 (January-December, 1964), 399–400.

10. Dictamen no. 17,756 of the Contraloría General de la Republíca, *Boletín de la Contraloría General de la República*, 41 (March, 1969), 149.

was replaced by Article vii of Law 15,021, and the new language specified two types of real estate in Chile, agricultural and non-agricultural. Agricultural real estate was no longer subject to licensing, and chicken farms were considered an agricultural enterprise. The municipality could still prohibit the establishment of a chicken farm under other provisions, such as the General Law on Construction and Urbanization, which empowered municipalities to prohibit the establishment of such an enterprise in a residential or hospital zone.[11]

These brief illustrations have underscored the extent to which municipal functions were taken over by agents of the national government through complex regulations and provisions. The discussion will turn to another, and perhaps more limiting, kind of control over the municipality: direct control by government agents over municipal operations per se.

Intendente and Contraloría: Checks on Municipal Autonomy?

According to the Chilean Constitution, municipalities were to be checked by another decentralized administrative organ, the *asamblea provincial* (provincial assembly). Provincial assemblies were supposed to be constituted by representatives from all municipalities to exercise a "correctional and economic vigilance" over municipalities.[12] This means that the assemblies would have been able to suspend within ten days the execution of ordinances and resolutions of a given municipality if these were considered to be contrary to the Constitution or laws and prejudicial to the interests of the province or state. Constitutional lawyers in Chile disagree as to whether this action would have been final.

Whether this be the case or not is a moot point, because the Chilean legislature never saw fit to pass a law creating these provincial assemblies. Instead it passed a law granting the intendentes or provincial governors much of the authority to supervise municipalities which the Constitution granted the assemblies.[13] However, this law specifically prohibited the intendente from dissolving the municipality and limited him to exercising those faculties of the assembly dealing with the "authorization, approval and regulation of municipal governments."[14]

11. Dictamen no. 49,530 of the Contraloría General de la República, *Boletín de la Contraloría General de la República*, 37 (July, 1964), 563–64. The General Law on Construction and Urbanization is Law 14,171, and the article in question is xciii.
12. See Law 11,860, art. cvi, sec. 1.
13. See Law 7,164 (1942).
14. This law has been criticized as unconstitutional by Chilean legal experts. See Silva, *Tratado*, vol. 3, p. 482, and Mario Gonzales Bernaschina, *Derecho municipal*

On paper this provision would seem to have given the intendente enormous powers of control and supervision of the municipalities. In practice the intendente rarely exercised this power.[15] Ordinances and municipal budgets could be sent to him for his approval, and in the overwhelming majority of cases were approved automatically. If changes were made, these were usually minor corrections of errors made in the application of a particular law. Indeed, many intendentes did not even require that the municipalities send them anything more than the municipal budget for their approval. In fourteen municipalities that were studied by the author, municipal secretaries and local officials could not recall one instance of a severe clash with the intendente over the latter's refusal to approve a budget or municipal resolution. Indeed, many local officials thought that the intendente was required by law to review only municipal budgets, and not all municipal resolutions and ordinances.

The reason for this lack of stringent supervision of the municipalities is twofold. In the first place, intendentes wished to avoid controversy. It was their job to be the personal representative of the president of the republic in the province and it would have been politically damaging for the chief executive to be accused of "violating municipal autonomy" by objecting to a small matter relating to internal municipal administration. Not only could this have led to attacks on the president from opposition parties and elements within the community affected, but it could have contributed to controversy within the president's own party or other parties of the governing coalition. The intendente was particularly cautious in these matters because his own position depended exclusively on the will of the president. His job was already too sensitive (he was charged with overseeing law, order and personal security in his province) for him to become embroiled in a dispute over a patronage appointment in a small town far from the provincial capital.

---

chileno (Santiago: Colección de estudios jurídicos y sociales, Editorial Jurídica, 1952–54), vol. 1, 232–36. A subsequent decree law (Decreto con Fuerza de Ley no. 22 [1959]) synthesized in one place the many provisions dealing with "interior government." This "Ley organica del Servicio de Gobierno interior" underscored the task of the intendente as auditor of all government and government-sponsored corporations within his jurisdiction.

15. The next few paragraphs are based on interviews with one intendente and officials in two other *intendencias*. They were promised anonymity. The material was corroborated in interviews with Mario Ruiz, head of the Department of Municipalities in the Contraloria (August 23, 1969); Arturo Aylwin, chief counsel, [Fiscal General] of the Contraloria (August 22, 1969); Elena Lagunas, head of the Department of Municipalities of the Ministerio del Interior (August 11, 1969); Sergio Ceppe, former head of the Confederacion Nacional de Municipalidades (July 4, 1969); and interviews with local officials in fourteen municipalities during the summer of 1969.

In the second place, the intendente and his staff did not have the resources or expertise to analyze the complex morass of Chilean jurisprudence and judge whether a particular municipal resolution or ordinance agreed with the spirit and letter of the law. "The truth is that we have neither the time nor the personnel to study with care municipal ordinances and resolutions," one intendente told the author. The director of the Department of Municipalities in the Contraloría General was much harsher on the intendentes, saying that "in reality the performance of the intendentes is zero, or actually minus one. They do absolutely nothing with regard to the municipalities, and what they do is very poorly done. They have no idea of municipal jurisprudence and little knowledge or concern about municipal problems." Indeed, the Contraloría General took over the main task of ruling on whether municipal funds were properly spent, and the Contraloría constantly found errors in budgets approved by intendentes.

Before turning to a discussion of the position of the Contraloría in supervising internal municipal matters, it is necessary to point out that disputes between municipalities and an intendente or governor occurred over other matters, particularly over authorizations of public functions. For example, in the case of the municipality which had secured permission to set up a loudspeaker system for entertainment, a conflict arose when municipal leaders permitted the broadcasting of political speeches. The governor objected, claiming that the municipalities could only broadcast entertainment, not politics. The minister of the interior asked the Contraloría for its opinion on the matter, and the Contraloría agreed that the governor had the right to prevent such broadcasts, if necessary by turning to the director of the Dirección General de Servicios Electricos y de Gas to force a suspension of service.[16]

A similar conflict left bitter feelings in one of the municipalities where the author did field research. The mayor had authorized several political parties to hold demonstrations in the community square. In order for these demonstrations to proceed he had to ask the police force to stop traffic for the duration of the program. However, the governor of the department ordered the police not to stop traffic, but to prevent the demonstrations instead. When the municipality complained to the Contraloría about this incident, the Contraloría made it clear that the governor was correct and that the municipal officials were in error. According to Chilean law, municipalities were not political bodies, but administrative bodies. Thus they could not

16. Dictamen no. 49,530 of the Contraloría General de la República, *Boletín de la Contraloría General de la República*, 37 (January-December, 1964), 563–64.

authorize political functions, which were within the purview of the minister of the interior and his subordinates.

In another town, prior to the festivities for a religious holiday, the mayor issued a traffic decree specifying where visiting buses and trucks could park. Those vehicles which paid higher permit fees were given more desirable parking places. Bus owners were particularly anxious to secure parking around the plaza, assuring them of full buses for the return trip. However, the commander of the police force brought in from the provincial capital to supplement the local force decided that the mayor's instructions were inadequate. In his "orders of the day" he issued a new set of regulations governing parking. This led to confusion and anger on the part of bus and truck owners who complained that they were going to lose business by being forced to park their vehicles in outlying districts of town. Many demanded refunds of their money. The mayor was extremely upset with the police action. Not only did it invalidate weeks of careful planning and work, but it put the mayor in a very embarrassing position vis-a-vis the bus operators and owners who twice a year brought in substantial revenues for the municipal coffers. This embarrassment was aggravated by the fact that the mayor could not return the money because permit fees were paid to the local treasury and not directly to the municipality. The treasurer not only was not authorized to return the payments, he could not be found to explain this fact to the aggrieved party.

The mayor sought to reach the intendente of the province. He received no response. In desperation he decided to contact the minister of the interior himself. He sent several telegrams to the minister and called a couple of prominent politicians of his party, asking them to intervene on his behalf. After almost a day's delay, the minister of the interior's office finally called the commander of the police force, ordering him to bring his "orders of the day" into line with the mayor's decree.

Chilean intendentes and other presidential officials, while charged in theory with broad regulation and supervision of the muncipality, did not really exercise that function. Conflicts which arose between the local government and provincial or departmental authorities stemmed not so much from formal control as it did from jurisdictional disputes over internal security and public order.[17]

17. It should be noted that Peter Cleaves gives an erroneous impression in discussing the powers of the intendente in auditing municipalities. While he makes the point that intendentes do not use the veto power very often, he gives the impression that the veto power is final. This is erroneous. The municipality can overrule the veto in administrative matters and when laws or the Constitution have been allegedly violated, it is up to the Supreme Court to pass final judgment. This fact may give pause to intendentes

As the previous discussion implies, the Contraloría General de la República took over many of the control functions given by law to provincial executives. Even in the most remote community, local officials were very aware of the existence of this agency and fearful that it might call them to task for wrongdoing. Though municipal officials were not always familiar with the auditing authority of the intendente, the opposite was true of the Contraloría. Contraloría was viewed as omnipotent in its ability and authority to catch violations of the law. Mayors interviewed were impressed with the efficiency of the agency in answering their requests for interpretation of legal matters regarding the municipality's operation. The word of the Contraloría was viewed as final.

Local government employees, in particular, were wary of Contraloría scrutiny. As one municipal secretary who had been in office forty-six years put it, "The Contraloría sees in every functionary a thief." Another complained that Contraloría inspectors were "more interested in preserving carbon paper than in seeing to it that the municipality undertake projects for community improvement."

The Chilean Contraloría General de la República was created in 1927 at the recommendation of a United States mission advising the government on financial matters, and given constitutional status in 1943.[18] The Constitution charged Contraloría with the final inspection of all administrative acts carried out by organs of the state, both centralized and decentralized. This included juridical control as well as auditing of accounts. With respect to the first point, the Contraloría was given the power to rule on the legality and constitutionality of all decrees issued by the president and the various public agencies. The president of the republic could overrule the Contraloría's objection on general decrees by obtaining the signature of all of his ministers, in turn subjecting them to possible congressional censure. In decrees dealing with public expenditures not specifically authorized by law, the Contraloría's word was to be final.[19]

wishing to exercise their veto. See Peter S. Cleaves, *Developmental Processes in Chilean Local Government*, Politics of Modernization Series, no. 8 (Berkeley: Institute of International Studies, University of California, 1969).

18. The Contraloría was created by DFL No. 400 of March 26, 1927, and was incorporated into the Constitution through Law 7,727 of 1943. The "texto refundido" of the Contraloría is found in Decreto Supremo no. 2421 of July, 1964. Article xxi of the Constitution deals with this agency. It is an autonomous branch of government, though it is dependent on the Ministry of Finance and the Congress for its budget. In 1962, according to an INSORA study, the Contraloría had 705 employees. See INSORA, *Recursos humanos de la administración pública chilena: Informe Complementario* (Santiago: n.p., 1965), p. 43.

19. Ronald McDonald has exaggerated the powers of the Contraloría by suggesting that it "could constitutionally indict the President for failing to implement the required

With respect to the second point, the Contraloría was authorized to examine and judge the legality of the accounts of all public agencies, including municipalities, and carry the general accounts of the nation. The Contraloría was consequently charged with overseeing all the provisions of the various laws governing municipal finances, including the Organic Law of Municipalities, the Statute on Municipal Employees, the Law on Municipal Income, and the Regulations on Municipal Budgets, so as to prevent theft, fraud, and other anomalies.[20] Inspectors from the Contraloría could check expenditures to determine whether the documentation in question was authentic, the arithmetic and accounting procedures sound, and the laws regarding tax stamps and seals enforced. In addition, they could study whether an expenditure was properly computed in the budget, and whether it was in accord with the purposes stated in the authorization. Finally, they could judge whether the expenditure was carried out by a competent person within the allotted time period.

Likewise, inspectors examining revenues of the municipality were required to investigate whether taxes conformed with laws, ordinances or decrees that determined their size and form of application.[21]

Usually the Contraloría could initiate an investigation of a particular municipality in response to a denunciation by a third party, often one of the municipal councilors or a deputy. If an objection was raised concerning a particular account, as a result of denunciation or regular inspection, a suit or *juicio de cuentas* could be instituted. It should be made clear that if there was a delinquent or criminal act involved, then the proceedings were stopped and the case turned over to the criminal court. In other words, in the juicio de cuentas criminal sanctions for illegal behavior were not sought or applied. Rather, the guilty party was required to replace by a certain date the funds that were illegally allocated. A public functionary who within a month did not meet requirements for repayment could be suspended from his job. Public agencies could also be ordered to take the necessary funds out of the functionary's own salary.[22]

---

reapportionment, but such action would needlessly divide the nation on an apparently dispensable issue." He is also wrong in saying that the Contraloría was created in 1943. See "Apportionment and Party Politics," p. 458.

20. See Enrique Silva Cimma, *Derecho administrativo chileno y comparado* (Santiago: Editorial Juridica, 1961), vol. 2, 318–20; Lionel Bastías Romo, *Responsabilidad en el régimen municipal* (Santiago: Editorial Jurídica, 1966), p. 70.

21. Bastías, *Responsabilidad*, pp. 76–78.

22. The same is true of the Cour de Comptes in France. This court is concerned neither with the responsibility of persons authorizing expenditures nor with the subjective responsibility (i.e., guilt) of the accountants for any errors or irregularities they might discover. If an error is found, the accounts are declared in debit and the

Aside from the juicio de cuentas, the Contraloría could order a *sumario administrativo* (administrative indictment) by proposing that a certain disciplinary measure be instituted against a municipal employee. However, it was up to the municipality or the mayor to see to it that disciplinary action was carried out.[23] Bastías Romo notes that often inspectors from the Contraloría would spend months of work and research in order to suggest a disciplinary action, only to find that it was completely ignored.[24]

The foregoing discussion suggests that Contraloría actually had little authority in controlling *elected* municipal officials. While it could hold that a given action, such as the use of a municipal truck for the mayor's personal errands was illegal, the Contraloría could not punish a mayor or municipal councilor. Contraloría could denounce an illegality before the courts, but the courts would consider it only when a crime was committed, and not when an administrative infraction had been incurred. Since, as the vice-director of the Department of Inspection of the Contraloría noted, the greatest number of irregularities resulted from actions undertaken by the mayors themselves, the lack of enforcement of administrative indictments is not surprising. The only way in which Contraloría might have punished a mayor was after retirement by tapping retirement funds to pay back an illegal expenditure. However, Contraloría officials could not recall one instance in which this had in fact happened.

When financial matters were out of order in a municipality, either the municipal secretary or the treasurer was held responsible. The municipal secretary was the "ministro de fe" of the municipality and could be forced to reinstate payment from his own salary. According to the chief counsel of the Contraloría, mayors or councilors have at times pressured the secretary to make an illegal transfer of funds from one item of the municipal budget to another. In most of those cases the Contraloría was lenient with the municipal employee.

The Contraloría was also limited by the fact that it could not declare a municipal agreement or resolution illegal as it could declare executive decrees illegal. This fact led to some interesting interpretations on the part of the Contraloría which can be illustrated by the following case.

Ministry of Finance can determine the liability of a functionary. If fraud is discovered, then the matter is turned over to the criminal courts. For a discussion of this see F. Ridley and J. Blondel, *Public Administration in France* (London: Routledge & Kegan Paul, 1964), p. 185.

23. Bastías, *Responsabilidad*, p. 67.

24. Ibid., p. 90, and interview with Manuel Valencia, subchief, Department of Inspection of the Contraloría General, August 26, 1969. An inspector told the author: "Municipalities rarely do what they are told to do because they are more concerned with helping the party and the friend."

An inspector of the Contraloría found that the municipality of Maipú had authorized the establishment of two private slaughterhouses. Since Law 5,611, Article i specifies that municipalities should have a monopoly over slaughterhouses, the inspector asked the Contraloría to rule whether municipalities could be allowed to turn over this responsibility to private parties. The Contraloría ruled that municipalities couldn't establish their own slaughterhouses. Only the president of the republic could authorize the establishment of a non-municipal slaughterhouse. However, the Contralor went on to say: "This organ cannot issue a pronouncement on what would happen to private slaughterhouses in the commune of Maipú, in case the authorizations granted by the Illustrious municipality of Maipú were illegal, since it does not belong to the Contraloría General to pass judgment on the legality of municipal resolutions as is prescribed in Article cxv of Law 11,860."[25] In its ruling the Contraloría clearly declared that the municipal action was illegal in general terms. However, the Contraloría disclaimed authority to judge the legality of the specific action of the municipality in question.

The Contraloría's ability to control municipalities was also hindered by a lack of resources and personnel to investigate more than a handful of local governments. The Department of Inspection of the Contraloría in 1969 had a total of fifty inspectors, and only eight dedicated themselves exclusively to municipalities. Consequently, routine inspections were performed infrequently and mainly in large communes. Most inspections were made as a result of specific denunciations.[26]

While only one municipality among the fourteen studied by the author had received an inspector during the past two years, local officials continually expressed apprehension that any error or minor indiscretion could lead to trouble with the Contraloría. The most important factor in reinforcing this apprehension was the widespread publicity given to the few instances in which the Contraloría had been successful in pressing a case against local officials in the court. During the winter of 1969, for example, newspapers across the country featured as frontpage news a case concerning the mayor and all of the councilors of the municipality of Aysen who spent fifteen days in jail for authorizing an illegal Christmas bonus for municipal employees.[27]

25. Dictamen no. 46,244 of the Contraloría General, *Boletín de la Contraloría General de la República*, 37 (1964), 540–44.
26. Interview with the director, Department of Inspection.
27. The mayor and councilors from the municipality of Aysen were denounced by the Contraloría before the court in Ancud. The court ruled that they were guilty and sent them to prison. They spent fifteen days in prison, until the Court of Appeals of Valdivia ruled that the payments were not made for personal profit but with good inten-

Because they feared being caught for illegal activity, and because they lacked the education and resources to interpret the complexities of the many laws affecting municipal government, local officials relied heavily on the Contraloría's rulings. In 1968, the Contraloría issued 1,109 opinions on legal and financial matters directly related to municipalities in response to requests from municipalities, government agencies and private parties. An example of the requests for a ruling which the Contraloría received from municipal officials is the following letter from the mayor of Collipulli:

> This mayoralty takes the liberty of formulating the following consultation:
> The municipality recently acquired a truck for its services which it already possesses.
> The problem concerns how to pay for the driver of said vehicle, since the position has not been created.
> One could opt to hire him under the rubric of new projects, but since he would be an employee for the service of the municipality, that is, for all municipal services, he could not be considered only for "new projects."
> Because of these considerations, and in view of the need to have a driver for the use of this vehicle, I am taking the liberty of soliciting from you a prompt opinion.
>
> Saluda Atte. a Ud.
>
> Luis H. Risso
> Alcalde
>
> Julio Vivanco Yañez
> Secretario

Al Señor Jefe de la Contraloría General de la Republica, Oficina Zonal Concepción

The head of the regional office of the Contraloría answered as follows:

> The reiterated jurisprudence of this controlling organ has held that the necessary tasks for a stable and permanent municipal service, such as sanitation service, can be performed only by permanent personnel of the Corporation; workers can only be hired for specific tasks, charged to the relevant budget item, and when the tasks are completed, employment must end.
> Nonetheless, this Contraloría has accepted as an exception that in the case of a new project, understood as the creation or extension of a municipal service which satisfies in a direct and immediate fashion the needs of the people, municipalities may hire personnel to handle the new project.
> The creation or extension of sanitation service is considered a new project and consequently there would be no objection to the municipality's hiring a truck driver to engage in that service, provided naturally that such an assign-

tions and ordered them released. The Congress then approved, bypassing the committee stage, a bill giving the municipal officials amnesty while declaring the payments legal, so that municipal employees would not have to return the funds. For some of the Senate debates on this question, see *El Mercurio* (Santiago), June 27, 1969, p. 13.

ment be only for that service and that the municipality not have another functionary who could assume it, and in any case the appropriate job must be created at the legal time.

In accordance with the foregoing, then, the exceptional situation referred to is the only one which would permit the Illustrious Municipality to resolve the problems which it brings to the attention of the Controlling Organ.

Saluda Atte. a Ud.

Hector Benitez Freyhofer
Contraloría General de la
República
Jefe, Oficina Zonal Centro

For the information of local officials, the Contraloría published a monthly "Boletín de Jurisprudencia Municipal," a compilation of *dictámenes* or opinions of the Contraloría which local officials used as guidelines in performing their duties. These advisory opinions were written in a special office in the Contraloría which the Christian Democrats set up to deal specifically with municipal problems.

The creation of this office represented an attempt on the part of the Christian Democrats to put more emphasis on the "advisory" and educational function, as opposed to the punitive "control" function. As the head of this office told the author, "Officials must be helped; we are trying to change the idea of the Contraloría as a policeman standing on the corner, ready to beat people with his nightstick." Aside from informational material sent to municipalities and answers to requests for a judgment on specific problems, this department also sent auditors to various municipalities to advise civil servants on methods for improving local administration. The auditors are not sent in in response to a denunciation, but as advisors. If they find errors, they try to educate the local officials rather than present them with an indictment for illegal activity. An indictment would result only from repeated violations. The creation of this special auditing section within the "subdepartment of municipalities" led to internal conflict and rivalry with the older and larger Departamento de Inspección (Department of Inspection). The inspectors feared that if various offices dealing with substantive areas set up auditing sections, their function might very well be replaced. They also scoffed at the "educational" approach. Because of this internal rivalry and scarce personnel, the auditors of the Department of Municipalities concentrated their auditing activities in the province of Santiago alone.[28]

28. The above paragraphs are based on interviews with the heads of both departments, auditors in both departments, and the Fiscal of the Contraloría. The subdepartment of municipalities can also be understood as an attempt by the Christian Democratic government to influence the Contraloría General. Since only the top officers of the

This brief review of the role of the Contraloría General de la República has suggested that that agency did not possess extensive direct authority over Chilean municipalities. Its jurisdiction over municipalities was quite limited and it lacked the personnel and resources to engage in a thorough control of municipal actions. Nevertheless, in an indirect way the Contraloría did exercise much influence over Chilean local governments. Highly publicized instances of the Contraloría's indictment resulting in punishment of functionaries as well as elected officials gave the agency an awesome reputation for efficiency. Moreover, the Contraloría's interpretations of the complex municipal jurisprudence were essential to the routine functioning of local government.[29]

This chapter has reviewed the fact that agencies of the national government took over several areas within the competence of local governments. At the same time it has suggested that the Intendencia, which in formal terms had a great deal of control over municipalities by virtue of its inspection powers, in practice did not exercise much of a limiting role. The Contraloría took over most of the auditing and review function once entrusted to the intendente. However, the Contraloría's influence over the elected municipal officials is more symbolic than real. It is based on fear resulting from highly publicized indictments and on its ability to interpret the complex municipal law.

If national agencies had taken over important functions formerly under the jurisdiction of local government, did Chilean municipalities retain any important responsibilities? An examination of the activities which municipal governments were still called upon to perform reveals that in the late 1960s they were still charged with the following functions:

1. Functions dealing with community health
   a. Garbage pick-up
   b. Enforcement of the law on alcoholic beverages
   c. Regulation of stables, sewers and drains
   d. Enforcement of norms of hygiene and public health determined by the Servicio Nacional de Salud, following Article xxvi of the Código Sanitario (Sanitary Code) established by Law 10,383 of August 8, 1952

---

agency are appointed by the president, most of the functionaries do not owe their allegiance to the government but to the institution. It was easier to create a new department and staff it with Christian Democrats than to change time-honored practices of other employees.

29. It must be noted that the Contraloría, while providing the most comprehensive and authoritative legal interpretations for municipalities, is not the only agency sending municipalities information on municipal jurisprudence. The National Confederation of Municipalities sends periodic mimeographed circulars to municipalities with legal information.

2. Functions related to urban development
   a. Elaboration upon guidelines set up with the Ministerio de Vivienda y Urbanismo, the "plano regulador" for the community determining zoning patterns
   b. Approval of plans for the formation of new housing developments conforming to D.F.L. No. 224 of August 5, 1953, and administration of them once built
   c. Regulation of construction of buildings on public thoroughfares and inspection of same with authority to order repairs or demolition of buildings presenting a hazard
   d. Naming and numbering of all streets
3. Functions involving community services
   a. Building and servicing of public lighting facilities
   b. Authorization of commercial stands in public areas, such as magazine stands and open markets
   c. Regulation of commercial signs and political propaganda on building walls
   d. Building of sewers, potable water systems, cemeteries, slaughter-houses, etc.
   e. Paving of streets in conjunction with the Dirección de Pavimentación Urbana
4. Functions related to community recreational activities
   a. Building of plazas, sports arenas, parks, theatres, etc. and maintenance of same with municipal budget
   b. Provision of subsidies for theatres, sports clubs, and other wholesome diversions
   c. Granting of permits for dances and popular fiestas in public or private places where admission is open to public
5. Functions related to community education and culture
   a. Creation and maintenance of schools, libraries, museums and other institutions
   b. Granting of prizes and subsidies to promote education
   c. Organization of celebrations of patriotic holidays and other holidays such as Christmas and New Years
6. Functions related to mass transit and transportation
   a. Regulation of the use of public thoroughfares, determination of traffic flows, parking, etc.
   b. Granting of licenses to individuals and vehicles
7. Functions related to public safety and public order
   a. Establishment of rules to guarantee order in public places
   b. Regulation of begging
   c. Prohibition of gambling establishments and regulation of horse racing[30]

This compilation of municipal functions shows that, while agencies of the national government had involved themselves increasingly in all aspects of national life, local governments retained, at least on

30. This chart combines the lists presented by Jorge Reyes, "Las limitaciones y perspectivas de la Accion municipal en Chile," *Boletín informativo PLANDES*, p. 34, and Ramirez, Salazar and Zunino, *Sistema de gobierno local*, pp. 28–30.

paper, wide-ranging responsibilities. Indeed, if they were capable of fully carrying out their mandate, it would be difficult to dismiss these functions as "administrative matters of minor importance." Most of these municipal activities were basic to the quality of life of the local community. They involved direct administration or indirect control and regulation of crucial services. Indeed, it can be argued that the whole range of municipal services directly affects the average Chilean town dweller more than national policy decisions on matters of national importance.

And yet it is still not clear whether Chilean local governments possessed the resources and capabilities to carry out those functions still under their jurisdiction. Were Chilean municipalities too poor to do justice to their responsibility, as many observers have suggested? An answer to this question can be obtained by examining the general financial condition of local governments in Chile.

The Scarcity of Financial Resources in Local Government

Mayors, municipal councilors and municipal secretaries were almost unanimous in stating that the basic problem of the municipality is the lack of adequate resources for municipal programs. They complained that it is the lack of funding that has put them at a disadvantage with the national government and led to increasing involvement of national agencies in local affairs. One *regidor* (municipal councilor) remarked: "The state harasses the municipalities too much; a large sum of resources, for example, must be turned over to the Junta de Auxilio Escolar (Committee for Student Aid), and the municipality has no say in their expenditures." Another remarked bitterly: "The government has taken billions of pesos away from the municipality."

Municipal funds were collected through the treasury of the central government, and certain percentages were due to be returned each year. "We are subject to an inventory. All of the funds go to national coffers. It is not fair that the municipality not get more money back."

In different municipalities different complaints were heard about services no longer administered by the municipality. Thus Rosario,[31] which used to collect large sums of money from licensing buses coming to the religious festival, could no longer set ticket prices in public transportation, a function taken over by the Under-Secretariat of Transportation. Taxis were also eliminated from municipal control by the Under-Secretariat. By 1970, local government re-

31. The names of municipalities have been changed to protect the identity of persons interviewed.

ceived only thirty-three percent of the income from automobile licenses, a traditional source of municipal funds.

One of the most serious complaints raised in several municipalities was that community residents were not paying their license fees. Citizens just simply did not have the money, and mayors and regidores found that it was unpopular to force people to pay. The mayor of Manzanal noted that in his city sixty percent of the people had not paid their license fees because other debts took first priority. In Colinas a large deficit of 80,000 escudos awaited the collection of licenses and permits to be settled. For the same reason, Puente was two months behind in the payment of salaries. Since municipal employees' salaries made up the bulk of the budget, very few resources were available for much else.

Municipal officials also complained that funds which they had coming to them were not returned by the national government. Taxes, collected through local treasuries, were sent to the Tesorería General de la República (National Treasury). It was up to the Departamento Financiero (Financial Department) of the Ministry of Finance to return the appropriate amounts to each municipality. In Quille the state returned only 500 escudos of the total sum of 15,000 escudos which the local officials said was coming to them. Indeed, Chilean municipal officials argued that the government owed municipalities over 100 million escudos. This figure was based on Law 15,764, Article viii, (provisional) which specified that municipalities were entitled to seven percent of the income tax in relation to urban assessed value. Central government authorities would always underestimate what this seven percent would yield and turn over to municipalities only the estimated figure. Thus, in 1970 the government turned over the estimated 160 million escudos when the tax actually yielded 327 million. Officials of the National Confederation of Municipalities (CONAM) strongly questioned the legality of that practice and took their case to the Contraloría for a ruling. Though Contraloría ruled that the Ministry of Finance was required to make the funds available to local governments, the head of the Financial Department of the Ministry of Finance strongly disputed that decision. He argued that budget laws, approved each year by the Congress, automatically modified any previous legislation including Law 15,764.[32] Contraloría had no authority to compel the Ministry of Finance to channel funds into municipal coffers when other areas received greater priority.

32. Based on interviews with the general secretary of CONAM, the head of the Department of Municipalities of the Contraloría General, the head of the Departamento Financiero, Ministerio de Hacienda, technical experts in the Ministerio de Hacienda and local officials. The minister of finance by mid-1970 was forced to argue that the government did not owe municipalities funds. See *El Ilustrado*, August 5, 1970, p. 4.

Often, however, municipalities did not receive the funds that were coming to them because mayors or regidores failed to request the appropriate amounts once the decree authorizing payment was enacted. The Departamento Financiero did not inform municipalities when the corresponding decree was issued and it was up to local officials to be on the lookout for the decree.[33]

A final problem mentioned by several local officials concerned the fact that Impuestos Internos (Internal Revenue) had fallen behind in its property assessment. Particularly in rural areas the legal value of property was often extremely low, thus depriving municipalities of potential income.

An analysis of the general financial situation of Chilean municipalities clearly raises serious questions regarding the capabilities of local government. Financial resources, as reflected in the municipal budgets, are extremely meager, and the share of governmental expenditures corresponding to municipalities is only a fraction of national government expenditures.[34]

In the last twenty-five years, the per capita funds available to Chilean municipalities have been minuscule and have remained constant despite a dramatic rise in urbanization and in the need for municipal services. In 1967 the per capita budget of Chilean municipalities was $8.18 (U.S. dollars). By way of contrast the per capita budget of local governments in the State of California in 1967 was $121.10 or thirteen times greater than the Chilean figure.[35] The lack of resources of local governments in Chile can be further appreciated by contrasting them with the resources available to the central government. Table 2.2 gives the percentage of the national government budget which corresponded to Chilean municipalities.

Table 2.2. Municipal budgets as a percentage of governmental expenditures.

Year	1896	1937	1945	1956	1963	1967
Percentage	11.40	9.66	9.22	6.90	6.93	6.40

Source: Data for 1896 from Chile, Oficina Central de Estadísticas, *Sinopsis Estadística y Geográfica de la República de Chile en 1897* (Santiago, n.p., 1898), calculated from information on pp. 61 and 209; data for 1937 calculated from information in Chile, Dirección General de Estadísticas, *Finanzas, Bancos y Cajas Sociales* (Santiago, n.p., 1937), pp. 2, 142–43. The rest of the figures are from Cleaves, *Developmental Processes*, p. 27.

33. See chapter 6 for further references to this problem.
34. In a study of these budgets DESAL showed that from 1952 to 1958, per capita municipal income remained virtually the same. See DESAL, *Antecedentes y Criterios para una Reforma del Gobierno municipal* (Santiago: DESAL, 1967), p. 166.
35. Cleaves, *Developmental Processes*, table 5, p. 29.

The table shows that municipal budgets have constituted approximately one tenth of the national budget for decades and have actually declined to less than seven percent starting in the decade of the 1950s.[36] By contrast, in 1960 state and local governments in the United States accounted for forty percent of all governmental expenditures and local governments alone for twenty-six percent. Using the same measure utilized in examining Chilean municipal budgets, this means that the budgets for local governments in the United States constituted 44.2 percent of the national budget in the year 1960.[37]

A more specific analysis of municipal expenditures will help to complete this examination of the resources available to Chilean local officials. Turning to investment funds, the evidence presented in table 2.3 suggests that these have increased at a much slower rate than national government investments. The growth of investment of the national government from 1960 to 1965 was by 351.98 percent, whereas the growth in municipal investments amounted to only ninety-three percent.

More significant is the fact that most municipal resources were not used for projects to improve the life of the local community but were used to meet the operating expenses of municipalities. Indeed, a clear trend can be discerned in table 2.4 which examines the proportion of the budgets expended for salaries and social benefits. Expenditures for these items have increased considerably over time. In 1896 they represented less than seventeen percent of all expendi-

Table 2.3. Comparison of investments of the central government and municipalities in selected years.

Year	Growth of central government investment	Growth of local government investment
1960	100.00	100.00
1961	134.83	97.70
1962	218.26	121.97
1963	295.21	142.38
1965	451.98	193.16

Source: Ramirez, Salazar and Zunino, *Sistema de gobierno local*, p. 16. Data was compiled from the Dirección de Estadísticas y Censos, *Anuarios*, for the respective years.

36. Most analyses of the finances of municipal government imply that this situation represents a serious deterioration of the place of local government in national life. What is striking, however, is that in 1896, five years after municipal autonomy was introduced, the municipal expenditures as a percentage of government expenditures was only 11.4 percent. For a discussion of municipal budgets during that period see chapter 8.

37. Herbert Kaufman, *Politics and Policies in State and Local Governments* (Englewood, N.J.: Prentice-Hall, Inc., 1963), p. 21.

tures, while in 1966 they represented sixty percent. The largest increase came about during the 1960s.[38]

These municipal expenditures on wages and other benefits have come under severe criticism from Chilean students of local administration who have argued that local posts are merely created to accommodate political pressures.[39] They have noted that there has been a parallel decline in expenditures on new projects, ongoing projects, and property acquisitions. Table 2.5 confirms that only a very small fraction of municipal budgets goes to investments in new projects and ongoing projects of the municipality.[40]

Table 2.4. Proportion of municipal budgets expended on salaries and social benefits in selected years.[a]

Year	1896[b]	1935	1940	1950	1960	1963	1966
Percentage	16.9	33.1	49.6	39.3	59.1	61.7	58.9

[a] Calculated from figures given in the following publications: *Finanzas, Bancos y Cajas Sociales* (1941), pp. 142–43; *Finanzas, Bancos y Cajas Sociales* (1966), pp. 47–48; *Sinopsis Estadística y Geográfica de la República de Chile en 1897*, p. 61.

[b] Includes amounts spent on office expenses as well.

Table 2.5. Percentage of municipal budget spent on new projects and projects in progress and property acquisition.

Year	New projects	Ongoing projects and property acquisition
1960	8.55%	4.54%
1963	6.65	3.89
1966	5.23	3.48

Source: Finanzas, Bancos y Cajas Sociales (1966), p. 48.

38. The table shows that in 1940 the percentage of the budget devoted to salaries increased substantially over the 1935 figure, but dropped again in 1950. This was probably due to the advent of the Popular Front government of 1938 and the large earthquake of 1939. Social benefits increased after the Popular Front by a few percentage points, but the rise was due more to the great increase in wage laborers hired by municipalities. In 1936 regular salaries represented a larger proportion of the budget than wages. By 1940, however, wages took one-third more of the municipal budget than salaries. See *Finanzas, Bancos y Cajas Sociales* (1941), p. 143. It should be noted that the law prohibits the expenditure of more than fifty percent of the municipal budget on salaries, but this prohibition does not extend to other welfare fringe benefits. Some municipalities spend as much as eighty percent on wages and other benefits.

39. For example, see Jorge Reyes, "Las limitaciones y perspectivas de la acción municipal en Chile," *Boletín Informativo PLANDES*, 23 (September-October, 1967), 35.

40. It was not possible to obtain figures for the earlier dates because it was not possible to determine whether similar budget items were placed in similar categories.

In 1966 salaries and benefits accounted for the highest expenditures, followed by payments for the utilities of the municipal building. The rest of the expenditures were earmarked for such items as subsidies, travel expenses, and maintenance. These items as well as "new projects and investments" fluctuated around six percent each. In general terms, Chilean municipalities had very slim resources to meet their constitutional mandate.

Obviously some municipalities were even in more difficult straits than the national figures would imply. For example, the small rural municipality of Achao in the province of Magallanes had, in 1960, a population of 11,900 and a per capita income from ordinary sources of E°1.3. In 1966 Achao spent seventy-two percent of its budget on salaries and social benefits for its employees. The second largest item in the budget, representing twenty-one percent of total expenditures, was devoted to payment of pending accounts. No resources whatsoever were budgeted for new projects or even for the maintenance of old projects. Another impoverished municipality was Santa Juana, located in the province of Concepción, only a few miles from the city of Concepción, the third most important metropolitan center in Chile. Also a rural municipality, Santa Juana's per capita income in 1961 was E°1.00. Sixty-three percent of its budget in 1966 was expended on salaries and social benefits. The total amount of money set aside for new projects for the entire year was E°400.00 (or approximately $46.00).

In sharp contrast is the case of Las Condes, a wealthy suburb of Santiago. With a population of 86,000 in 1960, Las Condes had a per capita income of approximately E°80.00. It invested less of its income in salaries and wages and social benefits than its poorer counterparts, with 42.2 percent invested to this purpose. A small percentage – only 8.2 percent – of the budget was invested in new and older projects. However, this sum amounted to E°1,053,160, enabling the municipality to carry out tangible new programs. The great disparity between a few wealthy municipalities and the many poorer ones is detailed in table 2.6.

The table reveals that sixty-seven percent of Chilean municipalities with forty-two percent of the population of the country had per capita incomes of less than E°4.00, whereas four percent of the municipalities with thirteen percent of the country's population had per capita incomes which fluctuate between E°16.00 and E°27.00. Put in other terms, municipalities with 42.3 percent of the population

---

However, there is some indication that the figure for these items was never substantial. Thus in 1950 a category for projects and purchases of real estate represented only seven percent of the total budget. See *Finanzas, Bancos y Cajas Sociales* (1951).

50 · Political Brokers in Chile

received 14.1 percent of ordinary municipal income, while those
with 77.4 percent of the population receive 45.5 percent of the
resources. Those with 86.7 percent of the population receive 62.8
percent of the income.

DESAL students and others have argued that agricultural municipalities in agricultural communes have the greatest difficulty.
While it is true that richer municipalities are invariably urban,
multiple regression analysis with per capita income as the dependent
variable and various socioeconomic characteristics as independent
variables shows that in general agricultural communities are slightly
better off than their more urban counterparts. Particularly in the
Santiago, Valdivia-Osorno, and Chiloe-Aysen-Magallanes regions
agriculture correlates positively with per capita income. Only in the
Concepción-Arauco region is the relationship negative, even if
slightly. Table 2.7 presents the simple correlation coefficients for the
nation and by region between two income variables and one expenditure variable. Multiple regression analysis shows that socioeconomic characteristics of communities explain little of the variance
in these same variables.

The financial situation of Chilean municipalities became so critical
by mid-1970 that the head of the National Confederation of Municipalities sought relief for local governments from the president himself.[41] Several municipalities literally went bankrupt.[42] By the end
of the year the government was forced to accede to these demands
by dipping into the two percent margin in the national budget set

Table 2.6. Distribution of municipal income among four categories
of Chilean municipalities in 1966.

Income per capita	No. of municipalities	Percent	Population	Percent	Percent rural
E°0–3.99	180	67.41	3,261,294	42.30	71.2
E°4–7.99	58	21.72	2,707,390	35.12	11.6
E°8–15.99	19	7.12	717,032	9.30	9.0
E°16–27	10	3.75	1,023,546	13.28	4.4
Total	267	100.00	7,709,262	100.00	

Source: compiled from data in DESAL, Antecedentes y Criterios, pp. 175–80.

41. Interviews with officials of the Confederación Nacional de Municipalidades in
August 1974. See also El Siglo, November 9, 1970, p. 9; La Nación, August 24, 1970,
p. 10.
42. See La Nación, January 5, 1971, p. 7; Ereilla, February 3, 1971, p. 34–36, El
Diario Ilustrado, October 29, 1970, p. 6.

aside for national catastrophes.[43] The Frei administration also allotted $10 million dollars from its ample fund of currency reserves for municipal equipment.

Commissions set up at the end of the Frei administration and at the beginning of the Allende government to introduce reforms in municipal government and finance simply did not get very far. In the tur-

Table 2.7. Simple correlations between political, social and economic variables and two income and one expenditure variable for Chilean municipalities by regions and national total.

		Size	Urb	Agr	Ming	Indst	Serv	Comp	Part	Paving
Region I	Income	−26	−28	26	−	−12	−	−14	−34	−05
Tarapacá-	Ex. Inc.	−23	−30	27	−	−13	−	−13	−32	−06
Coquimbo	New Work	−22	−16	07	−	−13	−	−25	−03	−05
Region II	Income	−29	−38	19	−	−21	−	−26	33	−13
Acongagua-	Ex. Inc.	−33	−53	46	−	−36	−	59	18	08
Valparaiso	New Work	−19	−09	13	−	−	−	−11	09	06
Region III	Income	−31	−45	43	−	−37	−	−29	−	16
Santiago	Ex. Inc.	−14	−30	22	−	−13	−	−25	20	−17
	New Work	−23	−08	21	−	−23	−	−21	11	−01
Region IV	Income	−13	−10	14	−	−12	−	−27	−15	03
O'Higgins-	Ex. Inc.	−13	−14	13	−	−05	−	−29	−18	−08
Ñuble	New Work	−35	−18	23	−	−25	−	−23	07	14
Region V	Income	17	12	−18		53	−	29	06	−10
Concepción-	Ex. Inc.	−44	−68	68	−	−55	−	−23	−37	−53
Arauco	New Work	−33	−49	49	−	−35	−	15	−25	27
Region VI	Income	−12	−07	−04	−	09	−	−00	16	09
Bío-Bío	Ex. Inc.	−33	−40	39	−	−34	−	−49	−21	25
Cautín	New Work	−29	−34	46	−	−38	−	−07	−26	06
Region VII	Income	−44	−45	44	−	−40	−	−30	−54	−27
Valdivia	Ex. Inc.	−44	−45	44	−	−40	−	−30	−54	−27
Chiloe	New Work	−29	−31	30	−	−19	−	−29	−40	−33
Region VIII	Income	−29	−49	60	−	−17	−	−45	−21	−31
Aysen	Exc. Inc.	−29	−49	60	−	−17	−	−45	−21	−31
Magallanes	New Work	−25	−46	54	−	−50	−	−42	−50	−10
Nation	Income	−09	−13	14	−05	−09	−13	−09	−09	−00
	Exc. Inc.	−16	−19	14	03	−12	−19	−16	−30	−05
	New Work	−18	−28	28	−13	−19	−23	−20	−26	−02

Note: 'Income' is the total income of the municipality; 'Ex. Inc.' is extraordinary income from loans and grants; 'New Work' is expenditure on new projects. The independent variables include indicators of size, urbanization, agriculture, mining, industry, services, party competition, electoral participation, and an index of government per capita investment in paving.

43. *El Mercurio*, December 11, 1971, p. 26.

bulent Allende years municipal government did not come to occupy a position of priority. When the coup overthrew the constitutional regime, municipal governments were as poor as ever.

The growing involvement of government in Chilean economic and social life resulted in the take-over of agencies of the national government of functions which the Constitution placed under the jurisdiction of municipal governments. However, for legal, financial and political reasons, direct control over municipal affairs by the intendants and the Contraloría General de la República has not been as significant as might be expected at first glance.

The erosion of municipal functions should not, however, obscure the fact that Chilean local governments retained primary jurisdiction over vital matters affecting the community. The problem was not so much a loss of functions as a great scarcity of resources. Municipalities had meager per capita incomes and most of their funds were expended on salaries and fringe benefits; only a small fraction was spent on new projects.

The scarce resources of municipalities combined with the reduction of municipal jurisdiction leads to the conclusion that the stakes in local politics were quite meager. These findings, combined with the findings of the previous chapter, lead to a curious paradox: competitiveness to achieve local office was very keen; and yet, local office did not seem to involve significant stakes. An in-depth study of a sample of local communities is necessary in order to clarify this ambiguity and provide a fuller picture of the dynamics of Chilean local politics. However, before turning to such a study, the next chapter will continue to use national level data to probe one possible explanation for the paradox in question. That explanation, derived from the Chilean literature on local government as well as more theoretical literature on Latin American politics, suggests that localities are competitive, despite low resources, because the attainment of local office was a basic stepping-stone in a national political career.

3. Local Government and Political Recruitment: The Test of an Hypothesis

Students of local administration have speculated widely on the causes of what they view to be poor performance on the part of Chile's municipalities. Though problems of financial deficit and waning jurisdiction were attributed to many factors, such as misguided centralism and scarcity of resources, a substantial portion of the blame was placed on the neglect of municipal business by local elected officials. According to this interpretation, municipal councilors and mayors were simply too busy with "politiquería" or politicking to concern themselves with local planning and programming. One of the principal papers at a conference on the "crisis" of local government in Chile attributed this to the fact that "councilors tend to consider the municipality as a mere stage in their political career culminating in the National Congress, and not as an entity through which they can contribute to the welfare of the community."[1] Similar conclusions were reached in a study on "Urban Leadership in Latin America" by two U.S. scholars. In their report, D. A. Chalmers and D. H. Riddle noted that "the local leader functions primarily as a party member rather than as a local official, thus diverting his attention from local problems to those of his party in strengthening itself at the national level. Political careers are not built on success in local government, except through winning elections. Consequently, there is a very strong tendency for the local official to see his personal career in national and party terms rather than in terms of success in governing the city."[2]

The proposition that attainment of local office was a fundamental stepping-stone in structuring a national political career may help to resolve the paradox observed in the previous chapter. A serious lack of resources for municipal governments may not have prevented a highly competitive race for local elected posts simply because the

1. See Jorge López R., "La crisis municipal chilena en enfoque bajo el concepto de eficiencia," *Boletín Informativo PLANDES*, 23 (1967), 49. For similar sentiments see the summary remarks of the convener of the conference, Juan Astica, pp. 31–32. See also Diógenes Ramírez Arriagada, *Autoridad, communicaciones y estabilidad en la administración municipal* (Santiago: INSORA, 1968, mimeographed), p. 58, and Arturo Aylwin A., Hugo Alfonso L. and Patricio Oyaneder V., eds., *Análisis crítico del régimen municipal y proposiciones para una nueva legislación* (Santiago: Editorial Jurídica de Chile, 1971), p. 106.

2. Douglas A. Chalmers and Donald H. Riddle, "Urban Leadership in Latin America: Report of the Eageton Institute of Politics to USAID" (n.d., mimeographed).

objective of the race was not successful local governance but the achievement of a position that would lead to higher office. According to this interpretation, the primary function of local government was not policy formulation and implementation but the provision of the first stage in the political recruitment process.

James Payne, in studying Colombian politics has made similar observations about the importance of local office holding as an end in itself. Payne, however, has gone further in attempting to provide a theoretical explanation for this phenomenon. Resorting to a cultural approach, he argues that a "status orientation," as opposed to a "program orientation," is the leit-motif of Colombian politics. Colombian politicians avoid cooperation and planning and concentrate on obtaining political positions for the prestige they bestow on the occupant. Since Colombian politics is supposed to be open, individuals could easily move up the political hierarchy.[3] A lack of municipal resources in a society with a "program orientation" might diminish the competitive drive to control local office. This would not be the case in a society such as Colombia where "status orientation" predominates.

Payne's distinction is a central one to the literature on political culture. Sidney Verba, for example, argues that in some societies the "expressive" side of politics predominates over the "instrumental" side. He notes that "this is perhaps the most significant general distinction that can be made about political beliefs. It is essentially a distinction between, on the one hand, beliefs that stress political activity carried on for its own sake or political institutions that are valued for their own sake and, on the other, beliefs that focus on political activity or political institutions in terms of their usefulness for producing other satisfactions."[4] The expressive-instrumental dichotomy has been widely used by scholars who have studied extreme competitiveness and factionalism in other parts of the world. In a review of some of that literature Norman Nicholson notes that in many countries, primarily Asian, politics revolves around "the battle for status."[5] As he says, "factional systems typically have a political culture in which personal power and the rewards associated with it represent the main goal of political activity. In such a system,

3. See James L. Payne, *Patterns of Conflict in Colombia* (New Haven: Yale University Press, 1968), especially pp. 45–50. See also James L. Payne and Oliver H. Woshinsky, "Incentives for Political Participation," *World Politics*, 24, no. 4 (July, 1972), 524–28.

4. Sidney Verba, "Comparative Political Culture," in Lucian W. Pye and Sidney Verba, eds., *Political Culture and Political Development* (Princeton: Princeton University Press, 1965), p. 547.

5. Norman K. Nicholson, "The Factional Model and the Study of Politics." *Comparative Political Studies*, 5, no. 3 (October, 1972), 5.

one searches in vain among ideological disputes, policy disagreements, or class conflicts for credible justifications for the constantly
shifting alignments and the intense intraelite struggles."[6]

The purpose of this chapter is to explore the proposition derived
from the literature on local government in Chile that election to local
office constituted a key stepping-stone in structuring a political
career. An examination of this question will help to clarify political
recruitment patterns in that country as well as provide further insight
into the political functions of local government. It should be stressed
that the chapter will not explore the motivations of individuals in
seeking local office, but the importance of local office holding in
achieving higher office.[7] The conclusion to part II of this book will
return to a consideration of expressive and instrumental beliefs in an
attempt to characterize Chilean local politics.

Selection and Nomination: The Key Role of Political Parties

Before turning to the role of local government in the recruitment
process, it is necessary to make a few preliminary remarks about the
legal and political context of candidate nomination and selection in
Chile. This is crucial, because the formal procedures set the param-
eters of the recruitment process.[8]

The most salient characteristic of these formal rules is that they
encouraged the nomination of candidates presented by strong party
organizations. This is not surprising: the legal aspects of the electoral
and nominating system favored the stronger party organizations
precisely because strong parties contributed to the shaping of the
formal rules. Especially in recent years this reciprocal relationship
has worked to the disadvantage of weak parties and independent
candidacies.[9]

6. Nicholson, "The Factional Model," p. 301.

7. These factors are closely interrelated. Perceptions of local officials must have some
congruence with reality to develop in the first place, and must be reinforced if they are
to last. In other words, objective opportunity for advancement must exist if this is the
primary motivating factor in seeking local office.

8. Austin Ranney, in his study of political recruitment in Britain, has noted the
importance of distinguishing between "candidate selection" and "nomination." The
latter refers to the legal declaration of candidacy before government officials, whereas
the former refers to the extra-legal procedures utilized by individual parties in choosing the candidates which they will nominate. This distinction is rarely made in the
United States, where direct primaries sanctioned by state law make candidate selection
and formal nomination one and the same process. In Chile, as in Britain, it is essential
to keep this distinction in mind. Austin Ranney, *Pathways to Parliament: Candidate
Selection in Britain* (Madison and Milwaukee: University of Wisconsin Press, 1965),
pp. vii–viii.

9. See chapter 8 for a discussion of some aspects of the history of electoral legislation.

While Chilean law recognized independent candidacies, the nominating procedures made it very difficult for independents to seek electoral office. This is the case because independent candidates had to obtain the signatures of a relatively large number of registered voters pledging support for their candidacies. What made it particularly difficult to obtain these signatures was the legal requirement that registered voters declare their support for the candidate in person, before departmental officials. Independent candidates for deputy and senator had to obtain 2,000 and 5,000 such signatures, respectively.[10] The difficulty of this requirement can be illustrated by the fact that in the 1969 election the average number of votes received in the country as a whole by each candidate for deputy was 4,200. If the Santiago area with its larger population centers is excluded, the average number of votes received was 3,700.[11] The required signatures for candidacies for the municipal councils varied according to the size of the commune in question, and obtaining the appropriate number of signatures was equally difficult.[12] Furthermore, and in spite of the fact that Chile had a multimember district electoral system, registered voters could patronize only one independent candidacy.[13]

In order to protect against "political adventurism," Chilean law also prescribed that an individual couldn't file an independent candidacy if he belonged to any political party for at least 180 days before the declaration of candidacy.[14] Finally, all candidates had to be nominated long before the election itself. As Alejandro Silva Bascuñan noted, this provision was designed to "contribute to the discipline and prestige of political parties and avoid last-minute surprises and alliances that discredit political life and introduce confusion and skepticism on the part of the electorate."[15] Candidates for deputy and senator had to be nominated at least 120 days before ordinary elections were held.[16]

While the filing of independent candidacies was made difficult by the formal rules, these rules clearly encouraged the party organiza-

10. Alejandro Silva Bascuñan, *Tratado de derecho constitucional* (3 vols.; Santiago: Editorial Jurídica de Chile, 1963), vol. 2, p. 169.
11. Calculated from preliminary election returns in Senado, Oficina de Informaciones, *Boletín de Información General*, 48 (April 10, 1969).
12. According to Charles Parrish, Arpad von Lazar and Jorge Tapia, in at least one commune the required signatures amounted to twenty-five percent of the registered voters. See *Chile Election Factbook* (Washington, D.C.: Institute for Comparative Study of Political Systems [ICOPS], 1967).
13. Silva, *Tratado de derecho*, vol. 2, p. 169.
14. Ibid., p. 170.
15. Ibid., p. 167.
16. Ibid., p. 168.

tions' recruitment functions. Thus parties could file as many candidacies as allowed by law without obtaining signatures from registered voters. Furthermore, the law encouraged unity and central authority in party structures by requiring that nominations be filed by the "central directives of the political parties," and not by local units or individual party leaders.[17] In 1969, out of 768 candidates for deputy in the country, all but two were nominated by political parties.[18]

The law also discouraged the formation of parties by independent elements or disgruntled members of established parties. For a party to be legally recognized it had to register at the Dirección del Registro Electoral. Written applications included the party statutes, the names of members of the executive committees, and, most importantly, the notarized signatures of at least 10,000 registered voters supporting the new political organization. Furthermore, new parties could not apply for legal status after 240 days before an election, dampening the possibility of last-minute political movements' being formed for an electoral contest. Strong party organizations were also favored by the provision that if a party lost representation in Congress, it ceased to be a registered political party. This was the case even if the party in question controlled many local governmental posts.[19]

The foregoing discussion of the formal nominating procedures in Chile has made it clear that legal requirements encouraged political parties to be the principal recruiters of candidates for political office.[20] How then did Chilean parties select those candidates for nomination?

In general, as in British politics, the candidate selection process in Chile was closed rather than open. The decision on the selection of candidates for different political posts was made by party organs privately, in contrast to the United States practice of selecting candidates in public primaries.[21] Whether candidate selection was per-

17. Ibid.
18. Dirección del Registro Electoral.
19. Silva, *Tratado de derecho*, vol. 3, p. 383.
20. The electoral requirements favoring party organization do not affect the conclusions of the first chapter, which stressed the high rate of party competition in elections of various kinds across the country. Certainly the fact that parties had the ability to present candidates in all constituencies, to the disadvantage of independents, provided the structural setting for party competition. But competition was dependent on the divisions of the community in response to party alternatives. Several parties could thus be presented in a given community, with only one receiving the overwhelming majority of the vote. This is illustrated by the fate of the PADENA in the 1969 congressional election. PADENA presented 119 candidates in all electoral districts but none were elected to the Chamber of Deputies.
21. For the United States, see Frank J. Sorauf, *Political Parties in the American System* (Boston and Toronto: Little, Brown and Company, 1964), pp. 101–2. On Britain, see Ranney, *Pathways to Parliament*, passim.

formed democratically within each party organization depended both on the type of election and the organizational characteristics of the party in question. Generally, in the selection of candidates for local office, local and especially provincial party committees were more influential. When it came to choosing candidates for the Congress, however, the national executive committees of the various parties were more important, often making the final decision on nominations from a list drawn up by regional and local committees. The executive committee's powers were enhanced by its ability to withdraw a nomination.[22]

By way of illustration the Christian Democratic party began its nomination of local candidates six months before municipal elections. Each potential candidate had to be sponsored by a *militante* (party activist) and had to submit an application with the following information:

1. Complete personal information.
2. Employment history for the previous two years.
3. Information on attendance at doctrinal and leadership training courses.
4. Offices held in other organizations, such as unions, cooperatives and social groups.
5. Offices held within the party and length of service in each office.
6. A statement discussing the areas of the commune in which the potential candidate had "electoral influence" and an estimate of the total vote he could command.
7. A brief exposition of his thinking with respect to the principal problems of the municipality and the particular "orientation" he intended to follow as a councilor.

Once this period of "precandidacy" was over, the candidates were selected by the local communal party organization or *junta communal*. A list of those receiving the greatest number of votes was sent to the *junta provincial* (provincial party organization) for final approval. This body had final authority to appoint half of all local candidates to appear on the local party list and could fix the order in which the candidates appeared on the ballot. It could also reject all of the names proposed by the local organization and designate other candidates, subject to appeal to the national council and the party president.[23]

The Chilean Radical party's *asambleas* had considerably more jurisdiction over matters of policy and candidate selection than the local units of other parties. The Communist party, on the other hand, was the most centralized organization, with rigid authority lines plac-

22. Silva, *Tratado de derecho*, vol. 2, 1970.
23. This material comes from the Partido Demócrata Cristiano, *Estatutos del Partido Demócrata Cristiano, 1963* (Santiago: Impresores el Imparcial, 1963), pp. 27–29, cited by Francis Giles Wayland Smith, "The Christian Democratic Party in Chile: A Study of Political Organization and Action," (Ph.D. dissertation, Syracuse University, 1968), p. 85.

ing candidate selection for all elections in the hands of the party's Central Committee.[24]

Another area where the influence of the national executive committee of the various parties became very important was in their ability to form electoral pacts with other parties. Before the electoral reforms of 1958, national party officials actually made agreements to present common lists. Though the 1958 and 1960 reforms prohibited such practices, pacts were still structured as one party agreed not to present candidates in a certain district in return for the other party's reciprocating in another district.[25] The electoral arrangements for the 1965 congressional election for the Chamber of Deputies are described by Parrish, von Lazar and Tapia as follows:

In the election for the Chamber of Deputies, the pacts were . . . complicated because of the number of voting *agrupaciones* (28). The results of the informal pacts were diverse. The Conservatives offered candidates in nineteen *agrupaciones*, and they supported the Liberal party in six and the Radical list in the three remaining. The Liberal party ran candidates in 25 *agrupaciones*, and, along with the Conservative party, supported the Radical list in the other three. The Christian Democrats ran candidates everywhere, except in the very far south province of Magallanes. The left is traditionally very strong there, and all of the parties outside of the FRAP, including the Christian Democrats, supported the Radical party list. Within the FRAP the Communists ran slates of candidates in three *agrupaciones*, having in these the support of the other parties of the FRAP. The Socialists nominated the only FRAP slate in eight areas while PADENA candidates ran alone in three. The Communists and Socialists offered candidates in six areas, the Communists and PADENA in two *agrupaciones*, and the Socialists and PADENA in one. All three FRAP parties ran together in five areas.[26]

As the authors note, these informal electoral pacts illustrate how the national party authorities sought to maximize their respective parties' voting strength through cooperation with other party organizations.[27] Candidate selection in Chile was consequently conducted almost exclusively by party organizations, with national party officials having considerable say. The phenomenon of self-recruitment was rare.

Local Politics and Political Recruitment

Given the nominating and selection procedures of Chilean parties, did they turn primarily to the ranks of local elected leaders in order

24. Interviews by the author in July, 1969, in Santiago with officers of political committees. See also Federico Gil, *The Political System of Chile* (Boston: Houghton Mifflin Co., 1966), ch. 6. This topic requires detailed empirical study.

25. Silva, *Tratado de derecho*, vol. 2, p. 171.

26. *Chile Election Factbook.*

27. This account deals almost exclusively with maneuvers of parties at the national level, and not with campaigning at the grass roots.

to find candidates for national office? In order to test the hypothesis that local office is primarily a stepping-stone in a national political career, this analysis will focus on recruitment patterns to the Chamber of Deputies, the lower chamber of the Chilean Congress. Since in Chile there were no elected positions between the office of municipal councilor and the Chamber of Deputies, the local arena was a logical recruiting ground for candidates for deputy.[28]

The 150 Chilean deputies were elected in twenty-eight multi-member districts, all of which consist of several departmental units. Since departments were made up of several communes, this meant that electoral districts did not cut through the jurisdiction of individual municipalities. Such an arrangement facilitated the candidacies of local officials in the plural-member districts. The candidacies were further aided by the Chilean practice of scheduling congressional elections two years after the municipal elections. This reduced potential confusion on the part of the electorate and made it possible for local incumbents to run for national office in the prime of their terms, and not after their terms had ended. While Chilean law did not permit the French *cumul*, the holding of local and national offices concurrently, it did permit local officials to run for national office without resigning from the municipal council. Mayors, however, had to resign from the mayoralty if they decided to seek higher office.[29]

An examination of the political backgrounds of Chilean deputies elected in 1969 provides some support for the general hypothesis. Seventy-four or half of all of the 150 members of the chamber had served on a municipal council before being elected to the chamber.[30] Though a majority of all deputies did not have municipal experience, almost fifty percent of their number did come up through municipal ranks. This suggests that while the status of local office holding was not a fundamental requisite to a national career, it did provide a primary recruiting ground for advancement. But, is data on successful candidates enough to evaluate the impact of recruitment patterns on the average councilor? An examination of the backgrounds of 150 successful candidates for deputy tells us little about the objective

28. Thus the "political opportunity rate" was much lower in Chile than in other countries with more elected positions. For an elaboration of this concept see Joseph Schlesinger, "Political Careers and Party Leadership," in Lewis Edinger, ed. *Political Leadership in Industrialized Societies* (New York: John Wiley and Sons, 1967), pp. 269–73.

29. See chapter 5 for a discussion of the legal basis of this prohibition.

30. This data was gathered in the Oficina de Informaciones de la Camara. Local office holding for each deputy was further checked by examining lists of local officials going back two decades. Lists were obtained in the Departamento de Municipalidades, Ministerio del Interior.

chances of the large number of councilors in the nation's 276 municipalities. The focus of the analysis must switch away from the small
group of elected deputies and focus on the larger pool of candidates
for deputy. What was the general likelihood that the average Chilean
councilor would be selected to run for national office? To what extent
did parties turn to municipal ranks in selecting their candidates?

Common sense suggests that since Chile's municipalities had a total
of 1,628 municipal councilors in 1969, the number of councilors that
could be selected as candidates would of necessity have been quite
small. An examination of the local office-holding background of all
candidates confirms this expectation. Column 4 of table 3.1 shows
that in the 1969 congressional race only 9.2 percent of all municipal
councilors were selected to run for the lower house of parliament. The
overwhelming majority of councilors had little prospect of becoming
candidates for higher office.

But to what extent did political parties turn to the ranks of councilors
over individuals with no local government experience in selecting
candidates? Though in general few councilors were selected, it is
still conceivable that Chilean parties sought most of their candidates
from municipal ranks.

Column 5 of table 3.1 provides such information. It shows that even
when incumbent congressmen are excluded, councilors were chosen
as candidates less than one third of the time by the major Chilean
parties.[31] Two thirds of the choices of candidates for the Chamber
of Deputies had no municipal experience.[32]

The table reveals further that there was significant variation among
the parties both in the general likelihood that councilors would be
selected and in the extent to which parties turn to municipal ranks for
recruitment. In general, councilors who were members of parties on
the left had a much greater chance of being selected to run for national
office. The highest number of councilors running for deputy is found
in the Socialist party where a total of 22.2 percent of the parties'
councilors served as candidates. The Communists in turn looked to
15.6 percent of their councilors for the honor of running for the lower

31. It is assumed that incumbents seeking reelection were favored in the recruitment
process by political parties. This assumption is supported by evidence revealing that
106 or 70.6 percent of all incumbents sought reelection in 1969. The focus of the table
is on the *major* Chilean parties because the inclusion of minor parties provides misleading results. This is the case because a minor party, PADENA, presented candidates
for deputy of which only three were municipal officials. But, PADENA had a very small
pool of local officials, only 36, to draw on in nominating candidates.

32. It is conceivable that a candidate for national office who was not an incumbent may
have held local office in a previous term. This possibility was verified by examining
earlier lists. Only one instance was found of an ex-municipal official chosen to run for
deputy.

Table 3.1. Percentage of all Chilean municipal councilors selected as candidates for deputy and percentage of all nonincumbent candidates for deputy with previous municipal service in the 1969 congressional race, by political party.

Party	Column #1 Total number of councilors	Column #2 No. of councilors selected as candidates for deputy	Column #3 No. of candidates for deputy (nonincumbent)	Column #4 Percent of councilors selected as candidates	Column #5 Percent of nonincumbent candidates for deputy who served as municipal councilor
Socialist	194	43	142	22.2	30.3
Communist	135	21	51	15.6	41.2
C.D.	658	26	87	4.0	29.9
Radical	333	27	103	8.1	26.2
National	270	25	133	9.3	18.0
Subtotal	1590	141	509	8.7	27.7
Independent & others	38	8	152	23.6	5.3
Total	1628	149	661	9.2	22.5

Source: Calculated from unpublished lists of municipal councilors elected in 1967 and lists of candidates for deputy selected in 1969, available at the Dirección del Registro Electoral, Santiago, Chile.

chamber. By contrast, the Radicals and the Nationals turned respectively to 8.1 and 9.3 percent of their councilors for a candidacy role. The Christian Democrats paid least attention to their councilors in selecting candidates as only 4.0 percent were selected.[33]

Parties on the Left were also more likely to turn to the ranks of councilors rather than elsewhere in selecting their candidates. This was particularly the case with the Communist candidates, 41.2 percent of which held municipal posts. The Socialists followed with 30.3 percent. The Christian Democrats, however, were close to the Socialists with 29.9 percent. Most likely to turn away from the municipalities for candidates was the rightist National party, with only 18.0 percent of all candidates with municipal experience. The Radicals, with 26.2 percent, were in an intermediary position. However, in no case did a party turn primarily to the ranks of lower level officials in selecting their candidates for national office. Even the Communists selected almost 60 percent of their candidates from nonmunicipal ranks.

The general findings from table 3.1 suggest that the hypothesis that experience in elective local office was a basic stepping-stone in a national political career cannot be fully supported. At the same time, and by implication, it suggests that the objective pattern of political recruitment could not in itself support a generalized pattern of belief among local officials that local office holding was a sure avenue to higher office.

And yet, the evidence presented thus far is too contradictory to venture any firm conclusions. It will be recalled that almost fifty percent of all deputies serving in 1969–73 had municipal experience. Though local office holding did not seem to be an important criteria in becoming a candidate, it is quite significant in actually being elected to public office. An examination of the "success rates" of candidates with municipal experience confirms this impression. Table 3.2 shows that while incumbents were by far the most successful candidates, among the nonincumbent candidates, councilors were almost twice as likely to be elected as noncouncilors.

These findings suggest the possibility that councilors who were selected to run for deputy were not representative of the average councilor and, indeed, that there may be a certification process among local officials themselves which separates those who succeeded in receiving a nomination from the majority who did not. An analysis of the "deviant cases," those municipal councilors who were selected

33. Despite the assertion made by Federico Gil, municipalities did not, by the late 1960s, serve as "schools" for rightist politicians. See Gil, *The Political System of Chile*, p. 250.

to run for higher office, should provide further information in evaluating the status of local office holding in the Chilean recruitment process. Was selection as a candidate a random process? Or were some councilors better certified to be selected than the majority of their peers?

In the absence of social background data for municipal councilors, it is necessary to turn to another kind of data in order to discover whether there are any general uniformities characterizing the deviant cases. This data is aggregate data on the characteristics of the municipalities themselves.

One can hypothesize, for example, that parties were much more likely to recruit candidates for national office from the ranks of councilors in large cities rather than small ones. Presumably, in a larger community, the members of the municipal council had large followings which could make them attractive to parties competing in a highly urbanized society. Analysis of recruitment patterns of local officials in small as opposed to large municipalities confirms this view. In communities of less than 20,000 inhabitants with a total of 63.1 percent of the nation's local officials, only 28.2 percent of the local officials were selected to run for deputy. By contrast, cities with over 20,000 inhabitants provide 71.8 percent of all candidates selected from municipal ranks even though they account for only 36.9 percent of all local officials.[34]

Size, however, is only one of many variables which might play a predominant role in differentiating communities with national candidates from communities without national candidates. And, indeed, other variables may be more important in discriminating between the two types of communities once size is held constant. In order to deter-

Table 3.2. Success rates of incumbents, regidores and other candidates for deputy in the 1969 congressional election.

	Number running	Number elected	Percent elected
Incumbents	106	72	67.9
Regidores	149	32	21.0
Others	513	46	9.0
Total	768	150	

34. Figures on size of communities are from the 1960 Chilean census and are published in Armand Mattelart, *Atlas social de las comunas de Chile* (Santiago: Editorial del Pacífico, 1965). The twenty thousand cut-off point is an arbitrary figure.

mine whether other variables are important and their degree of importance, it is necessary once again to expand the scope of the analysis.

To this end, eleven additional variables will be considered for each Chilean municipality. The variables can be divided into two principal groups: political variables and socioeconomic variables. The first, political variables, are two measures of party competition—one for a local election and one for a congressional election. The inclusion of these variables is suggested by the hypothesis that the more competitive a community the greater the likelihood that parties will turn to that community to select their council candidates.[35] The assumption behind the hypothesis would be that candidates in more highly competitive communities might have greater political skills. Another political variable, political participation, is closely related to the preceding ones. The argument could be made that, where the citizenry participates more, political activity is more intense, and office holders in those areas might be more attractive to party recruiters than candidates from communities where there is less interest in the political process.[36] The fourth and final political variable refers to the level of political importance of the municipality. Municipalities in Chile were divided into three general groups: communal capitals, departmental capitals, and provincial capitals. Clearly, the provincial capitals were more important administrative and political centers than the other two, and departmental capitals were more important than communal capitals. The intendant of the province had his seat in the provincial capital, and party headquarters for the province and provincial branches of government agencies were also located there. The hypothesis can be advanced that the political prominence of a community might very well give officials serving in its local government greater visibility in political circles. In turn, that would contribute to improving the chances in the competition for nomination.[37]

The second category of variables consists of several different measures of the socioeconomic development of the country's communities. Included are measures such as the level of educational

35. An index of party competition was calculated for each commune for both elections. For a discussion of the index, see chapter 1.

36. Participation is the percentage of eligible voters (citizens over 21 who could read and write) who actually voted. Population over 21 literate was calculated for each commune with unpublished data provided by the Dirección de Estadísticas y Censos. Voting data for the 1967 municipal election is from the Dirección del Registro Electoral.

37. A provincial capital was also the capital of the department and the commune where it was located. A departmental capital was also the capital of the commune where it was located.

attendance,[38] the level of medical care,[39] and the per capita expenditures for paving of streets and roads.[40] These indicators focus on different types of indicators of community well-being. Again, one can hypothesize that communities which have been more successful in developing services, either on their own or through state action, might serve as a more likely pool from which to select national candidates. Finally, indicators of occupation can be added to the analysis. These include the percentage of the population in a given community in each of three categories: mining, industry, and services.[41] Particularly the latter two might be related to the growth of a community's economy, bureaucracy, and services and thus provide further distinguishing characteristics. Two final variables, both of a more summary nature, were also included—size and urbanization.[42]

In order to conduct the analysis, it is necessary to turn to a technique capable of determining which of these variables are important in defining differences between communities where local officials are recruited for national office and those where they are not. The most appropriate technique for this purpose is a multiple discriminant function analysis. The technique is valuable because it permits the combination of multiple variables in a line function that will best discriminate between two or more a priori groups. In other words, it permits an evaluation of the relative power of each variable when all variables are considered simultaneously. A variable that might seem important when considered alone may very well be unimportant when all other variables are considered simultaneously. The reverse is also true; a variable that is weak in a univariate comparison may become important when covariance among variables is considered.

In actual analysis, the program takes the variable which discriminates most among the two or more groups and considers it first. Because it can discriminate the groups and the intercorrelations with all other items, each of the rest of the variables is then considered in order of its contribution to explaining the difference between groups.

38. This indicator is the percentage of the population between the ages of 7 and 14 attending school in 1960. The indicator was calculated by Jorge López, Francisco Salazar and Diógenes Ramirez at the Instituto de Administración, University of Chile.

39. This indicator is the percentage of all babies born with the help of a doctor. The source is the same as that for the previous indicator.

40. This index was calculated by the author and is the per capita expenditure by commune dedicated to paving of streets. It was calculated from unpublished data provided by the División de Pavimentación Urbana of the Ministerio de la Vivienda y Urbanización. Population figures are from Dirección General de Estadísticas y Censos, "Poblacion estimada al 30 de Junio y 31 de Diciembre de 1968 por provincias, departamentos y comunas" (mimeographed, 1969).

41. Data from the Chilean Census of 1960 reprinted in Mattelart, *Atlas Social*.

42. The urbanization variable is in Mattelart, and the size variable was calculated from data in the same source.

The program makes use of F-values at each stage to evaluate the discriminant and aggregative power of each function.[43]

Table 3.3 presents the results of the multiple discriminant analysis employing the variables mentioned and three separate a priori groups. The first group consists of all municipalities where municipal councilors were not chosen to run for national office. The second and third groups consist of municipalities where respectively one or more than one candidate was recruited from the municipal council to make the race for the Chamber of Deputies.[44] The results presented in the table

Table 3.3. Multiple discriminant function analysis[a] for municipalities without candidates, with one candidate, and with more than one candidate recruited from the ranks of municipal councilors.

Variable entered	F at entry	Stepwise Multiple F	Percent correctly grouped
1. Political Importance of Municipality	77.47°°	77.47	64.3
2. Medical Assistance	8.36°°	39.53	57.0
3. Industry	3.50°	27.74	59.4
4. Party Competition 1967	2.79	21.63	59.1
5. Size	2.58	17.92	59.8
6. Services	1.52	15.21	61.9
7. Paving	1.01	13.18	61.9
8. School Attendance	0.63	11.60	62.6
9. Urbanization	0.59	10.30	61.9
10. Party Competition 1965	0.58	9.37	62.9
11. Mining	0.34	8.53	62.2
12. Participation	0.17	7.81	62.2

[a] The variables are listed in the same order as they appeared in the stepwise discriminant function. "F at entry" is the F-value of each variable at entry into the function; "Stepwise Multiple F" is the Multiple F of all variables at each step; "Percent correctly grouped" refers to the percentage of cases correctly placed given the number of variables involved at each step. N = 286.

° Significant at $< .05$
°° Significant at $< .01$

43. Allan Kornberg is one of the few political scientists who has used multiple discriminant function analysis. See Allan Kornberg and Mary L. Brehm, "Ideology, Institutional Identification, and Campus Activism," *Social Forces*, 49, no. 3 (March, 1971), 445–59; and Allan Kornberg and Robert C. Frasure, "Policy Differences in British Parliamentary Parties," *The American Political Science Review*, 65, no. 3 (September, 1971), 694–703. For an account of the statistical procedures, see Harry E. Anderson, "Regression, Discriminant Analysis and a Standard Notation for Basic Statistics," in R. B. Cattel, ed., *Handbook of Multivariate Experimental Psychology* (Chicago: Rand McNally, 1966).

44. One hundred ninety-five cases fell into the first, 54 into the second, and 37 into the third group. Since the program requires the size of the smallest group to be one more than the number of variables, there was no difficulty running the program.

include both the F at entry for each predictor variable and the values of the stepwise Multiple F as well as the percentage of observations correctly grouped on the basis of all variables included in the analysis at each particular point.

The analysis reveals that of the twelve variables examined simultaneously, only three differentiate significantly between the three different groups of communities. These variables are the political importance of the community, the level of medical attendance, and the percentage of the population employed in industry. Of these three factors, the political importance of the community is by far the most discriminating variable, alone accounting for most of the correct placement of communities in the three groups. In other words, the addition of other variables did not increase the proportion of cases correctly grouped. The administrative and political importance of the municipality accounted for 64.3 percent of all correctly grouped municipalities.

These findings suggest that councilors elected to the municipal council of provincial capitals had a much greater chance of being selected by political parties to run for national office than their counterparts in communal capitals. Councilors elected in departmental capitals stood in an intermediary position. An examination of all candidates selected from the ranks of councilors supports this conclusion as it reveals that 40 percent served on the municipal councils of the 25 provincial capitals.

Multiple discriminant function analysis further shows that the three groups have significant aggregate differences on two other variables. The fact that medical attendance is one of them suggests that communities with a higher standard of welfare are more favored in the selection of candidates.[45] The other variable, which is significant at a lower level of tolerance is the percentage of the population employed in industry. Communities with higher levels of industrialization are more likely to have candidates from their municipal councils selected to run for national office.

The program shows conclusively that a variable such as size, which as noted earlier is associated in a univariate analysis with the deviant cases, turns out to have a negligible effect in discriminating between the groups when all variables are considered simultaneously.[46] Political characteristics of communities are also not important in differ-

45. Medical attendance is not highly related in Chile to the level of educational enrollment. Thus, the correlation between the two variables is .27. Medical attendance is highly related to only one other independent variable, services with a correlation of .60.

46. The simple correlation between size and political importance of communities is .39. Correlations between political importance and other variables are all smaller.

entiating between groups. Though competitiveness in local elections discriminates more strongly than competitiveness in national elections, neither variable is significant.

In conclusion it is clear that the deviant communities, those in which municipal councilors were selected to embark on national political careers, were predominantly communities of greater political and administrative importance as defined by law. The likelihood of being selected to run for national office was consequently not random among all councilors nor was it primarily restricted to those in large, more urbanized, communities. Rather, selection is biased in favor of those fortunate enough to serve in communities of political importance.

The analysis presented in this chapter casts doubt on the validity of the proposition that achievement of local office was a necessary and viable first step in a successful national political career. Fifty percent of the deputies in the 1969 chamber had no municipal experience. Those local officials who were recruited for higher office came predominantly from communities of political importance. Furthermore they may have had qualifications which the average regidor did not share, such as higher educational attainment.[47] Thus, the chances for the average regidor to rise in the political hierarchy were not good. It is thus difficult to argue that the competitive struggle to achieve a local office was motivated primarily by a desire to move up the political ladder. If this was the primary motivation for achievement of local office there probably would have been a clearer pattern of advancement to higher office for this motivation to be reenforced.

The examination of a highly competitive struggle to achieve local office, the review of scarce municipal resources, and the analysis of the functions of local government in the political recruitment process has provided a general overview of local politics in Chile. However, this study of Chilean municipalities in global terms has raised more questions than answers. If local office was not primarily a stepping stone in a national career, why was it so competitive? What were the stakes and resources in local politics? Did local leaders engage in instrumental activities, or were they merely concerned with the ex-

47. It should be noted that it is likely that party leaders don't look consciously to certain types of communities in recruiting candidates but rather look for individuals with certain skills or personalities. An analysis of the biographies of all successful deputies in 1969 shows that 60 percent had university degrees. Furthermore, 40 percent of deputies with municipal experience had university degrees. Since few councilors have university training, a university degree may have been an important criteria in candidate selection. To be elected to local office in politically important communities might very well entail special qualifications. This is what Lester Seligman refers to as "candidate certification." See his "Political Recruitment and Party Structures: A Case Study," *American Political Science Review*, 55 (March, 1961), 77–86.

pressive side of politics? How important were programs, issues and ideology at the local level? Given the low level of resources, was there any point to collective action in the municipal council? A more detailed examination of local politics in Chile, based on field research in a sample of communities is necessary in order to begin to answer some of these questions.

Part II

4. The Centrality of Particularistic Demands in Chilean Local Politics

The scarcity of financial resources available to municipalities in Chile did not prevent local officeholders from leading extremely busy lives. And yet, extensive interviews with local leaders, and close observation of the operation of 14 different municipalities in a five province region, revealed that *alcaldes* and *regidores* dedicated relatively little time to the operation of the municipal government per se.[1] Collective action at the municipal level was quite rare; municipal councilors and mayors were primarily individual political entrepreneurs. Their principal goal was to satisfy a multiplicity of demands from their personal constituents. The small favor, or *gauchá chica*, was the dominant characteristic of municipal life in Chile, particularly in the smaller communities which constituted the vast majority of all communities in the country.[2]

Pedro Canales was a Communist regidor from the fairly large city of Colinas in the province of Bío-Bío. He is without a doubt one of the most dedicated and hard-working local officials interviewed. In conversation he stressed his belief that the socialist society he envisioned could come about only through class struggle; at the same time he dedicated most of his energies to performing in a masterly fashion the traditional small favor for his constituency.

Canales was a well-dressed man with a secondary education and further training as a public accountant. His home was a large wooden structure strategically located in the center of town. It had two entrances, one to the home proper, and the other to a small office consisting of two rooms. The councilor held regular office hours, attending the public at 9:30 A.M. and at 2:30 P.M. Every day of the week a small crowd could be seen, waiting as early as thirty minutes before office hours, to see Canales. On occasion members of the party cell sat in on conferences with petitioners and were instructed to do much of the footwork involved in meeting people's demands. The author was asked to come at 9:00 A.M. on March 18, 1969 to conduct his interview. Already at nine o'clock seven people were waiting to see him. I called at the main entrance of the house and was politely ushered into the living room. I was told the councilor had gone off to do

1. See Appendix II for a description of sampling techniques and interview procedures.
2. The term *gauchá chica* was used more often than the term *gauchadita*, but both are interchangeable.

some errands and would return shortly. At 9:45 he walked in and apologized for being late, asking me whether I would mind waiting for a few more minutes while he attended to some urgent business. He then disappeared into the patio of the house. A few minutes later the regidor's voice and voices of several other people were clearly audible in the office next to the living room. In a very soft and diplomatic fashion he asked a group of about three or four people what their problem was. A spokesman for the group answered that they wanted to legalize the possession of the property on which they were living, property which belonged to the municipal government. After inquiring about some details of the property as well as personal facts about the members of the group, Canales agreed to look into the matter and bring it up before the proper authorities. He then dispatched one of his lieutenants with the group to get specific details of the location of the properties.

After the little group left, a woman entered the office and asked Don Pedro if he had received from Santiago the social security papers which he had promised to obtain for her. Canales informed her politely that the information had been dispatched to Santiago to party people, and that he should be hearing from them shortly; he then told the woman to come back the following week.

The next client was a young boy who had apparently been arrested by the police for drunkenness and fighting the night before. He was due to appear before the Juez de Policía Local (local judge) and was wondering if Canales could speak to the Juez in order to convince him that he should be given only a small fine. Canales in very strict terms reprimanded the boy for his behavior and made him promise that he would no longer engage in such "degenerate" activities. He promised the boy nothing except to say that he would think about the matter.[3]

The next man to come into Canales' office was very shy and had a hard time expressing the real purpose for his visit. Finally it became clear that his son was getting married, and he needed some witnesses

3. I later found out that the two Communist regidores were not on good terms with the Juez, a lawyer appointed by the municipality to handle small cases of this nature. In fact, two people had voted against giving him a good recommendation to the Corte de Apelaciones (Court of Appeals), which each year asks the municipality to comment on the performance of such officials. The municipality had agreed by a vote of four to two to inform the court "that the official performance of the Juez de Policia Local, Señor Luciano Prieto, is not open to question because of his efficiency, zeal and morality in the discharge of his responsibilities." Canales and the other Communist regidor, Reinaldo Cabezas, argued that the judge did not fine employers who illegally dismissed workers, nor did he accept testimony from union members. Colinas, *Actas del consejo municipal*, December 23, 1968.

for the civil ceremony. The regidor promised that witnesses would be provided.

As I was writing down this last interview, Canales finally appeared in the living room of his home, at eleven o'clock, for my petition, and granted me a two-hour interview.

While Regidor Canales was exceptional in his organization and dedication to his job, which he combined with his role as leader of the Communist party in the commune, his handling of small personal favors for people in the community was by no means a rarity. Many regidores from all parties spent an enormous amount of time on such matters.

Clearly regidores in certain occupations were freer to devote more time to such pursuits. In Viña Verde, Regidor Julián Toro, a retired policeman, owned an old Model A Ford and spent his waking hours doing favors for the people of his community. Toro's proudest accomplishments, however, were the services he rendered the people of Ensenada, a small village of 1000 families high in the Andes at the other extreme of the commune. This community, about three hours away by automobile, was virtually isolated, with only weekly bus service as a link to the outside world. Toro was able to obtain a radio for the community and carried out the necessary negotiations in the provincial capital to obtain a piece of land for a first-aid center. However, his greatest contribution to the people of Ensenada was his willingness to take care of their *trámites* and *papeleo* (red tape and paperwork) in the provincial capital and in Santiago. With the aid of his political contacts, Toro was able to obtain, in countless trips, necessary information and documents to update social security, pension and tax papers. He also helped people when they needed to go to court by advising them on how to behave and by putting in a good word with the judge, who was a friend.

A final case is that of Regidor Rubén Alves from Quille, who specialized in helping many of the small vineyard growers in his area. As director of a small rural school, he had learned many of the intricacies of the trade and had helped his constituents survey grapes for disease and frost damage. When I arrived to interview Alves he was not at home. He had taken his old vehicle into town with a dead child in the back seat, a child he himself had fetched out of the well. No one else could have taken the body to the morgue. The day before, Alves had made another trip to the provincial capital to arrange with a friend who worked for the Department of Highways to send a bulldozer to smooth out a stretch of dirt road, which had badly deteriorated.

These three examples illustrate the types of particularistic transactions which engaged Chilean regidores. In the majority of cases, when I arrived at the home or business of a regidor, several people were waiting to see him. The *gauchás chicas* which he was called upon to perform fall into three main categories: the first two derive from his role as broker, either before the municipality or the government bureaucracy; the third involves a favor which he bestowed directly.

The first type of favor, involving the regidor's municipal role, was the most prevalent kind. It included presenting before the municipal council petitions for licenses to open commercial establishments, register vehicles, build houses or businesses, hold social functions, and other formal grants of authority within the jurisdiction of the municipal council. Some of the routine petitions in this category came directly to the municipality, addressed to the mayor. An example of such a petition is the following letter in the files of the municipality of Puente, in the province of Malleco:

Miscellaneous petitions

[E° 1.00 tax stamp placed here]
                                                             Puente
Danilo Antagnori Escobar, Identification Card 69451 of Manzanal residing in that city, at Sargento Alda No. 533, engaged in commerce, to Senor Alcalde of the Commune with all due respect expresses and requests:

That since the 1st of November is the day in which families go to cemeteries to offer posthumous homage to their deceased families and friends, I come to implore of you that you grant the undersigned the necessary permission to sell refreshments, beer and food in the vicinity of "Cementerio Cato," in the Sector of Santa Rosa of the Commune of Puente.

                                                          Es gracia

                                                        [Signature]

Puente, October 25, 1968
To Sr. Alcalde of the Commune of Puente—Presente

A major portion of the municipal council sessions were devoted to a consideration of such petitions. Though all petitions had to be written in accord with a standard format and had to carry a tax stamp, only a few petitions went directly to the municipality. The overwhelming majority of petitions were cleared in advance outside of the municipal building with one of the regidores. The practically unanimous response of local elected officials was that people, when faced with a problem or a petition, did not simply go to the municipal building to see "someone," but rather went directly to the official they knew best and asked that he intercede on their behalf. One municipal secretary was indignant about this practice and remarked that "regidores function as political brokers; things don't enter the municipality as they should, but rather through the regidor. . . . It's a political vice."

The second type of petition involved intercession with an agency outside of the municipality, the local judge or local bureaucrats. Often regidores were called upon to interpret complex law and regulations before intervening directly with public agencies. In numerous cases regidores had to turn to contacts developed in local bureaucratic agencies and party contacts in the provincial capital or in Santiago in order to aid constituents.

The importance of this function cannot be stressed strongly enough. Small but vital transactions could often be carried out only in the capital city. It was not unusual for a school teacher from a poor rural community to spend months trying to convince government authorities to pay an overdue salary. Many teachers and other public servants had to borrow money to make ends meet until the government check finally came through. Ironically, obtaining a loan often required Santiago approval as well. Securing a job, admitting a child to school, releasing a loved one from jail, transferring a grandparent to a larger hospital in a major city, more often than not, involved authorization from the center. Without the aid of local officials or their political contacts, many community residents simply could not have successfully finished their *trámites*.

The most common favors in this category related to the complex Chilean social security and welfare system. Local officials would thus initiate the *trámites* for retirement or disability benefits, or would help to up-date social security or medical insurance papers. The author continually heard of cases of constituents who were actually living in Santiago at the time, either with relatives or in a *pensión*, working full-time on *trámites* for basic benefits, with the political aid of contacts provided by local officials. Rarely did a mayor make a trip to Santiago on municipal business, without also looking into the status of the affairs of several clients.

Closer to home, municipal councilors spent an enormous amount of time interceding on behalf of constituents before a judge or before local public officials. A Socialist *regidor*, serving his first term of office, was simply shocked to find that his people were primarily interested in this kind of particularistic help. He recalled that when he was running for office, he asked the head of the local Communist party for the names of Communist party members who would support him in the campaign — since the Communists were not presenting their own slate. Repeatedly he was asked, in the homes he visited, whether he knew where one of his rivals, a Conservative, could be located — since he was then helping everyone obtain the tax stamps for social security papers which were up for renewal. "The people simply don't have a political consciousness," he remarked despairingly. "All they think of is the personal favor." The Conservative regidor was much less charitable: "One spends most of one's time in public offices doing tramites for the poor. They can't go because the functionaries are not patient with their ignorance."

The third category of small favor includes those which regidores did on their own rather than as brokers between individuals and third parties. Regidores were constantly asked to settle small disputes between two or more parties, often over land boundaries and property. On occasion they were even called upon to serve as mediators in marital squabbles, especially by aggrieved wives. The higher status of regidores and alcaldes, in the eyes of many of the people, especially those in small towns, meant that their opinions and advice were sought and respected. Local officials thus served adjudicating functions apart from those performed by the Chilean court system. One regidor summed up many of his duties in the following manner: "I am dad, mom, lawyer, judge, etc. . . . I have to solve problems in the first instance. They come with everything. They even want me to help them with marital problems. Country people ask me to help resolve disputes over land ownership. . . . Since I have many friends and contacts [cuñas], people ask me for letters of recommendation for employment. . . . I have to go and have tea with the old ladies of the Centro de Madres. . . ."

Another regidor found that his personal duties taxed him in a different way. He told the author, "I have thirty-one *compadres*. . . . so that I have many responsibilities as a witness and at parties." His main problem was staying sober. Most regidores were able through their own occupations, or because of their background, to offer special help to constituents. More than half of the regidores interviewed were engaged in agriculture or in commerce. Only three of the regidores engaged in agriculture were large landowners; most were middle to small landowners. Even so, they were able to provide employment, loans, a truck, and even goods to many petitioners. The merchants were able to provide credit. One regidor, for example, operated a slaughterhouse and gave credit on animals not yet ready for slaughter. The two lawyers in the sample were in a particularly effective occupation for helping people, because of their detailed knowledge of welfare laws and their ability to intervene in civil and criminal cases on behalf of constituents. One of these regidores, a Radical, remarked with a deprecatory tone, "I help my people as a lawyer; the Socialists take care of social security papers and do other stupid small things."

The four accountants were also very effective in dealing with large numbers of people because of their ability to help out with tax and salary matters.

In Minas where the Socialists and the Communists had a virtual political monopoly over the municipal council, the personal favor was equally important. However, in that town citizens were less likely to get in touch with the regidores directly and more likely to contact party leaders for the *gauchá chica*. One of the Communist regidores described the procedure as follows: "People come to the party first, then the party brings the matter to the attention of the regidor for solution." This phenomenon occurred because the regidores were dependent on party leaders for nomination and election to a greater degree than was the case in other communities. In Minas the regidores used party headquarters to see the people. A young Socialist regidor told the author: "I take care of the people in the party headquarters, and there we take charge of helping them build houses and other small favors. I turn over commissions and permits to the comrades, and at party headquarters we give out light bulbs."

While, as part III will show, particularistic transactions had their origin in an earlier period, and were a traditional feature of Chilean politics, their ubiquity was reenforced by two important and continuing characteristics of Chilean society: centralization and scarcity. The centralization of the political system not only cut back on the autonomy of municipalities, seriously curtailing their jurisdiction and finances; it transformed local officials into brokers between the distant offices of an omnipresent government and community people who became dependent on its regulations and services.

These services were essential in a society of meager resources. Rural areas were particularly hard hit by poverty. In the Maule region, contiguous to the region where field work was conducted, the per capita monthly income in 1966 was only E°63, compared to E°180 for the nation as a whole.[4] The importance of particularistic favors in the context of economic deprivation can be illustrated by reporting the results of a survey administered to rural and urban dwellers in the Maule region. Respondents were asked what criteria should be used in selecting a school teacher for the area and were given a choice between two applicants. The first was highly qualified, but well-off economically. The second was not very competent, but needed a job badly. Sixty-three percent of the sample said that it would be pref-

4. See DESAL, *Tenencia de la tierra y campesinado en Chile* (Buenos Aires: Ediciones Troquel, 1968), p. 54.

erable to hire the needy applicant, despite the fact that the quality of the education of their children was at stake.[5]

Scarcity and centralization are interrelated variables. Lack of resources in the society as a whole contributed to the trend of the more powerful political forces in the center taking over an increasingly large share of the nation's resources for central dispensation. Both scarcity and centralization contributed to the durability of the role of the broker. Centralized institutions, financially overcommitted, would simply not meet their responsibilities unless pressured by politically influencial elements. The more centralized the system, the more difficult to generate such a pressure, the more important the role of the broker.

The basis of political pressure, and thus the basis of the politics of the *gauchá chica*, was the democratic politics of accountability. At no time was this clearer than during local campaigns when the essence of the particularistic style was paramount. For several weeks before each election, local incumbents and their challengers would visit friends and neighbors as well as community people of equal and lower status reminding them of the favors which they, or their contacts, had performed in the past, and promising better performance in the future. Few regidores kept a written account of these many transactions, but all remembered what they entailed. Especially in smaller communities the followers of a particular local official consisted of a very specific group of individuals which regidores referred to as "mine," "my people," or "my clientele." In larger communities face-to-face contact was just as important, although candidates had to rely on half a dozen friends to do much of the legwork. Advertisements clearly took

Table 4.1. Distribution of responses of the regidores to the statement: "Some say that electoral propaganda does not influence much the results of an election, since it is more or less decided by the work and influence of the candidate's collaboraters."

Very much in agreement	29
Somewhat in agreement	16
In disagreement	10

5. The survey was conducted in Talca, Maule, Linares and the northwest portion of the province of Ñuble by researchers from DESAL. DESAL, p. 91.

second place to this personal approach in the eyes of regidores, as the answers to the question in table 4.1 reveal.

In general, regidores' clientele was made up of individuals representing a cross-section of the population, and was not drawn from a particular organized group. Sometimes, however, the diverse clientele was located in a given geographical area, such as a small community in a rural area or a neighborhood in an urban area. There are two exceptions to this pattern in the communities sampled. In communes with mining or manufacturing industries which were organized, some regidores drew their strength on the support of syndicate members and in several cases were themselves syndicate leaders. The second exception concerned two regidores in the sample who were Protestants and had been elected primarily by fellow church members.

If personal contacts and appeals were predominant, one would expect that elections for local office would rarely have dealt with national issues. One regidor noted that "in this town there are no public meetings during the electoral campaigns . . . and national issues are not discussed. What is important is the personal contact between the candidate and his people." Indeed, only three out of the sixty respondents to the structured questionnaire said that national issues played some role in local elections. At the same time, when they asked whether people in the region voted more often for the man than for the party, the overwhelming majority said that citizens voted for the individual. (Out of the sixty respondents, only three said that people voted for the party, and seven said that they did not know, or gave no answer.)

Chilean electoral mechanisms clearly encouraged individual candidates to seek personal clienteles. Candidates for the office of regidor ran on party lists, but voters could vote for only one candidate on a ballot containing all party lists. The total vote for each list was computed in order to determine the number of seats to be given to each party, if any. If a list was given two seats, then the candidates on the list obtaining the two highest pluralities were elected. In effect this meant that candidates ran against fellow party candidates as well as against opposition elements. Each candidate attempted to win the largest plurality on his particular list in order to increase the likelihood of winning a seat on the municipal council. Especially in smaller communes, which make up the majority of the country's communes, personal contacts were further strengthened by the fact that each party could nominate as many candidates as there were seats on the council. Thus, in elections where seven parties competed for five commune seats it was possible to have up to thirty-five candidates on the ballot. In a commune such as Santa Barbara in the province of Bío-Bío, with approximately 2,500 voters, this meant that there was an average of only seventy-one voters per candidate. Since the front runners of a list often polled large numbers of votes, it was conceivable for a candidate to be elected with a very small clientele if his list did well.[6]

Though particularistic orientations were a major feature of local politics, the importance of the role of party organizations within that system must not be minimized. Individual candidates sought their own clienteles, but as chapter 3 made clear, the electoral system made it virtually impossible for independent candidacies to appear and thus encouraged the formation of party-structured lists. Most of the local elected officials interviewed had been active in local party organizations before being selected by the party to run for local office. Aside from ideological, emotional and social attachments, it was the political party which provided local officials with vital contact in governmental agencies, both in the provincial capital and the province. We will show, in later chapters, how parties performed this crucial function of organizing linkages to the center. In return for rewards from the center, local officials helped mobilize the vote for their party in other elections, or, more precisely, attempted to deliver their clientele to the national candidate of their party who helped them most. In sum, while local politics did not revolve around national issues, and local leaders maintained that the small favor was paramount, political parties structured the competitiveness of the community.

It should be mentioned that just because officials perceived that local politics revolved entirely around the small favor, it does not follow that Chilean voters responded solely to particularistic transactions. Whether they did or not is an empirical question which can only be answered by extensive survey research. Preliminary evidence suggests that a large number of voters in Chile had party attachments passed down by the family or acquired recently, no doubt in part, through the influence of an important local leader. The survey of 751 rural and small-town males in the predominantly agricultural Maule region revealed that twelve percent of the respondents were registered members of a political party. Another thirty-eight percent had some degree of party identification. Since sixty-one percent of the sample was registered to vote, most of the registered voters

6. Excluding the first district of Santiago, there were 8,068 candidates in the municipal elections of 1971, and 3,341,414 registered voters. The average was consequently 416 registered voters per candidate. If one were to eliminate the dozen or more cities over 100,000, the number would be reduced considerably. For a discussion of the complicated Chilean D'Hondt system of proportional representation, see Federico Gil, *The Political System of Chile* (Boston: Houghton Mifflin Co., 1966), pp. 215–19.

probably had some degree of party identification.[7] Though it is not possible to make a firm judgment on the relationship between party identification and the nature of voting behavior, from personal observations this author thinks that in local elections the small favor was fundamental in determining the selection of a candidate, though many voters probably selected their candidate from only one party list. Delivering the clientele to a national candidate is another matter. While regidores boasted that they could deliver many of "their voters" to the congressional candidate of their choice, they also admitted that many times clients did not follow their directives. The authors of the survey mentioned above attempted to determine the criteria which the sample used in selecting candidates. They found that fifty-two percent used only particularistic criteria, such as personal acquaintance with the candidate, whether he was recommended by someone, or whether he did favors.[8] This means that a surprisingly large number of voters thought of nonparticularistic criteria in justifying their vote. In particular, local notables had a particularly hard time delivering their clienteles to a national candidate after their party had lost a presidential election. Thus the Radical and National regidores did not have much success in electing Radical and National candidates for deputy after the overwhelming Christian Democratic victory in the presidential election of 1964. Indeed, the impact of this election was such that in the municipal election of 1967 the Christian Democrats made substantial gains.[9] While many voters may have turned to Christian Democratic candidates under the assumption that the party in power could best deliver the small favor, it is likely that the national political climate influenced many others who did not follow the same reasoning.[10]

Performing small services for the people of the community was the

7. DESAL, pp. 38–49. In this area thirty-seven percent of the males are illiterate and thus cannot vote. See Armand Mattelart, *Atlas social de las comunas de Chile* (Santiago: Editorial del Pacífico, 1965), p. 125. According to another study conducted by the Centro de Estudios Socio-Económicos, seventy-five percent of urban dwellers have party identifications in Chile. See DESAL, *Tenencia*, p. 40.

8. DESAL, *Tenencia*, pp. 91–92.

9. On the other hand, the fact that local elections revolved essentially around local issues and personalities is probably most responsible for the Christian Democrats' not doing as well in the local election of 1967 as they did in the parliamentary election of 1965. From this perspective it is misleading to suggest that the fortunes of the Christian Democrats went down in 1967. Comparisons of voting percentages across elections for different offices should be approached with great caution in Chile.

10. While local officials may not be able to stem a national tide, it is clear to this author that local officials were influential in contributing to the recovery of the Radical and particularly the National party in the 1969 parliamentary elections after the debacle of 1965.

most important and time-consuming activity of Chilean regidores. Regidores for the most part were resigned to performing individual favors for constituencies because of the importance of service to their electoral clients. However, at the same time, they expressed some resentment and frustration over this chore. One regidor summarized this view by saying: "All of the problems in this town are of a personal nature, such as licenses, fights, tickets. . . . Problems and solutions of a general nature must be sought by the regidor on his own. People are concerned only about themselves. This is very annoying. . . ." This remark, though stressing the importance of the *gauchá chica*, is significant because it introduces a fundamental corollary phenomenon: local politics in Chile was characterized by a dearth of organized group activity aimed at influencing municipal authorities.

The Absence of Organized Interests in Chilean Local Politics

In one of the few studies conducted in small town and rural Chile researchers from DESAL discovered that very few people belonged to secondary associations of the type that might have exerted pressure on the municipal government. According to DESAL, only eleven percent of the salaried population belonged to a labor union, only twenty-eight percent belonged to an association of small farmers, and only eleven percent belonged to a cooperative. Indeed, over forty percent of all respondents had never heard of such organizations. By contrast, a larger percentage of the population belonged to organizations which would not normally exert pressures on the local government—namely, religious organizations and sports clubs.[11] The same study revealed that participation in political party activity was relatively high. Twelve percent of the sample said that they were registered members of a political party while another thirty-eight percent said that they had definite party preferences. Still, fifty percent of the respondents did not express any party preferences.[12]

Research in the various communities visited during the summer of 1969 also revealed the scarcity of organized groups and, more importantly, the almost complete absence of any identifiable group pressures on municipal governments. Collective interests were rarely expressed, the feeling being that it was the responsibility of the municipality to initiate programs of a general nature. The result of this pattern was the isolation of the decision-making body: there were

11. DESAL, *Tenencia*, pp. 38–39.
12. Ibid., p. 40.

no important organized constituencies who could have provided a regidor with key political support in pressing for a given project, nor could a regidor sponsor a certain project for a powerful group. Initiative came from the government body itself. While council meeting rooms invariably had a few extra seats and sessions were open to the public, these seats were rarely occupied.

When local officials were asked whether any groups or associations took an active interest in the functioning of the municipality, the general response was negative. Forty-one stated that no groups or organizations took an active interest, while fourteen said that they did. Five regidores did not seem to know what the question meant.

Those councilors and mayors who said that some groups did take an active role in municipal affairs were asked to name the groups in question. Juntas de Vecinos were mentioned seven times, Centros de Madres were mentioned twice, social clubs once and sports clubs five times.

And yet, the Juntas de Vecinos, created by the Frei administration in an effort to mobilize political participation, were modestly active in only two of the largest municipalities in the sample. As with many other programs of this type, the Juntas de Vecinos were concentrated in the Santiago urban area and in a few other major cities and did not effectively reach peripheral areas.[13]

It is noteworthy that none of the officials interviewed mentioned labor or peasant unions or employer associations when referring to organized elements within the community. This, in spite of the fact that two communities had strong and prominent labor unions. In Aseradero, workers in a large saw mill were organized under the direction of communist and socialist unions. In Minas, a mining town, miners were also organized by parties of the left. In both cases, however, the unions concerned themselves primarily with labor management relations and paid little attention to local government. The unions had their own linkages with political leaders in the center, both directly and indirectly through labor federation auspices. The

13. Incomplete unpublished statistics from the Oficina Regional de Planificación (ORPLAN) for the Bío-Bío region confirmed the low membership of Juntas de Vecinos in other communes not studied by the author. Likewise, Centros de Madres, while organized in most communities had very small active membership. A survey conducted in rural areas of the province of Colchagua revealed that approximately 50 percent of heads of families belonged to an association such as a church or sports club. Between 9.5 and 15.7 percent, depending on the size of the community, belonged to associations such as Juntas de Vecinos, rural unions, cooperatives, political parties, etc. See Armand Mattelart et al., *La vivienda y los servicios comunitarios rurales* (Santiago: ICIRA, 1968). As with other studies of this kind, the reporting of the methodology is much more extensive than the reporting of results. It is difficult to draw firm conclusions.

political strength of the unions was such that they did not have to turn to local leaders as brokers for organizational matters.

In one sense, however, the unions did involve themselves in local politics. Union leaders in both communities stood for election as municipal councilors and were elected. But, rarely did the councilors receive instructions from the union and rarely did they intercede on behalf of the union as an organization. Instead the councilors functioned very much as the other councilors in the municipality—taking care of the small demands of individual constituents.

Peasant unions have a long and arduous history in Chile, having achieved legal recognition only in 1967. Though by 1970 they had over 120,000 members, in only one of the communities sampled had peasant unions achieved any significant strength.[14] In that community, the union had succeeded in getting its leader elected to the municipal council. As a councilor, however, he sought primarily to fulfill the traditional particularistic aims of his fellow campesinos rather than to use the municipality as a vehicle for group goals. In his estimation, the group goals such as land expropriation were goals that went beyond the perview of the municipality—and had to be negotiated in the center with the aid of the union's political sponsors. Rural unions in the municipalities studied had very little autonomy in 1969, and were primarily instruments of party organizations seeking to maximize their electoral fortunes. As such, they had little interest or means for pressuring local municipalities, despite the fact that municipalities generally neglected the rural area of the commune in favor of the urban enclaves. Only during the Allende period, when large portions of land were taken over by peasant unions and groups, did rural laborers achieve a measure of political power and independence from party organizations. Even then, however, their goal was land, not municipal services.

While organized rural and urban laborers would turn to the municipality as individuals to seek particularistic demands, large landowners had very little to do with the municipality at all. Though two mayors were large landowners, the large landowner by 1969 was not a dominant force in municipal politics. During the congressional campaign of 1969 several patrones trucked peasants to outdoor parties or *malones* in order to woo votes for conservative candidates for the National Congress. The fact is that for his own needs, and those of his colleagues, the landowner could readily turn to the regional or national agricultural association, or to his own national party and

14. See Brian Loveman, "The Transformation of the Chilean Countryside," in Arturo Valenzuela and J. Samuel Valenzuela (eds.), *Chile: Politics and Society* (New Brunswick; Transaction Books, 1976).

personal contacts in the center, without having to turn to lower level brokers. I tried to interview one landowner only to be told by the maid of the impressive rural house that the *patrón* had left for Santiago that morning. Thinking that I had lost an interview, I turned to leave when I was informed that he would return that afternoon. My disbelief at this impossible feat dissipated when I realized that the field behind the house was an airport and that the landowner had gone to Santiago in his own twin-engine plane on a routine business trip.[15]

In general then, Chilean municipalities faced little organized pressure group activity. It is thus not surprising that not one regidor and alcalde mentioned any outside group or organization when asked, "Who takes the initiative in this town in the presentation of new projects?" This does not mean, however, that associations such as clubs did not approach the municipality. On the contrary, the municipality was constantly being petitioned by organizations as well as individuals. However, as was the case with petitions from individuals, the organizations also sought particularistic dispensations from the local authorities. They were concerned with obtaining permits from the municipality for the conduct of their activities and subsidies for financing their programs. As one regidor said, "Certainly there are many groups in the town, but they don't take much interest in the workings of the municipality—rather they ask the regidores for things so that they may be approved during council sessions. . . . For example, the sports clubs want subsidies and prizes, and a Centro de Madres asked for a little tree."

An example of the kind of petition such groups brought to the municipality is reflected in the following handwritten letter sent to the mayor of Puente by the local choir:

The directorate and members of the Polyphonic Choir of Puente solicits of the mayor and councilors of the commune permission to hold a benefit party [malon de beneficio] Saturday, the 18th of the current month, on the ground floor of the parish house.

Realizing the spirit that guides us, we are confident that our petition will be favorably received.

Es gracia

[Eight signatures]

Al Senor Alcalde of the Commune

Occasionally groups fought each other and the municipality was asked to choose between opposite positions. Thus in Viña Verde a dispute

15. For a discussion of landowner associations and other associations of private interests see David Cusak, "The Politics of Chilean Private Enterprise Under Christian Democracy" (Ph.D. dissertation, University of Denver, 1972).

arose between the parish and the Centro de Madres. The *parroquia*, upset over drunkenness and rowdiness in religious festivals, wanted the municipality to prohibit the sale of alcoholic beverages on the day of Saint Sebastian. The Centro de Madres, on the other hand, wanted to sell alcoholic beverages on that occasion. Interestingly enough, representatives of these groups did not come and speak to the council about these matters. Rather, the priest, as well as the Centro de Madres, after consulting several regidores privately, sent written *solicitudes* to the municipality detailing their respective positions. After some discussion, the council agreed to accede to the request of the *parroquia*. The Radical regidores backed the priest. The issues involved in this controversy were quite specific and particular.

While many petitions for permission to hold these events come directly to the mayor or the municipality, when organizations sought a subsidy they often turned to one of the regidores. Lively and sometimes bitter fights took place over small items in the municipal budget allotted for subsidies. Regidores, at the behest of the mayor, either tried to come to agreement before the session was held to consider the municipal budget, or they had a long drawn out argument over which *futbol* club would get more money this year for its sports equipment and to finance the championship. Indeed, the complex budget, drawn up in accord with the rigid specifications set by law, was usually approved in a pro forma manner, except for a determination of the items dealing with subsidies. It was even easier to agree upon budgetary allotments for special projects than it was to agree on subsidy matters. While members of the same party occasionally sought subsidies for organizations made up mostly of party members, more often than not, individual regidores either had supporters and friends in certain clubs, or sought to build a greater following by promising that they could provide the most generous benefits.

The overwhelming majority of petitions and demands made upon the municipal government by groups in the community were equivalent in nature to the demands made by particular individuals. Organized pressure for community projects for collective advancement was virtually nonexistent. Time and time again regidores complained to the author about this lack of interest or involvement in local politics. One noted that "in effect there are no groups or persons who take an active interest in the workings of the municipality; nevertheless, people expect the municipality to solve all their problems for them." Another concurred in a bitter tone: "The problem in this town is that there is too much apathy; people could participate, but they don't want to. How can they expect one to do a job if the people themselves don't cooperate?"

The result was the isolation of local government from community demands and pressures for general projects and community-wide services. Because of this lack of community interest in municipal activities, mayors and regidores stressed that much more responsibility was placed on them to come up with projects for local progress. Indeed, local officials told the author that the people *expected* them to come up with solutions to municipal problems and to suggest innovations for community betterment.[16]

The Importance of Projects and the Absence of Collective Action in Chilean Municipalities

The belief on the part of local officials that the people of the community expected them to come up with projects and programs lead, in turn, to an interesting phenomenon. Local officials acknowledge that they had to spend most of their time performing *gauchás chicas* for their constituents. At the same time, they emphasized that success in local government was also dependent on their coming up with popular projects for community-wide betterment. Indeed, many regidores argued that the two responsibilities were incompatible and that the time spent in "taking care of the clientele" detracted from what they themselves considered to be their legitimate role. While the *gauchá chica* was the stuff of politics, they condemned it as an aberration. Regidores complained that the preoccupation with small favors was a "vicio de los chilenos" or a "vicio de la gente," and that

16. It must be stressed that the absence of collective pressures on the municipal government does not warrant the conclusion which DESAL reaches, that individuals are "marginal" and alienated from society. The DESAL evidence itself suggests that respondents participate in organizations of a religious or recreational nature and are connected with the larger society, even if this connection is of a particularistic nature. Indeed, one should avoid placing a negative value judgment on particularistic transactions. It may very well be that the aggregate of such transactions is more positive in providing for individual and community progress. At the same time, one can argue that face-to-face contacts with leaders are a viable form of political participation which may integrate individuals more into the larger society than community-wide action where the individual may feel that he is only one of many. It is this form of political participation, where an individual may indirectly obtain access to the highest policy-makers through a network of contacts, that is not tapped by studies of political participation. Thus, for example the political participation scale constructed in one study includes talking politics, contacting local authorities, contacting national authorities, involvement in electoral campaigns and membership in political organizations and political parties. Such a scale would not adequately measure participation in a system where individuals approach local brokers who in turn can approach brokers at other levels of government for a resolution of a problem. The study referred to is Norman H. Nie, G. Bingham Powell, Jr., and Kenneth Prewitt, "Social Structure and Political Participation: Developmental Relationships, Part I," *American Political Science Review*, 63 (June, 1969), 361–78.

their time could and should be spent working on concrete projects. This attitude was expressed despite the contradictory fact that local officials took pride in their record of helping people meet particularistic demands. They would observe that "I take care of my own well," or that "my constituents never have problems with the stupidity [*payasá*] of their *trámites*." Pride in serving people well was kept separate, however, from their conception of what local officials should be doing at their job. They should be working on *obras* (projects) and leave till election time the *politiquería*.[17]

This emphasis on the importance of municipal *obras* and the disdain for the ubiquitous *gauchá chica* contributed to considerable tension in Chilean municipalities, primarily between the alcalde and the regidores, but often among the regidores themselves.

The conflict between the regidores and the alcalde can be appreciated by the fact that a large percentage of regidores stated that the alcalde was not the prime initiator of local projects, whereas the alcaldes unanimously disagreed with that verdict.

Table 4.2 reveals that all of the alcaldes and the overwhelming majority of the municipal secretaries held that the mayor was the prime initiator of new projects in the community.[18] On the other hand, only twelve, or approximately thirty percent, of the regidores mentioned

Table 4.2. Distribution of answers by local officials to the question: "Who takes the initiative in presenting new projects?"

	Types of official responding		
Initiatives taken by	Alcaldes	Municipal secretaries	Regidores
The alcalde	14	11	12
All the same	0	0	21
Regidores of my party	0	0	5
Me and the alcalde	—	2	4
Me	—	1	3
There are no initiatives	0	0	1

17. This attitude is reflected in the fact that the vast majority of regidores prefer to think of themselves as engaging in "administration" rather than "politics." When asked, "Do you consider yourself a politician or an administrator?" only nine local officials out of sixty said that they were politicians. On the other hand, thirty-four regidores and alcaldes said that they considered themselves to be primarily administrators, while fourteen refused to accept either label.

18. A couple of municipal secretaries take equal credit, while one chose to take complete credit.

that the mayor was the prime mover of new initiatives. The largest plurality of regidores, twenty-one (forty-five percent) sought to minimize the importance of any one individual's role by noting that all of the members of the municipal council, including the mayor, took equal initiative. Five regidores argued that only the members of their particular party took the initiative. Seven others made it clear that either they alone, or together with the mayor, were moving forces in their communities. In sum, seventy percent of the regidores either sought to minimize the importance of the mayor by attributing to all colleagues, to party colleagues or to themselves the role of initiator of new projects. It is interesting to note that community groups were not mentioned at all.

This theme, that initiative in local government in Chile did not come from the mayor but came essentially from everyone, is related to a similar but contradictory theme—that many initiatives in local government were not very successful. Regidores and mayors were asked to name the projects which their municipalities were undertaking or about to undertake, and sixteen of the forty-five regidores actually said that no projects were being undertaken or were contemplated. With the exception of the mayor, most of the regidores stressed that little was being done and that much more could be done.

Time and again regidores made it clear to the author that local projects planned by the municipality failed to get off the ground because regidores feared that the mayor, or one of their colleagues, would take sole credit for the project in question. As one of them put it, "In this municipality new projects are not being carried through because it's impossible to function as a team . . . there are many personal quarrels." In another municipality a regidor, commenting on the reason why sessions of the municipality had not been held for more than three months, said, "Here nothing can be done because of disunity; there is no consensus and no teamwork." Another said that this disagreement was due to the fact that "each one wants water for his own mill." A mayor of another town stated with pride that "politics in this town is done outside of the municipality, so there is no opposition from political parties. Instead it is difficult to make progress because others are opposed to one's running away with the glory."[19]

Personal conflict and rivalry to gain credit for certain initiatives is further revealed by the constant complaint of regidores that they in fact were responsible for certain ideas or projects, and someone else (usually the mayor) stole the idea and reaped all the benefit. One municipality, for example, had obtained a large E°30,000 loan to

19. See chapter 5 for a fuller discussion of the role of the party in local government.

make improvements in the local swimming hole. Two of the Christian Democratic regidores claimed to have done all the work to obtain the loan, but now were blocking the project with support of several colleagues because the mayor was not making it clear that the initiative was not exclusively his. As the municipal secretary put it, "The swimming hole has not come along because of financial problems, but because of a lack of unity of opinions. It's a political problem—no one wants others to get the laurels for the project."

Regidores are somewhat contradictory in their assessment of this problem. One very articulate councilman told the author: "If one puts aside political views, much can be done in the municipal council." But then in the following sentence, without reflecting on the implications of his words, he added: "I, for example, was the one who achieved the municipal library." Another remarked bitterly: "The vice of the Chileans is that there is too much personalism. . . . People want to work alone. . . . I, for example, introduced a motion to create a stadium, and another stole the idea."

Regidores who had served as mayors previously reinforced this theme by expressing the conviction that in their administration significant things had been accomplished. One said, "I solved the potable water problem when I was mayor. Now no one is doing a thing."

Interviews with local officials on projects carried out in their community revealed, however, a significant paradox. The sixteen respondents who noted that no projects were underway in their municipality did not cluster in the same communities; they were spread across the entire sample. In other words, in no municipality was there unanimity over the proposition that projects were not being undertaken. As noted above, the mayor always claimed that some projects were under construction and others were on the drawing boards. Most councilors agreed.

Compounding the paradox, the author's attendance at municipal meetings, and his reading of the minutes of meetings held during the year 1968 in all fourteen communities, revealed that municipal councils rarely dealt with large projects. The notable exceptions were the common effort to beautify the *plaza* (central square) and to set up a *balneario* (swimming hole). Collective action to obtain other projects was quite rare. The mayor, as the next chapter will show, invariably dominated the municipal sessions despite the contention of many regidors that initiative was shared. Little debate and consultation over matters of substance (as opposed to the multiplicity of small duties such as permits or licenses) took place. And yet, in all but three of the communities visited, the author was struck by the fact that significant projects were underway, confirming the statements of each mayor.

Potable water systems were being built or expanded, electric light was being extended to outlying communities, streets and roads were being paved, hospitals and schools were under construction, and bridges or small dams were being built. Table 4.3 summarizes the responses of fourteen mayors and thirty regidores, who noted that projects were underway, to the question "What projects is this municipality carrying out now or will carry out in the near future?" In each of the municipalities visited, the author was able to confirm the validity of the answers.

How does one explain the existence of these projects, the source of great pride to mayors and some regidores, given the lack of collective action in the municipality oriented at creating projects? And why did a large number of regidores refuse to recognize the existence of the projects and stressed the bickering of local politics?

It became clear, after spending only a short time in several municipalities, that the most important projects obtained by the mayor, and occasionally by enterprising councilors either with or without his approval, were projects "extracted" from central government agencies. The municipality's own resources were too meager to carry out comparable activities. Mayors consequently spent a great deal of their time mobilizing their political contacts in the center to obtain national investments in the locality. No collective action at the local level was required to obtain those investments, in the same way that collective action was not necessary for the satisfaction of most *gauchás chicas*. As with the satisfaction of particularistic demands, mayors and councilors would agree to mobilize their electoral constituencies in support of the congressman or senator who helped in extracting resources from the center. In turn, this meant that each local broker was

Table 4.3. Distribution of answers to the question: "What projects is this municipality carrying out now or will carry out in the near future?"

1. Recreational facilities	18
2. Paving streets or roads	17
3. Installation of new lighting	9
4. Sewers and potable water	7
5. Hospitals and schools	4
6. *Plano regulador*	2

Note: Sixteen regidores said that no projects were being carried out; the rest, fourteen mayors and thirty regidores, at times mentioned more than one project.

under considerable pressure to demonstrate that his personal and party contacts were the best, and that his constituency and the community at large should credit him and his allies for the benefits. This competitive system, in which projects were traded for votes in individualistic transactions, clearly mitigated against collective action, and encouraged jealousy at the local level. Since the mayor had the greatest advantage, because of his formal powers and his more prestigious position, regidores would vigorously compete to achieve the mayoralty.

Many councilors told the author that they hoped that they would become mayors next time around, and were not about to support too vigorously the current incumbent. Many intended to keep ideas and projects they had in mind secret, until they succeeded in being elevated to the highest municipal post. Several councilors who were scheduled to succeed to the mayoralty as part of a political agreement told the author confidentially of their plans. A few had already made trips to Santiago to obtain commitments from national political contacts for future aid. One regidor, had in fact finalized arrangements for a loan for various public works projects, and was patiently waiting for his turn to become the chief executive of the locality.

The reluctance to recognize projects, then, stemmed from a certain degree of resentment at the more dominant position of the mayor, and the feeling of frustration derived from a system where local action was irrelevant to the enactment of important programs for community betterment. In probing regidores, and observing the interaction between them, it became clear that family or cliques did not structure disagreements, though occasionally party ties did. For the most part the principal cleavage was between mayors and councilors. Earlier, this conflict was illustrated by the unwillingness of councilors to recognize mayoral initiative. Mayor-councilor cleavage is further illustrated by the responses summarized in table 4.4. The table shows

Table 4.4. Distribution of responses to the question: "Do you find that between the mayor and the municipal council there is much, some, or no tension?"

Responses	Mayors	Regidores of mayor's party	Regidores of other parties	Total regidores
Much tension	0	3	9	12
Some tension	0	7	8	15
No tension	14	7	13	20
Total	14			47

that while the mayors saw themselves as working well with "their" councilors, the councilors took a much dimmer view of the relationship with the mayor. Of the fourteen mayors in the sample who were interviewed, all said in response to the question, "Do you perceive much, some or little tension between the mayor and the municipal council?" that they perceived no tension. The regidores, by contrast, were more likely to express the view that tension existed between them and the mayor.

Almost sixty percent of the regidores perceived much or some tension between themselves and the mayor. While regidores who did not belong to the same party as the mayor were more likely to see tension, regidores both of the mayor's party and opposition parties divided equally in expressing the view that there was some tension. It is interesting to note that the number of regidores not of the mayor's party who said there was *no* tension between regidores and mayor is larger than the corresponding number who were members of the mayor's party.

Tension thus existed in municipalities over the attribution of local community projects and much of it occurred between mayors and councilors. The latter resented the fact that they engaged mostly in performing small favors while the mayor, as the next chapter will show, clearly had the upper hand in the formulation and implementation of policy.

The mayor was not a traditional notable who could exercise authority because of his personal status; his prestige derived from his elective position. Regidores interviewed by the author were asked to evaluate the prestige of various roles in the community. In every case the mayor was ranked two or three positions above the regidores and ranked first in the minds of thirty of the forty-seven regidores interviewed. The rest placed the mayor second only to the doctor, except for three who ranked him third after the doctor and the priest.[20]

Local politics in Chile was characterized by a significant lack of

20. It is important to note that large landlords most often were placed at the bottom of the list and never appeared in the top three categories. The large landlord used to be the key notable and political leader in rural and small town Chile. However, with the rise of political parties and government bureaucracy, his role as patron has been taken over by individuals occupying positions of formal authority or with links to such individuals. Field research revealed that landlords who retained considerable influence also occupied a local or national office. Only four of the regidores interviewed can be described as wealthy landlords. In an interesting and unfortunately unique study of one community over time, Andrés Pascal has documented the decline of the latifundista and the rise in his place of bureaucrats and local officials as the new *hombres-nexos* (linkage men). However, Pascal's study is seriously impaired because he neglects to consider the impact of political parties in this transformation and the function of parties as key linkage-networks today. See Andrés Pascal, *Relaciones de poder en una localidad rural* (Santiago: Icira, 1968.) A diachronic comparative study of community

collective action in municipal government for the purpose of designing and creating major projects. This was to be expected, due to the
serious lack of resources at the disposition of the overwhelming
majority of local governments. However, field research revealed that,
contrary to expectation, a lack of collective action was not accompanied by a parallel lack of program orientation among individual
community leaders. It would be a serious mistake to conclude that
local politics was primarily "expressive" in nature and did not have
strong "instrumental" goals. The key was not a lack of effort in gen-
erating local programs, but the fact that local programs were simply
not generated by the municipality as an organization. Instead, projects
and programs were "extracted" from national government agencies
through the mobilization of political contacts in the center. As chapter 6 will note, government agencies with scarce resources responded
readily to political pressure generated by the locality, rather than
submit to questionable planning schemes. At the same time, field
research showed that local officials performed a second indispensable,
and also nontraditional, function: the satisfaction of particularistic
demands for clients. The centralization of the political system and
the precariousness of the economy meant that rewards generated by
local officials and their political allies were crucial to the well-being
of many residents of the community. Again this activity, though
particularistic in nature, had clear instrumental goals — the obtension
of tangible benefits for individual clients. The importance of *gauchás
chicas* was, in turn, reenforced by a lack of group pressure and group
activity in the community. Both functions, extraction of national resources and satisfaction of small demands, relied on the mechanisms
of democratic politics. Resources for individuals or the collectivity
were obtained in exchange for promise of political support and the
delivery of votes.

By discouraging collective action, local governmental functions,
intimately tied to a vertical face-to-face political network extending
to the center of the political system, encouraged rivalry and jealousy
among local elected leaders. This cleavage was particularly acute between the mayor, the dominant force in local politics, and the other
regidores. The position of mayor was consequently actively sought
by each municipal councilor. Climbing up the political ladder to the
National Congress was not much of a preoccupation with Chilean
regidores who spent a good deal of time jockeying to become the chief

---

power in a sample of Chilean municipalities is needed, however, to pinpoint with
precision the process of local elite transformation. For a general discussion of the rise
of parties and their impact in curbing the power of local notables see chapter 8.

executive officer of the commune. Because this was an important feature of local politics, the next chapter will focus more carefully on the battle to achieve the mayoralty and on the power of the mayor in the municipality. That discussion will be followed by a detailed analysis of the center-local linkages in Chile, which proved to be so important in shaping the nature of local politics.

5. The Predominant Role of the Mayor in Local Politics

Political Pacts, Mayoral Instability and Party Salience in Local Politics

During the months of May and June, 1969, major Chilean newspapers carried numerous news items detailing the election of new mayors in important cities across the country. Thus in the city of Arica, José Solari, a Christian Democrat, was elected mayor, replacing a Communist who stepped down from that post.[1] In San Fernando, Juan Cortés López, a member of the Radical party, resigned from the mayoralty to make way for Rafael López Bariones, another Christian Democrat.[2] In the province of Malleco new mayors came into office in the municipalities of Gorbea, Imperial, Lautaro and Loncoche.[3] In dozens of other municipalities all over Chile, mayors resigned their posts to make way for successors of the same or opposition parties.

What is significant about this rash of resignations and new elections is that they were taking place midway in the terms of municipal councils elected in April, 1967, and municipal statutes make it quite clear that mayors as well as councilors are to be elected for full four-year terms. Article ixxxix of Law 11,860 notes: "Mayors will continue to exercise their functions for the duration of the period of municipal mandate, subject to removal according to the law, and they will continue in office until the new municipality . . . designates successors."[4] Nor were the outgoing mayors being removed as a result of an epidemic of corruption which, alone under the law, would justify removal. Rather, mayors were stepping down to conform with extra-legal political agreements made by parties and regidores to give each other a chance to serve in the most powerful and prestigious office in local government. Before discussing the political power inherent in that post, these political pacts will be scrutinized.

The *pactos políticos* were the product of keen rivalries between regidores after the local elections were over and before the convening of the first session of the council. Because local electoral contests were so competitive, rarely did a single party obtain a majority of municipal seats. The election of the mayor became contingent upon the ability of two or more parties to agree to vote for the same person. In the vast majority of cases the agreement involved dividing the

1. *El Mercurio* (Santiago), May 13, 1969.
2. *El Mercurio*, June 2, 1969.
3. *El Mercurio*, June 1, 1969.
4. Alejandro Silva Bascuñan, *Tratado de derecho constitucional* (3 vols., Santiago: Editorial Jurídica de Chile, 1963), vol. 3, p. 470.

mayoralty into two terms of two years, though there were cases in which the mayoralty was divided four ways, with four different individuals serving one-year terms.[5] Sometimes *pactos* were elaborated at the regional or even at the national level by higher party authorities. These *pactos* usually applied to a select number of larger municipalities. Thus in 1967 the Christian Democrats made an agreement with the Communists through which they would order regidores of their respective parties to cast their vote for a member of the other party for mayor that year, in return for support of their own candidates in 1969.

The vast majority of agreements, however, were not subscribed to by higher authorities, but were elaborated in each community. Furthermore, in most instances they were not made by party organizations but by the regidores themselves, often breaking down partisan unity in the municipal council.[6] The nature of political pacts in Chilean local government can be illustrated by describing some of the agreements reached in several of the communities where the author conducted field research.

Generally speaking, in municipalities where a single party had a majority of seats, there was no great difficulty in electing the mayor. In Viña Verde, for example, where three Nationals and two Radicals were elected, the Nationals selected one of their own for the full four-year term. Likewise, in Quille the Christian Democrats, with three seats compared to one for the Communists and one independent, had no difficulty selecting the mayor. In Hueña, the Christian Democrats also obtained three out of five seats. However, in that community two of the Christian Democrats fought for the mayoralty. After considerable disagreement, they finally compromised with the concurrence of their third colleague. One became mayor for two years and the other was promised the remainder of the term.

In some cases, where there was no clear majority for one party, political groups did agree to elect one regidor for the full four-year term. This occurred both in Triunfo and Trigal. In Triunfo a departmental capital with seven rather than five regidores, both the Christian Democrats and the Radicals had three regidores and the Nationals had one. The Christian Democrats and the Radicals courted the National councilman vigorously, with some intimating that

5. In the municipality of Las Condes, a pact between two Christian Democrats and two Nationals called for each to have one year as mayor of the commune (interview with municipal secretary.)

6. The municipal election of 1971, reflecting the polarization of the system, was an exception. The parties of the U.P. structured an elaborate pact at the national level, which for the most part was respected. For details of the pact see *El Siglo*, May 16, 17, 1971.

money was used in bargaining. The National finally decided to side with the Radicals, without demanding a share of the mayoralty. In Trigal an alliance was formed between two Nationals and one Christian Democrat, all agreeing on the election of a National for four years. Another Christian Democrat and a Radical dissented from this arrangement and remained in opposition.

When alliances were instituted, it was much more likely that the mayoralty would be divided. In Quinral a curious alliance was formed between a Communist, a National and a Christian Democrat, all agreeing on the election of the National for two years. The Christian Democrat was selected to serve out the rest of the term. The Radicals had previously controlled the municipality and had engendered animosity. The more "logical" alliance, involving the two Radicals, was completely ruled out. In Minas, where two Socialists and two Communists as well as one Christian Democrat were elected, the Communists and Socialists agreed to split the mayoralty. The same thing happened in Aseradero where again a Christian Democrat was left out as two Radicals and two Communists agreed that one of each would serve two-year terms. Occasionally a lone regidor would drive a very hard bargain. Thus in Colinas, where Communists had succeeded in electing two out of the seven regidores, the opposition parties agreed to rule out any pact with them. Two Radicals, one National, one Christian Democrat and one PADENA spent days attempting to work out a viable formula. The lone councilor of the small PADENA party was adamant in demanding a share of the mayoralty for himself. His wish was finally granted. The Radicals each received one year and the PADENA the remaining two.

The desire to become mayor was so great that quite often the *pacto político* led to a breakdown of party discipline. An example of party breakdown is the municipality of Fuerte Viejo, where the Radicals, with a clear majority, should have had no difficulty selecting a mayor. Two of the three Radicals were determined to gain the mayoralty for themselves, though during the campaign, they had agreed that the one who received the largest plurality of the vote would be automatically supported by the others. When the election was over, the man who came in second had second thoughts about the agreement, and journeyed to the provincial capital to convince provincial party leaders that he should be mayor. The provincial leaders accepted his arguments and issued orders to the other two regidores to vote for him when the municipality was constituted. This of course infuriated his colleague who had obtained the largest plurality. Instead of following party orders he made an agreement with the two Christian Democrats to serve two years and then step down in favor of one of them. Both of the Christian Democrats, in separate interviews, told the author that they had been under intense pressure from all of the Radicals, each seeking their support "even with checks."

In Estero the Christian Democrats also split over the same issue. The people of Estero elected in 1967 two Christian Democrats, two Radicals and one Socialist. Trouble set in when the Socialist refused local party orders to structure a pact with the two Radicals. The Radicals would give him only a year or at most a year-and-a-half in the mayoralty, and he wanted a full two years. Again, after time-consuming bargaining with a variety of different formulas in mind, the Radicals convinced one of the Christian Democrats to side with them.[7] The Radicals agreed to give the Christian Democrat two years as mayor in return for his support for a Radical for the remainder of the term. In addition, he pledged support for the selection of a Radical municipal secretary to be chosen soon to replace the retiring secretary.

A similar incident took place in Rosario. In that departmental capital the Radicals had a majority of four out of seven regidores. Again they could not agree among themselves as to who should become mayor. Finally, one of the regidores journeyed to Santiago and convinced a senator, who was a close ally and a member of the National Executive Committee of the party, to have that body issue an order dividing the mayoral term between him and his colleague who had received the highest plurality of the vote. As in Fuerte Viejo, the man who received the highest plurality of the vote was not at all happy with the party order, and made a *pacto* with the three Christian Democrats. The agreement was kept secret until ten minutes before the council meeting. As can be imagined, the meeting was chaotic and left bitter feelings on all sides.

As the above examples illustrate, party orders from provincial and national authorities were often not enough to prevent the breakdown of party discipline and, indeed, party friendships took second place. Even in cases where higher party organs dictated how regidores should vote, in accord with a regional or even a national *pacto*, orders were often violated.[8]

An even more serious difficulty with the *pactos políticos* was ex-

7. The other Christian Democrat was on very good terms with the Socialist and refused to go along with this scheme, preferring instead an alliance with the Socialist. This was prohibited by party orders as well as opposed by the other Christian Democrat.

8. One of the most curious cases of low party discipline was the case of a Socialist who refused to abide by a local party order to vote for a National. The National had close ties with the Socialist party leadership and was able to engineer the directive.

pressed by a prominent national legislator in charge of the Municipal Department of his party, who told the author that "more destabilizing than the political pacts is the fact that the political pacts are often not respected once made." In Minas, for example, a serious dispute arose between the Communist and Socialist parties when the Socialists refused to make way for the election of a Communist as mayor in accord with their agreement. The refusal to "entregar la municipalidad" (turn over the municipality), as the regidores continually described the transition, was due to the fact that in a neighboring municipality the Communists had stepped down in favor of a Socialist regidor who had joined the Partido Socialista Popular, which had split from the Socialist party. Though technically that man was scheduled to become mayor under the terms of the *pacto*, the Socialists argued that the pact was voided by his leaving the party. In retaliation they broke the pact in Minas.

Shifts in coalitions occurred in Rosario, where after a year the three Christian Democrats supporting the mayor had a change of heart. The mayor was isolated both from his own party colleagues, whom he abandoned to become mayor, and from his supporters of convenience. Council meetings were rarely held; the mayor governed essentially by decree. In Puente the mayor, elected for the full term by two fellow Christian Democrats, one Radical and one PADENA, lost his original coalition after the first year. However, he was able to pick up the support of a different group: one Christian Democrat, one Socialist, two Nationals and a Radical.

The instability of the *pactos* was partly due to the fact, noted earlier, that they violated Municipal Law. On several occasions the Contraloría ruled that the pacts were null and void ("los pactos adolecen del vicio de nulidad").[9] Since pacts were illegal this, of course, meant that an aggrieved regidor could not complain through regular channels. Indeed, because pacts were illegal, an examination of the public record gives little direct hint of a pact, and various excuses were employed to account for the change. Thus, in several municipalities, including the wealthy and important municipality of Las Condes in Santiago, the outgoing mayors stated publicly that their resignations were due to illness. In other cases, the new mayor simply took over due to the "absence of the incumbent mayor."

On occasion regidores took elaborate precautions to insure that agreements not be broken. In Colinas the lone member of the Partido · Democrático Nacional had already had a bitter experience in a pre-

9. Dictamen no. 44,417 of the Contraloría General de la República, cited by Jorge Reyes, "Las limitaciones y perspectivas de la acción municipal en Chile," *Boletín Informativo PLANDES*, 23 (September-October, 1967), 35.

vious term. He failed to become mayor because the resignation of the first mayor was not accepted by the municipal council. Indeed, if the parties who subscribed to a pact had a bare majority, as was the case in Colinas, it was quite possible for a pact to fail even if all the regidores kept their word. The fulfillment of a pact depended on the willingness of some of the "opposition" regidores to accept the mayor's resignation, because the resigning mayor could not vote on his own resignation, and a tie vote was not enough to accept a resignation. The PADENA did not want to risk being deprived of the mayoralty again, so he obtained a dated letter from the person who was to serve as mayor first. The letter stated that the mayor was planning to run for deputy in the 1969 congressional elections, and was thus resigning a year before that race. While the mayor had no intention of running for deputy, his resignation for that purpose would have to be accepted by the municipality because the law so required.[10] Since this resignation of necessity would come a few months before his "term" as mayor was up, the agreement provided that the first mayor would stay on as "acting mayor" until the PADENA's "term" was to begin. When the former's resignation was accepted by the municipality and our man was finally elected, he sent out the following letter to the captain of police forces, the treasurer of the commune, the judge, and the governor:

This is to inform you that as of this date I have taken over the functions of mayor of this commune.

Saluda Atte. a Ud.

However, ten days later the previous mayor reassumed office in accord with the agreement and he sent out the following letter.

This is to inform you that as of today I have taken over the functions of mayor of this commune, as acting mayor, while the absence of the mayor lasts.

Saluda Atte. a Ud.

For a period of almost a year the PADENA did not attend municipal council meetings, because as "official mayor" he would have had to preside over the sessions. Occasionally, in the absence of the "acting mayor" he took over the mayoral duties.

10. According to the Contraloría in Dictamen no. 33,203 of May 23, 1964, "the mayor who is a candidate for deputy or senator in a regular election conforms to the requirements of Article vii of the General Law on Elections (no. 14,852), if he resigns at least twelve months prior to election day. When the resignation is based on this the Corporation is required to accept the resignation in the first session after the session in which the resignation was presented. The mayor who does not resign in the designated time period loses his social welfare benefits." See *Boletín de la Contraloría General de la República*, 37 (1964), 378–79. Dictamen no. 68,106 of September 14, 1964 had a similar intent.

This discussion of electoral pacts instituted in a sample of communities has shown how important the position of mayor was in the eyes of regidores and how often complex arrangements were instituted to divide up the mayoralty and accommodate the demand of regidores to become chief executive officers. Pacts occurred mainly when there was a lack of an absolute majority of regidores from any one party, though frequently pacts were structured by members of the same party and by members of different parties in violation of party orders. Table 5.1 summarizes the party strengths in the municipalities sampled and provides information on the alliances structured to elect the mayor.

Did these findings that year from a sample of communities in 1967 apply to other Chilean communities? In other words, was there any evidence that political pacts were just as important across the board? Unfortunately it was not possible to obtain data on political pacts for all municipalities or even for a national sample without studying each municipality in depth. Political pacts were a local matter and often did not conform to party distributions, but cut across parties. A simple comparison of lists of mayors with that of regidores would not adequately determine the nature of *pactos*. Furthermore, since pacts were illegal it would have been practically impossible to get full data on changes in the post of chief executive midway through a municipal term. The Department of Municipalities of the Ministry of the Interior and the Confederación Nacional de Municipalidades (CONAM) received letters informing them of changes in mayors, but their information was not complete and earlier lists were not preserved.[11]

In spite of these difficulties it was possible in a limited way to assess the impact of political pacts at the national level. If political pacts were pervasive, then, it would stand to reason that the position of mayor in Chile was extremely unstable. This hypothesis was tested by examining tenure rates of mayors, utilizing the available information.

The hypothesis is clearly confirmed. Data for 1967 reveal that seventy-six percent of all mayors were serving in that post for the first time. Furthermore, the data show that in Chile it was not indispensable to have previous municipal experience in order to obtain the position of mayor. Thus out of a total of 211 mayors elected to that

11. The author had a difficult time obtaining the lists of mayors and regidores used in this study. Regidores lists for several terms were finally provided by the Dirección del Registro Electoral, which has a limited number of mimeographed lists. Lists of mayors for a couple of terms were obtained from the Department of Municipalities of the Ministry of the Interior and cross-checked with information in the Confederación Nacional de Municipalidades.

Table 5.1. Summary of arrangements instituted in sample municipalities to select mayors.

	Council majority of one party			No council majority of one party		
	Municipality	Council comp.	Mayor	Municipality	Council comp.	Mayor
Mayoralty is not split	Viña Verde	3 N, 2 R	N	Triunfo	3 CD, 3 R, 1 N	N
	Quille	3 CD, 1 I, 1 C	CD	Trigal	2 CD, 2 N, 1 R	R
	Manzanal	4 CD, 1 N, 1 R, 1 S	CD	Puente	2 CD, 1 R, 1 S, 2 N, 1 P	CD
Mayoralty is split	Hueña	3 CD, 2 R	1 CD, 1 CD	Mimas	2 C, 2 S, 1 CD	1 S, 1 C
	Fuerte Viejo	3 R, 2 CD	1 R, 1 CD	Colinas	2 R, 2 C, 1 CD, 1 P	1 R, 1 P
	Estero	2 CD, 2 R, 1 S	1 R, 1 CD	Aseradero	2 R, 2 C, 1 CD	1 CD, 1 R
	Rosario	4 R, 3 CD	1 R, 1 CD	Quinral	2 R, 1 N, 1 C, 1 CD	1 N, 1 CD

Note: CD = Christian Democrat, R = Radical, N = National, C = Communist, S = Socialist, P = PADENA, I = Independent

post for the first time, forty-nine percent were serving on the municipal council for the first time. Of course, since 64 percent of the regidores were serving on the council for the first time, incumbents had a greater opportunity to be selected mayor than nonincumbents. Clearly, however, a long apprenticeship on the council was not an overriding criterion in the selection of mayors.

The extremely high turnover rates in the position of mayor in Chile can be appreciated by examining incumbency rates for mayors in comparison with incumbency rates for other political offices in Chile's highly competitive environment. Table 5.2 compares the percentage of incumbents and nonincumbents in the positions of mayor, municipal councilor and deputy.

The table shows that the mayoralty position was clearly the most unstable, while the position of deputy was the most stable. Incumbents in the Chamber of Deputies made up about half of the Chamber, whereas incumbents in the position of mayor represented only one quarter of all mayors.

These findings on Chile, like the previous findings in chapter 1 on party competition in local elections, contrast sharply with Mark Kesselman's findings for France. As Kesselman reports, mayors in France had extremely long tenure rates. The average French mayor was in office for a total of 9.6 years and, unlike his Chilean counterpart, was able to dominate effectively the politics of his locality by engineering compromises and stressing the value of consensus in the municipality's struggle with the central government.[12] In France, as in Chile, the mayor was elected by the municipal council from its

Table 5.2. Incumbents in the positions of mayor, municipal councilor and deputy in 1967 and 1969.

Type of official	Mayors		Councilors		Deputies	
	No.	Percent	No.	Percent	No.	Percent
Incumbents	65	24	611	36	72	48
Nonincumbents	211	76	1103	64	78	52
Total	276	100	1714	100	150	100

Source: Calculated by the author by comparing lists of regidores and deputies for several periods before the 1967 municipal election and the 1969 congressional election. Regidores lists were compared with a list of mayors elected in 1967. The lists of regidores and deputies were obtained from the Dirección del Registro Electoral. The lists of mayors were obtained from the Department of Municipalities of the Ministry of the Interior and cross-checked with names obtained from the Confederación Nacional de Municipalidades.

12. *The Ambiguous Consensus: A Study of Local Government in France* (New York: Alfred A. Knopf, Inc., 1967), p. 34ff.

ranks. However, electoral pacts designed to divide the mayoralty post did not occur in France, as the mayor was able to retain considerable authority.[13]

The data on mayoral turnover confirms that the intense drive to seek the mayoralty was a prominent feature of Chilean local politics. Political pacts to divide up the mayoralty made it possible for many individuals to share that post, thus contributing to the great instability of that position.[14] Furthermore, political pacts reflected the low salience of party discipline in municipal affairs once the political campaign was over. Despite the argument of commentators, such as Jorge López, who argue that party allegiance was paramount, the process of selecting the mayor confirms evidence presented in the previous chapter which showed that solidarity of party members with the mayor of the same party was not that much greater than solidarity between the mayor and councilors from other parties.[15]

Attendance at council meetings confirmed the reduced importance of party structured conflict. On major local issues, such as the approval of the construction of a new theater or stadium, or the expansion of the potable water system, distinct party alignments rarely materialized. Negative votes and sharp disagreements came from council members without regard to party affiliation. Indeed, as suggested in the last chapter, the mayor himself was often the center of much controversy, as regidores from all parties challenged the validity of his programs and actions.

13. Kesselman is not clear as to why the mayor in France has so much authority. He stresses that the powerful position of the mayor itself gives prestige, but that there is a complementary process which, in the words of Andre Degremont, an author Kesselman cites, means that "rather than the position of mayor actually conferring authority, it gives formal support to the informal authority a local *notable* already has because of his character and social position." See Kesselman, p. 41.

14. Did the widespread incidence of *pactos políticos* distort the voters' preferences in local elections? In other words, was there any evidence that at least in aggregate terms the political pacts led to the election of mayors of a particular party more than of others? This question can be answered by comparing the number of mayors which each party obtained during the first council meeting of 1967 with the number of councilors which they gained in the election of the same year. In some cases — specifically, those of the Communist, National and PADENA parties — the share of the mayoralty positions corresponded closely to the share of municipal seats. However, both the Socialists and the Radicals were able to obtain a greater number of local chief executives than their distribution of local councilors warranted. On the other hand, the Christian Democrats gained a smaller percentage of mayors than of council seats. These findings suggest that the Christian Democrats may have been deliberately excluded from many electoral pacts in municipalities across the country. On the other hand, the centrist Radical party and the Socialists were more often the beneficiaries of these pacts than either of the other opposition parties. Nevertheless, despite the pervasiveness of political pacts in Chilean municipal politics, in general, the distribution of mayoralties closely parallels the distribution of municipal council seats.

15. See "Problemas administrativos y financieros de la municipalidad chilena," *Boletín Informativo PLANDES*, 23 (September-October, 1967), 18–19.

These observations were supported by data obtained in structured interviews. When asked to evaluate the role of political and ideological discussions in council meetings, an overwhelming majority of the municipal officials said that they did not play an important role, as table 5.3 shows.

Similarly, when mayors and councilors were asked to compare the roles of party and ideology at the local level to the role of ideology at the national level, a substantial majority once again stressed the lesser importance of ideology at the local level. These findings are reported in table 5.4.

The general theme expressed by municipal officials was that the most important force in municipal government was not so much the party as the personality of individuals. As one Radical put it, "With the National we get along fine, he is a good friend; it all depends on the person." Another regidor notes that, "When I was mayor I worked well with a Communist and a Conservative. I could not work with two colleagues from my own party. In the locality it all depends on the person." A Communist regidor added that "I should logically be able to work better with my colleagues from the Socialist party, but in practice I get along well with all of them." A final regidor stressed emphatically: "Look, those who know something of ideology are three or four in a small town—the rest is domestic conflict." Indeed, when the sample was asked whether it was easier to work with people from their own or from other parties, fifty-six out of sixty respondents said that it depended on the "person" in question.

Table 5.3. Distribution of responses to the question: "In municipal council meetings, how much time is taken up by political and ideological discussions which are not directly related to the affairs of the municipality?"

1. More than fifty percent	0
2. From twenty to fifty percent	2
3. Less than twenty percent	27
4. None	31

Table 5.4. Distribution of responses to the question: "Do you believe that party ideology at the local level is more, equally as, or less important than at the national level?"

1. More important than at the national level	5
2. Equally important	14
3. Less important	36
4. Don't know	3
5. No answer	2

In one sense the lack of ideological controversy in municipal affairs is to be expected. Ideological controversy does not usually develop over an issue such as granting a license to a widow to operate a bakery or spending money for new lighting fixtures. However, while these issues are small and apparently neutral they can still be conceptualized in ideological or partisan terms by noting that they distort more basic priorities. But even granting a lack of crystallization of ideological positions consistent with national party platforms, local issues and projects could still generate a higher level of party discipline. And yet only a few incidents came to the attention of the author where internal matters divided the municipality along party lines, and these for the most part involved municipalities with more than one Communist regidor. In one case, for example, two Communist regidores objected to the municipal plan to remove squatters from a riverbed. Members of the other parties, following party orders, voted against or abstained from voting on the Communist proposal to oppose the government's plan. In another municipality the Communists opposed a move to give the local doctor a gold medal for meritorious service on the grounds that he was an "enemy of the poor."

In some cases larger municipalities became involved in heated discussion of issues not directly related to the municipality. For example, when several squatters were killed by the police in Puerto Montt in early 1969, the opposition regidores in a couple of municipalities condemned the government for the "massacre." In Manzanal, opposition members, in another incident, refused to support a motion to give the president of the republic a gold medal on his visit to the city. During the Allende government these sharp disagreements over national issues would become more and more important as national polarization filtered into the most remote locality.

Though partisan conflict was lively during campaigns for local office, the key is that partisan conflict was not fundamental in structuring local cleavages in the operation of the municipality as such. Particularistic demands, the struggle to become mayor, and rivalries between mayors and councilors were more salient characteristics of local government. Because of this primacy of the role of the mayor, the chapter will turn to an evaluation of the position of the mayor in local politics.

Initiative in Local Politics: The Dominant Role of the Mayor

Though the Chilean mayor was elected by the municipal council from its ranks, the Constitution and statutes dealing with municipal matters gave him broad powers making him more than just *primus inter pares*. Not only did he preside over council meetings, he was charged with executing all decisions and was the official community spokesman to the "outside" world.

The mayor's role as chief executive implied considerable control over the execution of resolutions of the council and final say in matters of internal administration. Thus, for example, the mayor alone had the responsibility for insuring that the many items in the budget were expended as required by law. Though most items were politically insignificant, some, such as municipal subsidies, even if not very large, were of considerable political value. Sometimes, the mayor would consult with regidores ahead of time to bargain over these subsidies. However, once the budget was approved, the mayor had maximum flexibility in authorizing expenditures in these cases. What some shrewd mayors did was to give out the money little by little. Because of inflation, this meant that organizations received less real money, and, in the end, may not have obtained all the allotted funds. As one mayor explained, "If a club has E°10,000 in subsidies, I give them E°1,000 now, and E°1,000 in a couple of months. If at the end of the year I don't have money left to complete the amount, too bad." Thus the mayor could insure that subsidies go to those individuals and groups he favored. Since the mayor signed decrees both for expenditures and the fulfillment of municipal decisions, he could stall final action by procrastinating his signature. Furthermore, proposals for modification of the budgetary law could come only from the mayor. The municipal council could not propose any such modifications, or approve increases beyond the amounts suggested by the mayor—it could only reject the mayor's proposals.

Just as important was the mayor's extensive authority over internal administrative matters. Not only could he freely spend his own five percent of the budget, but he alone was charged with hiring and supervising the staff. Municipal personnel included both wage-earning *obreros* (laborers) and salary-earning *empleados* (white-collar workers). The former were responsible for such tasks as garbage collection, street maintenance, upkeep of municipal property and small-scale construction projects. The latter did most of the clerical work of the municipality, including such things as the issuance of licenses and permits. While the law set general limitations on the number of employees a municipality of a given size could hire, in practice patronage demands often lead to larger staffs than technically permitted. The mayor had exclusive rights in personnel matters, with authority to hire staff, grant leave of absence or other types of permission, declare vacancies and so forth. The only officials who could not be dismissed by the mayor were the municipal secretary and the

Director of Public Works (in those municipalities large enough to have one), who enjoyed tenure by virtue of their civil service status. The mayor consequently had tremendous patronage advantages. In practical terms, of course, the mayor who consulted with some of his colleagues on important appointments would more likely retain the cooperation of other regidores in running the municipality. But cooperation and consultation were often not forthcoming.[16]

The direct relationship between the mayor and the staff was particularly significant with respect to the municipal secretary. Municipal secretaries usually had a much greater command of the complex statutes dealing with municipal governance and budgets than anyone else in the community. They were constantly dealing with the intricacies of local administration, and because they were career civil servants, they provided continuity from administration to administration. The close reliance of the mayor on the secretary gave the mayor a clear advantage vis-a-vis the other elected municipal officials who were less likely to benefit from the secretary's counsel.[17]

The mayor's preeminent position in the municipality was further strengthened by the fact that he could not easily be removed by his colleagues. Though an absolute majority of municipal councilors, with the mayor not voting, could vote to remove him, they had to provide specific instances of violation of the law on the part of the mayor. Then the Court of Appeals would hear the case and rule on

16. These paragraphs are based on information in Oficina Interdisciplinaria para el Desarrollo (OIDES), "El Regidor en el Régimen municipal chileno" (Santiago, 1967, mimeographed), and OIDES, "Manual sobre el Presupuesto municipal" ([Santiago], 1967, mimeographed), as well as on interviews with the General Counsel of the Contraloría and other officials. The specific provisions of Law 11,680 dealing with the mayor are as follows: (1) the mayor is the representative of the municipality and can act in the name of the municipality either as a result of municipal agreement or following the provisions in the law (article lv, sections 1 and 2; article xciii, section 5); (2) the mayor is empowered with the task of carrying out municipal decisions and enforcing various provisions of the law (article xciii, sections 6, 8, 10, 11, 12) and, depending on the size of the municipality, has some resources for *obras* (projects); (3) He is also charged with the administration of the municipal government, both with respect to supervision of personnel and with respect to internal financial matters (article xliv, section 3; article xciii, sections 4, 5 and 9); (4) he is charged with supervision and administration of the budget as well as responsible for the care of local government property (articles lxxix, lxxxiv, lxxxv and xciii, sections 11 and 15).

17. On the other hand, if a mayor was not careful he could easily become a captive of the municipal secretary, who by virtue of his knowledge of the intricacies of local government had enormous influence in his own right. In one extreme case, the commune of Trigal's municipal secretary literally ran the municipality. A highly educated person, he took many initiatives on his own, such as getting the mayor to sign letters and ordinances which he had written up. In several instances the secretary got the mayor to agree to certain actions which by law required the consent of the municipal council. The regidores of Trigal, ignorant of their duties and rights under the law, actually believed that these matters were not in their purview.

whether the dismissal of the mayor was in fact permissible. These
strict regulations meant that mayors could not be removed for merely
political or personal reasons.[18]

Chilean mayors interviewed by the author clearly defined their role
as the dominant one in municipal affairs. They repeatedly emphasized
that they alone were charged with providing leadership to the community through the initiation of projects and programs contributing
to local progress. "The mayor is in command here" and "The mayor
is responsible for the progress of his town" are typical statements.
By the same token, mayors minimized the role of municipal councilors. As one said, "The mayor takes the initiative in important
matters; regidores are useful in presenting small problems."

As such, the mayor was the moving force behind the municipal
council. Attendance at municipal council meetings in several municipalities revealed the mayor's central role. In larger municipalities,
with a separate room for council meetings, the mayor invariably sat
at the head of the table. In smaller communities council meetings
were often held in the mayor's office, with the latter dominating the
room from his position behind the desk.

In council meetings the mayor presented the agenda, with routine
matters for the council's approval, as well as suggestions for local
projects, either to be undertaken by the municipality itself, or obtained from the central government. Rarely did regidores themselves
present special projects to the municipal council for consideration.
They merely reacted to the initiatives proposed by the mayor. Regidores, however, did present to the council, usually at the end of the
meeting, during time set aside for incidental matters, petitions
from citizens in the community for favorable action by the council.
These petitions consisted of demands for personal benefits, such as
the granting of a license to open a small store, permission to build
on a certain property, permission to hold a sports event, etc. Occasionally regidores put forth problems of a more general nature,
such as flooding in a neighborhood, or the existence of a garbage
problem on a particular street. As noted earlier, these personal
petitions were brought to the attention of individual regidores
outside of the municipality.

The domination of municipal council sessions by the mayor was
confirmed by a systematic examination of municipal council minutes
in the fourteen communes. Minutes from five council meetings

18. Provisions for dismissal of the mayor appear in Law 11,860, art. xc, secs. 2ff.
The Contraloría has repeatedly emphasized that the Court of Appeals had the final say
in the matter. See Dictamen no. 95,889 of December 9, 1964, *Boletín de la Contraloría
General*, 37 (1964), 1018–19.

during the year 1968 were chosen randomly in each municipality. Each statement by a council member was scored with one point. In every case mayors spoke more often than any of the councilors, and in seven municipalities mayors spoke more often than all of the municipal councilors.

In order to illustrate more fully the role of the mayor, this chapter will conclude with a more detailed analysis of the role played by the chief executive officer in three different communities.

Cleavage and Accommodation: The Cases of Quille, Rosario, and Fuerte Viejo

Quille is a relatively small community of 15,000 not far from the industrial city of Concepción. Traditionally the community had been run by Conservatives and Radicals but in the 1960s the Christian Democrats made significant inroads. In 1967 they managed to elect three of their number to the municipal council. The Christian Democrats remained united in electing the mayor for a full four year term, resisting the temptation of structuring an alliance with the Independent and the Communist councilors. Though one Christian Democrat would have liked to have split the mayoralty with his more dynamic and forceful colleague, the party was able to convince the governor to appoint him "Sub-delegado"—the executive's authority in the commune. Though he complained that his position did not carry as much authority as the mayor's, he nevertheless enjoyed having his own public office where he could attend his clientele.

Quille's mayor was a relatively young small farmer with great energy and enthusiasm for his job. His popularity in the community was underscored by the fact that he had received considerably more votes than the runner-up in the municipal elections. Like many mayors he was resented by his fellow councilmen who complained that the municipality was not a collective enterprise. The mayor brushed off this criticism by noting that council meetings were designed primarily to bring the small matters of the community to the attention of the mayor and the municipality and that he as mayor was charged with executing the major projects.

There was little doubt that the mayor was extremely successful in obtaining projects. The streets of the community were being paved, a new hospital was on the drawing boards, a large bridge had been built over a flooding creek, and the sewer system was being expanded. In his biweekly trips to the capital, and in close contact with one of the active diputados of the region, he had managed to coax out of the national bureaucracy an amazing number of large investments.

Municipal council meetings were dominated entirely by the mayor either reporting on a past or prospective trip and on the status of projects. The independent regidor, while grudgingly recognizing some of the real benefits to the community obtained by the mayor — simply opted for missing municipal meetings. He noted that he did not want to waste his time in meetings when the people in outlying communities needed his help. The Communist tried to play the role of gadfly, noting that paving of central streets was not as much a priority as the situation of people living in substandard housing. He tried his best to satisfy small demands for his constituents through the municipality. He missed not having a Communist deputy in his region to help in that task. Nevertheless, he would occasionally journey to the city of Concepción to contact a prominent Communist senator for help. The other two regidores of the mayor's own party also tended to go their own way. The Subdelegado spent most of his time in his office — and was generally highly critical of the fact that his proposals for projects were not followed through. He had close ties with another Christian Democrat deputy who had assured him that several other investments could be made — including a new school. He was confident that next time around he would become mayor and have an opportunity to implement his ideas. The other Christian Democrat had been elected largely on the mayor's coattails. A barely literate person, he was happy to defer to the mayor on municipal matters — seeking only to obtain benefits for his mountain community.

Quille, though not functioning well as a collectivity, is clearly a good example of how a community could benefit from an active mayor who saw his primary role as one of extracting resources from the center. Though the municipal council as such had little input in major matters, the mayor saw to it that small items were expeditiously processed. Hiring of employees, licensing, the sale of municipal property was done fairly and with ample consultation.

By contrast with Quille, in Rosario latent tension broke out into the open. In Rosario, the mayor made little effort to obtain resources from the outside, but sought to use the resources available to him as mayor to leave an imprint on the community. Other regidores, in turn, sought projects from outside making interpersonal relations even worse. By mid-1969 it was no longer possible to hold municipal meetings because a majority of the seven council members in that departmental capital refused to attend the sessions.

The disputes in Rosario can be traced back to the election of mayor in the first session of the municipality in 1967. As noted earlier, in that session the Radical mayor instituted an alliance with three Christian Democrats violating a previous agreement made among Radical candidates that the candidate with the highest plurality should become mayor. The agreement involved the splitting up of the municipality with the Radical serving for one period, and a Christian Democrat for the other. The Christian Democrats were pleased with the arrangement — it divided the Radicals and made it impossible for the Radicals to split the mayoralty among themselves. The reason why they did not want the Radicals to split the mayoralty is that they resented the Radical who would have shared the mayoralty. An aggressive person, he had been mayor previously and had channeled all projects to a smaller urban center in the commune, to the detriment of the main town. The Christian Democrats claimed that they, "like everyone in the town of Rosario, wanted the town to come first."

The mayor decided early that he truly wanted to get many things done. He thus proposed that a tourist area near some waterfalls be established, that a *balneario* (swimming hole) be built for the town people's use, that the stadium be finished and that a *casa de la cultura* be created for cultural projects.

The mayor, however, was not able to make much progress on his projects. Outside financing simply did not materialize. As a Radical, the mayor was automatically at a disadvantage compared with a Christian Democratic mayor, whose national contacts were bound to be more successful with a Christian Democratic government. His problems were compounded by the fact that the local Radical deputy had supported his rival for the mayoralty and had disapproved of his violation of party discipline. He simply was not able to obtain the necessary contacts to the center to enact his ideas.

Gradually, in frustration, he attempted to carry out his programs with municipal resources and to assert his authority over the community. Regidores began to criticize him more as he increasingly took local matters into his own hands. Municipal sessions became more boisterous, as all of the mayor's activities came under the critical scrutiny of his colleagues. One of the most controversial acts was the mayor's decision to expand the number of *obreros* on the municipal payroll, adding three more to the twenty man staff. The regidores' disapproved of this move and criticized his choices as being "political." They also objected to his decision to promote one *obrero* because it violated seniority rules and involved a relative of the mayor. Other issues included the mayor's decision to give land titles to some squatters. Since the municipal land in question was on a hill, the action was viewed as irresponsible. Municipal services could not be extended to the area and winter flooding would create havoc. Though some of the regidores sided with the mayor on this issue, the opposition to the action was extremely heated. By early 1969 the mayor was voting one way on a whole host of issues and all of the councilors were voting the other way.

The final breakdown of the tenuous coalition which sporadically still supported the mayor came during the March 1969 religious festival in Rosario. The nationally prominent festival, which attracted tens of thousands of people to Rosario, was not only a source of considerable funds for the Catholic Church, but a good source of funds and patronage for the municipal coffers. Dozens of small merchants came from nearby towns and cities to sell food, clothing, religious articles, and a host of other things to the pilgrims. The municipality charged licensing fees for all of these activities, collecting substantial revenues.

In the past, each of the regidores was permitted to select four inspectors to license merchants. This was a considerable political plumb because inspectors received not only a good wage, but a percentage of the receipts. This time, however, the mayor ignored tradition, and with two remaining supporters, appointed all the inspectors himself. The three Christian Democrats, who had nominally supported the mayor at the beginning refused to attend municipal meetings. They were joined by one of the Radicals who had refused to support the mayor all along. In retaliation, the mayor lowered the quorum required to hold municipal sessions, a clearly illegal act. As one Christian Democrat noted, "he is a regular dictator." A Radical agreed: "The problem with this town is that the mayor glorifies himself too much." In response, the mayor noted that the council was against progress and that he alone was pursuing the welfare of the community as a whole.

Fuerte Viejo, like Rosario, had a Radical mayor. However, his town was more like Quille in that many projects were underway, and the tension among councilors was low. The mayor of Fuerte Viejo, like his counterpart in Quille, relied heavily on the extraction of national resources. Like his colleague in Rosario he was a Radical elected with the support of the opposition, not his fellow Radicals. Being a Radical he did not have good access to the bureaucracy, unlike the mayor of Quille, but made up for his deficiency by working closely with a Christian Democratic diputado. His task was also aided by the fact that he was able to structure a remarkable local consensus. Thus, when he journeyed to the capital city he went more as a representative of the municipality as a whole than as his own man. Fuerte Viejo, then, presented a sharp contrast to Rosario.

The greater harmony of Fuerte Viejo was aided significantly by the fact that each of the regidores was elected from different urban areas within the commune. Rather than struggle against each other, with the aid of the mayor, the councilors set up an elaborate log-rolling system in which each regidor was responsible for his community, and the mayor saw to it that each got some projects. As Mayor Blanco put it: "I have turned over a town to each of the regidores. They are the mayors of these towns and I give them what they want. They give the orders in their towns and direct all the projects they undertake." By dividing up the spoils, each was thus better able to serve his personal clienteles.

In municipal sessions and in private conversations with the mayor the different regidores brought out the problems only of their respective communities. "Each regidor worries only about his town, so that there is no real opposition," one regidor remarked. This of course in itself did not reduce potential friction. At first there was considerable controversy because some regidores thought that it would be best to concentrate on one town at a time so that "real progress" could be made instead of diluting efforts across the board. However, as the mayor put it, "the majority prefers to pick a little here and there." What resulted was a classic give-and-take situation where everyone realized that whatever he got for his town depended on the support of the mayor and the others. One regidor noted that this meant that there really was little control over the actions of regidores in the various towns. He implied that in some cases regidores did not account carefully enough for expenditures made in their communities, and noted that the mayor should have assumed more responsibility. The mayor, however, disagreed, saying that he had enough work to do making the necessary contacts with important agencies in Santiago for particular projects without supervising them himself; adding that this was also the only way to get genuine cooperation. The mayor consciously attempted to clear all of his initiatives with each regidor and sought to divide benefits equally among the communities. Thus in a council meeting in which the mayor detailed his plans for a trip to the capital city, the council did not object to his recommendation for obtaining a loan through the help of the Ministry of the Interior for the electrification of all four towns, even though the electrification could not go very far with a loan of only E°30,000. The expansion of the potable water networks in both the town of Fuerte Viejo and the town of Estacion was to be sought in the Ministry of Public Works, and the expansion of the educational system in all the schools of the commune was to be sought in a trip to the Ministry of Education. While the mayor clearly dominated the sessions and provided most of the initiatives, it was understood by all that the supervision and administration of new projects in each of the communities would go to the respective regidor.

The great instability of the mayoralty in Chilean local politics meant that that post was not occupied by individuals with authority based on traditional community status. Political pacts, structured as a result of intense competition to become mayor, led to the election of a long line of individuals depending on the political circumstances of the moment. Because of the dominant role of the mayor in Chilean localities, it was that political position which conferred status on its occupants, rather than vice-versa.

Observation of local politics in 14 different Chilean communities leads to the conclusion that the search for status was not the only, nor the most important, attraction of the office. An incumbent mayor, with his control over meager local resources and his access to resources in the center, was in a unique position to service his own personal constituency and obtain programs and benefits for the community at large. These benefits were not merely symbolic, but highly tangible and useful contributions to community life.

Since major programs were not obtained through collective local action, an inevitable tension ensued between the mayor, with easier access and authority to pursue programs, and councilors relegated to performing small favors. This tension was very apparent in Quille, a community where several significant projects were underway. Rosario experienced even greater tension as the mayor, unable and unwilling to extract resources from the center to fulfill his plans, sought to use his prerogatives in municipal matters to the fullest extent. After several local coalitions appeared and disintegrated, the mayor found himself acting alone in the face of a completely hostile municipal council.

But this kind of tension was not inevitable in local politics. Factionalism was not due primarily to general cultural patterns of Chilean society. In Fuerte Viejo, not far from Rosario, factionalism was kept to a minimum and a great deal of harmony was obtained by instituting a classic log-rolling system. Through this system, each councilor could service his own clientele and share in the obtension of major resources. There was little collective action due to the lack of real possibilities and resources to generate local programming through such action. And yet, the structuring of a log-rolling system made it possible to satisfy the very instrumental demands of local politics through individual action.

The difference between Fuerte Viejo and Quille or Rosario, was not a difference in cultural characteristics, but a difference in the ways in which relationships were structured to maximize political activity in a society of scarce resources and marked political centralization. A society in which local resources were obtained primarily through political networks extending from the locality to the center. These networks did not involve direct appeals to the "authorities." Rather, a political ally in the center would intercede with particular authorities on behalf of individual local officials. The next chapter will explore more fully these crucial "vertical linkages" between locality and center in Chile.

6. Linkages to the Center: Congressmen as Brokers for Local Progress

Mayors and local officials in Chile believed that one of their primary tasks was the "extraction" of resources and projects from national governmental authorities. They were convinced that if they did not continuously haggle with the national bureaucracy, they would not succeed in obtaining the necessary resources for their communes. Thus, when asked whether ministries took the initiative in aiding the municipalities, the overwhelming majority of mayors and regidores said that the initiative had to come from the municipality itself. The language used is instructive: both local officials as well as deputies used extractive imagery, such as "The potable water project didn't come out," or "I got out the sewage system," or "the petition was enough to get a little school out of the Ministry of Education." One enervated mayor in his first term of office made it clear that local officials, while resigned to this state of affairs, were not too happy with it: "This is very frustrating. One comes to the municipality wanting to undertake a constructive task, but finds that everything has to be sought in Santiago; even to hammer a nail it is necessary to go to Santiago to argue with the ministries."[1]

Contacting the Center: The Trip to Santiago

Getting the appropriate agency to agree to build a sewer system, a bank to provide credit, a quasi-autonomous agency—the Sociedad Constructora de Establecimientos Educacionales—to build a school, involved more than just getting in touch with the proper authorities by correspondence. In Chile it meant a special trip to the center, the capital city, to inquire in person and apply the necessary pressure to obtain favorable results. The usual procedure was for the mayor to go on his own or be accompanied by a small delegation made up of other regidores (those supporting him at the moment) and occasionally of

1. Most regidores perceive that the relationships which exist between municipalities and government ministries are not good, with nine saying they were good, twelve opting for "fair," thirty-six for "bad," and three for "don't know." Six of the regidores who said that relations were good were members of the Christian Democratic party. Thus more Christian Democrats than any other party felt that relationships with the ministries were all right. However, those who thought that relationships were bad exceeded the former groups, with thirteen Christian Democrats in that category. Only two Christian Democrats opted for "fair."

other important people in the community. Thirteen of the fourteen mayors interviewed by the author had made from four to ten trips to Santiago during the past year (1968). Thirty regidores had made at least one trip to the capital city, and twenty-five had made more than three trips.[2]

An illustration of the business which local leaders transact in Santiago is provided by the agenda of an Extraordinary Session of the Municipal Council in the commune of Fuerte Viejo, held on March 2, 1968. At that session the council supported the mayor's desire to make a special trip to Santiago "para gestionar"[3] with the following ministries:

1. Ministerio de Educación [Ministry of Education]: to convince the authorities of the need for a new schooling complex for the commune.
2. Ministerio de Obras Públicas [Ministry of Public Works]: to apply for an expansion of the network of potable water in urban centers of the commune.
3. Ministerio del Interior [Ministry of the Interior]: to enlist the aid of the ministry in obtaining a loan of E°30,000 for electrification of all four urban areas of the commune.

It was also agreed that the mayor would consult in the Ministerio del Interior about the status of two large hydroelectric plants located at least in part in the commune which paid all taxes to a neighboring commune and the provincial capital. In the opinion of the mayor, such taxes should have been paid to Fuerte Viejo. The mayor was also reminded by some of the regidores that progress on a new road and bridge to a developing community of the commune was very slow, and the mayor promised that he would also look into this matter at the Dirección de Vialidad of the Ministerio de Obras Públicas. It was also agreed that the intendente would be asked to supply some machinery for repairing other portions of the same road. The mayor was authorized to use the necessary funds for his trip.

On the sixth of April, 1968, in an ordinary session of the municipal council, the mayor gave a report of his trip to Santiago. As far as the

2. A glance at telephone communications in Chile confirms the centralized nature of the system. More calls were made in 1967 from Angol to Santiago than from Angol to Concepción. Concepción is the third largest metropolitan center in the country and the fastest-growing industrial area, and only 137 kilometers from Angol. By contrast, Santiago is 630 kilometers away. See Chile, Oficina de Planificación Nacional, *Kardex de Estadísticas Regionales*, May, 1968, Appendix T 28, based on information provided by the Compañía de Teléfonos de Chile.

3. The word *gestionar* does not have an exact English equivalent. The best approximation is given in *Holt Spanish and English Dictionary/Diccionario ingles y espagnol* (1955), where the term means "to take steps to attain or accomplish something." While close to the term "to bargain," it is different in the sense that *gestionar* implies bargaining for a specific thing in a situation of disparate resources, where the object of the *gestión* has more resources than the person engaged in the *gestión*.

potable water matter was concerned, the Jefe de Vialidad promised that within a couple of weeks he would notify him of his answer through Deputy Osvaldo Cantaro, who accompanied the mayor in his visits to all agencies. In the Ministerio de Obras Públicas the mayor was told flatly that he would have to submit a more detailed proposal for paving. The mayor was more pleased with the results of his visit to the Ministerio del Interior, where the subsecretary said that there would be no problem in recommending the loan. In the Servicio Nacional de Salud the mayor discussed the possibility of having another doctor appointed with promises that this would be looked into. In the Ministerio de Educación, however, the mayor met the greatest receptivity, and was able to get an interview with the minister himself. The minister was both a good friend of Deputy Cantaro and had lived in the area as a child on his parents' *fundo*. Not only did he promise some help, the minister offered to visit the commune and inspect personally its educational problems. On hearing the news, the municipal council voted to invite the minister officially to the municipality. Discussion ensued as to what kind of gift should be given the minister. A painting of a rural setting was proposed, but the council agreed on a gold medal. An extraordinary session was asked for in order to consider the matter in greater detail. The resolution sent to the minister read: "By unanimous agreement the municipality agreed to extend you an official invitation to visit the commune, at which time this municipality will designate you Illustrious Son of the Commune of Fuerte Viejo."

The mayor then reported that he was not able to bring up the problem of taxation of industries and suggested that the lawyer of the municipality study the matter and find out if the 3.5 percent tax which this industry paid to another commune should not go to Fuerte Viejo instead.

On June 10, 1968, the mayor and one of the regidores once again made a trip to Santiago to personally extend the formal invitation to the minister. The minister promised to come as soon as a teacher strike was over, and promised once again that a school for elementary-school children would be built in the community.

This account from the town of Fuerte Viejo revealed one of the most important features of center-local relations in Chile: the mayor did not go to the ministries to *gestionar* on his own; rather, he was accompanied by a member of Congress whom he knew well. In no uncertain terms the mayor told the author that he would not have been able to get an appointment with some agencies, let alone obtain positive results, if it had not been for the help of Deputy Osvaldo Cantaro. "If I had not gone to see the minister with Luis Martinez [a deputy] and Saúl Toro [a senator], I would not have been received," another mayor remarked. A third said, "The *parlamentarios* are the people who open doors; without them one is pushed around and ignored [a uno lo tramitan y no le hacen caso]."[4] The unanimous opinion of regidores and mayors interviewed was that the help of deputies and senators was indispensable in getting things out of the national government.

What is surprising is that deputies and senators acted as the key brokers for local officials while the intendant, the chief executive officer of the province, played only a minor role. The mayor of Quille noted that "the intendant is null, he does not help at all." Another mayor noted that he had given up seeing the intendant. Not only did it take days to get an appointment, but nothing ever came from it. An ex-mayor who presided over an incredibly productive municipality which was able to obtain antiflood control projects, a new high school, a new theater, a gymnasium, a hospital and expansion of paving said that he obtained it all with the help of *parlamentarios*. The intendant played no decisive role in his transactions. Indeed, only two mayors out of the fourteen interviewed said that the intendant could be of more help in getting things out of the national government than congressmen. The first of these was a member of a splinter party, the PADENA, and had no relationships with any deputies and had made no trips to Santiago during the past year on municipal business. Neither, for that matter, did he have any substantial projects in progress. The only project in the works was repair of the one-room municipal building. However, the intendant had seen to it that a bridge was repaired. The other mayor who said that the intendant was more helpful than the legislators was the Christian Democratic mayor of Manzanal, a provincial capital. The mayor had a close working relationship with the intendant, who lived and worked in the same town and was a member of the same party. The intendant was able to channel important funds for local community progress.

There are several reasons why the intendant did not play a more dominant brokerage role. In the first place, while in theory he had supervisory powers over all agents of the national government operating within his jurisdiction, in fact, all governmental officials were subject to the centralized authority in Santiago. This meant not only that initiatives for a project came from higher authorities in the capital, but also that governmental officials owed their position and loyalty to their superiors in Santiago, and not to the political appointee of the president in the capital city. As noted in chapter 2,

4. *Tramitar* is an interesting word, very often used in Chile, meaning literally to "be transacted," i.e., delayed and given a hard time.

the intendants were reluctant to cause any great controversy in supervising municipalities for fear of embarrassing the chief executive or endangering their own position.

On small matters the intendants could be helpful to municipal officials. He could, for example, send a grading machine to smooth out a road after a flood but, in major matters, the intendant did not have the authority or the political resources to be of much help to local leaders. These had to go directly to Santiago, to the top of the centralized system, where well-located congressmen could be of help.

A second reason why the intendant did not provide much help to municipalities is that he usually expended the limited funds at his disposition in the provincial capital. A politically ambitious intendant was simply not very anxious to give up some of his resources for municipalities in other areas of the province. By concentrating on the capital city and on general projects such as attracting industry he could have a broader impact on the province as a whole to the greater advantage of his own career.

Legislators, then, were much more helpful to local officials than the chief executive of the province in obtaining resources. The first part of this chapter will discuss how local officials approached deputies and senators, and suggest why their relationship was mutually beneficial. The second part will complement this one by discussing in more systematic fashion the range of services that deputies were able to provide the municipalities and how resources were in fact obtained from the bureaucracy.

When a mayor wanted to get a project for his community, the first thing he did was to get in touch with the deputy with whom he had the closest personal contact. Of course it helped if "his" particular *parlamentario* was influential. The mayor of Quille was successful in obtaining many projects for his town with the help of Deputy Luis Martinez, and described the procedure as follows:

I go very often to Santiago—one or two times a month. I always go to see Lucho Martinez first. He is very well placed and has many contacts all over. Generally he is followed around all the time by some ten persons, so it is good to know him well to receive preferential treatment. With Martinez I always go first to the Turkish baths, those that are located near the Ministerio de Obras Públicas, then we go to all the ministries, where Martinez asks for help for the municipality. I usually take several days in Santiago, from Tuesday to Saturday.

As noted in the previous chapter the community of Quille provided ample evidence that his efforts were not in vain. The most spectacular project under construction when the author visited the community was the paving of the main streets of the town. Strangely, the paving was being undertaken by the Dirección de Vialidad, dependent on the Ministry of Public Works, and not by the Dirección de Pavimentación, dependent on the Ministry of Housing. Normally the latter agency was charged with paving city streets for which local communities had to put up a percentage of the cost. Vialidad's task was to pave roads, not city streets. However, the mayor with the help of Martinez was able to convince Vialidad to pave the main street of the town because it happened to be tied into a road system—i.e., a road came in one side of town and left through the other. Another coup for the town of Quille was the building of a large concrete bridge over a stream which floods in the winter, making it difficult for the approximately 200 people who live in the mountains to cross on foot. Improvements in health care and electrification were also being handled by national agencies enlisted through the good offices of Deputy Martinez and the indefatigable work of the young mayor.

Another mayor noted that he went to Santiago once a month:

The first time I always went with a congressman—of course it has to be an exceptional congressman with plenty of influence. The personal factor is basic in Chile. Things must first be obtained with the chief, then one has to speak to the lower functionaries, including the engineer. Developing friendships at the lower levels is very important; then one can continue to bug without the help of the congressman. Of course family or friendship ties are very helpful. For example, the Jefe de Pavimentación [Chief of the Paving Department] was a relative of my wife's, and of course he helped a great deal. . . .

As noted above, the most common pattern was for the mayor to go alone or with a delegation from the community. In some cases, however, regidores would go on their own and get in touch with the deputy they knew best. This was particularly the case with Christian Democrats, who thought that they could get things for the community by bypassing the mayor of another party. A regidor from Triunfo had just returned from a trip he made to Santiago when the author spoke to him. With the help of his deputy he went to the Ministerio del Interior to see whether it could pressure the telephone company into installing an exchange plant in a particular neighborhood of the town. He then went to the Ministerio de Justicia to see about a *personalidad jurídica* (legal status) for the Fire Department. Finally, in Obras Públicas (Public Works) he saw about expansion of the water system. He was successful in both the Ministerio de Justicia and in the Ministerio de Obras Públicas. Needless to say, his previous initiatives of this kind had not been well greeted by the mayor and the majority coalition.

Occasionally an "opposition" mayor would see a deputy or senator of the Christian Democratic party to get his aid in securing projects, generally in conjunction with his own deputy. Renato Fuentes, a Christian Democratic senator, helped the mayor of Colinas to get a loan approved in the Central Bank. However, another opposition mayor said that he had been turned down when he went to see a Christian Democratic deputy. "He told us we had to ask Radical congressmen for things." Several Radical regidores noted that Radical deputies, while at a disadvantage in getting things in a Christian Democratic administration, were still very helpful because of their vast friendships in the public bureaucracy. Radicals were particularly influential in the Ministerio de Obras Públicas and the Ministerio de Educación. However, in the Ministerio de la Vivienda, a Christian Democratic creation, their influence was very weak.

Opposition mayors also relied more on getting to know subalterns within the bureaucracy. One Radical mayor said: "One always goes with congressmen to the ministry, and even though I am a Radical I recognize that it's best to go with government congressmen. Of course, after some time I try to establish my own contacts at lower levels. For example, I now know very well the engineer in charge of the studies for the dam, and go see him often." Opposition mayors also went more often with delegations than Christian Democratic mayors who went alone. In a couple of instances, mayors did not deal with *parlamentarios* in trying to get things done, but dealt directly with the ministries. Both cases involved Communist mayors. As one put it, "All the *tramites* we do at the municipal level without congressmen. We are well received but they never solve our problems—they don't follow through." The other was even more bitter, saying that he was rarely given an appointment when he went to the ministries.

Even in small towns close to large provincial capitals, regidores and mayors found it necessary to make trips to Santiago to get things done. In Estero the mayor observed: "There are only a few things that can be done in Concepción, and those are small things only—matters of significance must be processed in Santiago." Thus the regional office would make available some road leveling machinery to fix some holes in the main street, but when it came to wanting to pave an additional block, a special trip to the capital city had to be scheduled. In one town in Bío-Bío the mayor said that the provincial director of Vialidad was grateful to him and some *parlamentarios* for pressuring in Santiago for projects which he himself wanted to undertake. The mayor said, "The zonal chief told us that if it were not for the support which you and the congressmen were providing, nothing would be accomplished," adding, "One gets things from the authorities only by harassing them."

Though mayors were mainly interested in obtaining projects or improvements of local services in their trips to the capital city, they also spent considerable time seeing to it that the municipality obtain resources which it had coming to it from the Department of Finance. Accompanied by deputies, mayors and councilors visited that office to inquire both about the amount of total funds to be returned to their particular locality, and, more importantly, the payment schedule of those funds. The funds were distributed to the municipalities in March, June, September and December, but it was up to the Department of Finance to determine what proportion of the total would be given out in each payment. Municipal officials obviously wanted the largest amount to come in the first payment, not only so that they could move ahead with projects, but also so that they could stay ahead of the perennial Chilean inflation. The head of the department told the author that he made no preferential allocation of funds, but did take into consideration cases where a commune had been hit by a natural calamity of some sort. He did admit, however, that occasionally the minister or undersecretary intervened on behalf of municipalities desiring large advances. A legislator who is well placed with the government or with the minister had a greater chance of obtaining a more favorable distribution of resources for his municipal clients.

According to the mayors, most of the petitions were made directly to the deputies in person, either when the deputy came to the region or when the mayor, regidor, or delegation of regidores went to Santiago. Sometimes, however, mayors wrote letters to several deputies in an effort to get them to take action on a particular matter. Thus in Puente the mayor needed to get a loan to finance two of his projects and sent a letter to the State Bank soliciting the loan. He then wrote to all of his congressmen asking for help in getting the loan approved. Among the answers he received were the following:

República de Chile, Senado
Señor don Luis Rubio
Alcalde de la I. Municipalidad
Puente

Dear Mayor:

Immediately upon the receipt of your letter of the eighteenth of this month, I wrote to don Alvaro García, Vice-President of the Banco del Estado, so that he could handle the request for a loan which that Municipality brought to the consideration of that Bank.

I am enclosing a copy of that letter, hoping to be able to give you an answer soon on this matter.

Attentively your friend,

Ricardo Fernandez
Senator

The copy of the letter which the senator sent to the bank read as follows:

República de Chile, Senado
Señor don Alvaro García
Oficina Central
Banco del Estado
Santiago

I would be very grateful if you could handle the request for a loan which was sent to you by the Señor Alcalde of the Municipality of Puente, Don Luis Rubio, on the eighteenth of the present month by means of Oficio No. 146 of that Municipality.

This loan will be dedicated to the execution of projects, related to the electrical lighting of that locality. This is an old aspiration of the community of Puente.

Attentively your friend,

Ricardo Fernandez
Senator

At the same time, the mayor received the following letter from a national deputy Pedro Pardo:

Chamber of Deputies

Pedro Pardo greets very attentively his dear friend Sr. Luis Rubio, Alcalde of the I. Municipality of Puente. It is my pleasure to acknowledge your kind note of the eleventh of this month, in which you include a copy of Oficio No. 146 of that I. Corporation.

With respect to this matter I must inform you that immediately I initiated personal inquiries [*gestiones*] with the Banco del Estado.

Pardo takes this opportunity to submit himself to your pleasant orders,

Santiago, November 22, 1968

Another deputy wrote the following in a similar letter:

Chamber of Deputies

Gabriel Cortés greets very attentively his dear friend and mayor of the I. Municipality of Puente, don Luis Rubio, and manifests that with the greatest pleasure he is seeing to it that the loan solicited by that I. Corporation is being activated in the Banco del Estado.

Cortés takes this opportunity to reiterate himself your friend and servant. . . .

Santiago, November of 1968

Often congressmen advise municipalities of action taken by agencies after a successful intervention. For example, one deputy sent the following letter to the mayor of a municipality:

My dear friend:

I am enclosing the letter from the señor Manager of Operations of the Banco del Estado in which he tells me that the Executive Committee of that institution has agreed to authorize a loan from that corporation in the sum of E°30,000 to be destined as follows: E°10,000 for remodeling of the Plaza de Armas and E°20,000 to repair the municipal building.

I hope that it will be possible for me to do something later on to obtain the balance, which would total the sum requested by the municipality.

Greeting you attentively, your friend and servant,

Roberto Campos
Deputy for Malleco

Another municipality received a four-page letter detailing various activities that one prominent senator had done. The letter began:

Señor don Gaston Hormazabal
Alcalde de la I. Municipalidad
Viña Verde

Dear Mayor and friend:

Today I have spent the entire morning at the Ministerio de la Vivienda, CORVI, the Caja de Empleados Públicos, attempting to determine what can be done about the matters which you raised in your recent letter about the problems of Viña Verde, etc. . . .

Another example of a petition made to a deputy for intervention in getting a project under way is from the commune of Hueña. Vialidad was going to pave the road connecting two major cities. This municipality, several miles off the main road, wanted the stretch of road from the highway to the urban center of Hueña paved.

Oficio No. 37

Señor don Jorge Sanhueza
Chamber of Deputies
Santiago

I am pleased to send you a true copy of Oficio No. 35 of the fifteenth of this month, sent to the Ministerio de Obras Públicas where paving . . . of approximately two kilometers, is requested.

Since you are familiar with this area, and within a short time machines will come through, paving the road to Quintal and passing La Posta, this would be the only opportunity. For this reason I take the liberty of pleading with you to make the sacrifice of employing your good offices to obtain what is solicited.

Thanking you in advance for your kindness, I remain as always at your disposition, greeting you very affectionately,

Luis Abdul
Alcalde

Deputy Sanhueza went to the Ministerio de Obras Públicas accompanied by a prestigious senator from another region and was able to obtain approval for adding the two kilometers of pavement. In his reply to the mayor, Sanhueza said the following:

Chamber of Deputies

Jorge Sanhueza, deputy, greets you attentively and has the pleasure of informing you of the following:

1. That with Senator Saul Toro he has obtained that the entire length of the street Comercio in Hueña be paved.
2. That at the same time he has obtained together with Senator Saul Toro that the street Esmeralda be paved up to the plaza of Hueña.
3. That the *tramites* undertaken by this deputy and Senator Saul Toro before the Sub-Director of Vialidad don Rene Wirke and before Don Fortunato Calassiati have given happy results which will no doubt benefit Hueña.

Sanhueza is pleased to be able to give out this news and takes this opportunity to once again place himself at your orders as friend and servant.

The author happened to be in the area in March, 1969, just as the road-paving crew took some time out of its task of paving the main road to pave the small stretch from the main highway to Hueña as well as several city blocks.

Regidores and alcaldes not only brought to the attention of the deputies municipal problems and projects to be obtained from the bureaucracy; they also sought more personal favors for their constituents. As noted in the last chapter, regidores often served as local-level brokers in matters dealing with pensions and social security. However, they alone could not succeed in the *tramitación* of a *gauchá chica* without turning to the help of national-level brokers or congressmen.

Local officials made it clear that they expected help from their deputies in return for the work they had done in the deputy's campaign. They were convinced that the candidate for deputy needed the support of local regidores in order to succeed in their quest for national office. In visiting several municipalities in southern Chile during the 1969 Congressional campaign, the author was able to observe first-hand the active involvement of local officials in support of their respective candidates. What is particularly significant about their conduct during the campaign is that local officials generally made strong commitments to support a specific candidate from the many on a party list. As in local elections, congressional seats in Chile were allocated following a proportional representation formula which determined the distribution by party of seats in each multimember district. This meant that often competition between members of the same party sharing the same list was as intense as competition against candidates of other parties. Only those with the highest plurality in the list stood a good chance of getting into office. A candidate for Congress sought commitments from local people of influence who could mobilize their own supporters in his behalf. As one popular regidor put it, "We are the work tools of the *parlamentarios*." An influential mayor, Juan Rojas, said that "the municipality is the base of all political parties. People say that they will vote as Rojas tells them." Another remarked, "The political parties depend on the regidor – I tell my people how they have to vote."

A third regidor summarized the dominant campaign theme in Chilean localities by saying: "I tell my people that they must vote for Deputy X because he follows through. He attends his people well all the time, not just during electoral campaigns." A final regidor remarked, along the same line, "I got the first plurality for X by talking personally with the townspeople. I told them that he could get things for them."

The clientele will not always follow the directives of the regidor or mayor in voting for candidates for another office. One Radical, for example, complained that "my electors told me that in the campaign for Deputy they would not vote for a Radical, but rather would vote for the Socialist . . . who in turn received the highest plurality in town." In this case the Socialist was a fellow regidor and his electors were set on voting for the "town candidate." The close ties of regidores with one candidate from his party, rather than all candidates from his party is revealed in table 6.1.

Table 6.1. Distribution of responses of regidores to the question: "With which congressmen do you have most contact?"[a]

1. One deputy of the same party	36
2. Several deputies of the same party	10
3. Deputies of the same party and other parties	8[b]
4. With none	6

[a] Twenty-five of the regidores said that they saw the deputy at least once every two weeks (a few once a week). Others said that they saw him more infrequently. Only ten regidores saw deputies less than six times a year.

[b] Three Radicals, four Nationals, one PADENA.

Congressmen and the Ubiquitous Small Favor

In interviews with the author deputies confirmed that most of their time was spent doing errands for constituents and that electoral considerations were upper most in their minds. All twenty-nine deputies from the five-province region where the sample of municipalities was drawn were selected for interviewing. This proved to be an impossible task because deputies were constantly on the move, visiting their regions or running around to various ministries and agencies. The "Tuesday to Thursday Club," as it is called in the United States Congress, was the norm for all deputies from the five provinces in Southern Chile. For two-and-a-half months the author made phone calls from his office at the University of Chile and visited congressional offices and the Congress itself. On two occasions he went to the districts specifically to find the subjects. Invariably the deputies would leave for their districts on Thursday or Friday and would not come back to Santiago until Tuesday for commission and plenary meetings of the Congress. Secretaries of the deputies tried to be helpful in setting up interviews but these were rarely met as last-minute conferences at ministries or dinner engagements delayed the busy legislators. Staffs often did not know where their employers were and thus were rarely responsible for scheduling appointments. While a few deputies had office hours in Santiago, they were not very appropriate for conducting interviews. The author sat in vain for endless hours in countless offices, with dozens of people who had journeyed to Santiago to seek the help of their deputy. Successful interviews were set up at very odd hours — late at night or very early in the morning or just before a luncheon engagement. Every weekend for the two-and-a-half month period all deputies left for the region. The only exceptions were the vice-president of the Chamber of Deputies, who skipped a couple of weekends because of legislative business; two deputies who got sick; and one who had other business in Santiago. In total only fifteen deputies were interviewed from the 1965 Congress, though the author spoke to seven others informally and interviewed three former congressmen.

Deputies were extremely busy men, constantly running from party meetings, to the Congress to the Caja de Empleados Particulares, to an *almuerzo* with constituents, to office hours, to an interview with a minister, all before catching a plane back to *la zona*. Without question the most important activity of the *parlamentarios de provincia* was service for the *zona* and, more significantly, for individuals in the *zona*.

By their own testimony deputies reluctantly admitted that they spend up to ninety percent of their time in constituency-related activities of a very particularistic nature. The lowest estimate of time spent on *asuntos de la gente de la zona* was fifty percent. Legislative involvement was even smaller than might be expected, because *parlamentarios* also took an active part in party meetings and activities, both in Santiago and in the provincial capital. Most of the deputies decried and resented this pattern. "The Congress is in crisis," said one deputy. "Even though I wanted to be a good parliamentarian, I don't have time for legislative activities and must devote myself in full to constituency activities. It is a vice, but that's the way things are." Another noted that "unfortunately personal attention is the key — people vote for personal attention."

Congressmen agreed with local officials that the stuff of politics was the processing of small favors. They also agreed that regidores and mayors were important elements in their own political campaigns. As a deputy told the author, "one's base is made up of small caciques." Deputies stressed repeatedly that, particularly in small towns, local elected leaders were crucial to a successful bid for reelection. A prominent deputy put it this way: "The regidores are the big cheeses (los capos) in small towns. . . . They are the bosses (mandamases) and it is they who have the electoral base; after all, they are the ones who give permission for a local dance." Illustrative of the close relationship between regidores and deputies was the fact that in referring to local officials congressmen constantly used possessive pronouns. One deputy boasted that in a particular region "almost all the regidores were mine." A deputy from Ñuble enumerated his supporters by saying, "In Viña Verde I have one regidor, in Quinral I have another, etc."[5] Another deputy was particularly proud of "one regidor of mine in Viña Verde who is doing a great job." Finally, a deputy who lost his bid for reelection told the author that one of his biggest problems was that he did not have very many regidores — "They were committed to others."

Deputies unanimously agreed with the sentiment of regidores that the principal duty of the congressman vis-a-vis his local brokers was intercession before governmental agencies to obtain small favors and local projects. They noted that the municipalities clearly had to take

5. Interviews with the deputies, which were conducted after interviewing regidores in the provinces, served to check on whether in fact deputies knew the regidores well. In every interview the author pressed the deputies to identify by name regidores in towns where interviews were conducted. Since the author had spoken to many of the same regidores at length, he was able to confirm the fact that deputies had close working relationships with some mayors and regidores, though often they acknowledged not receiving support from all of the local officials from their own party in any given community.

the initiative in an attempt to obtain resources—lest they be completely abandoned, or lose resources to other more assertive municipal leaders.

Furthermore, all deputies agreed that their action on behalf of local officials was not only a duty—but a very necessary duty. Without their support, a few mayors of large cities might succeed in approaching the bureaucracy, but the mayors from the vast majority of Chilean municipalities would have a hard time approaching a ministry to seek new projects or to finish old ones. "Functionaries pay little attention [la dan poco boleto] to municipalities," or "Municipal councilors in Chile are not accorded respect," or "They don't listen to mayors in the ministries" were common assessments on the part of deputies of the relationship between public servants and municipal officials. In fact, deputies noted that most local officials would even have a difficult time getting an appointment. "Alcaldes and regidores, especially those from the provinces, have very little influence."

Clearly the greatest demand on deputies' time came from personal petitions dealing with the complex social security system in Chile. Deputies personally spent time in the Cajas or in the Servicio de Seguro Social, looking into retirement benefits, survivor benefits, etc. "One has to be an errand boy for the old ladies," said one deputy. "They are constantly bugging one with retirement and survivors' benefits—it's a rat's nest." "There is an incredible quantity of personal petitions in Chile—it's a real aberration," remarked another. And yet deputies recognize that their intervention was crucial. Sometimes the cajas took several years in processing the papers of certain individuals, and only when a *parlamentario* or some other person with direct contacts or influence interceded did the proper papers materialize and the benefits come. "The function of a parliamentarian is to see to it that the bureaucracy not forget or lose the papers of a little old lady." Another deputy remarked, "What the parliamentarian must do is open doors in the public administration—it's a bad habit, but that is life." A third said, "It's a real drag being a deputy. I spend my whole life pasting tax stamps on documents."

Regidores and mayors, especially in the smaller communities, served as brokers between the people and the deputies, channeling the former to particular congressmen for a resolution of their problems. In one town a mayor told the author that a friend of his had spent over a month in Santiago working on his railroad retirement and was getting much help from deputy so-and-so whom he had recommended. Often regidores themselves went to Santiago to *tramitar una jubilación* (process a retirement). Regidores, depending on their years of service, received a small retirement allowance upon leaving the municipality. One regidor was not interviewed because he was in Santiago at the time the author was conducting his field work. He was *tramitando* his retirement from the police force.

Many deputies felt that it was "the vice of public bureaucracy" which was to blame for their troubles. "If only bureaucrats were more efficient and gave people what was coming to them, then we would have more time to spend on local projects and legislative matters." *Parlamentarios* acknowledged, however, that their help in these matters contributed to keeping brokers happy at the local level and to gaining more voters. By pushing for exceptions and benefits for their clients and their local brokers' clients, they had contributed over the years to an overextension of the social security system. As noted in the previous chapter, the only way the system could avoid complete collapse was to delay and renege on many benefits. This in turn made the role of the deputy functional to getting some benefits processed. The administration was able to survive by not bending until forced to bend. As Parrish and Tapia have noted:

> The erratic growth of the social security system has often resulted in the granting of new benefits and privileges without adequate provision to pay for them. Under pressure from clients and politicians the *Cajas* have been encouraged to use funds intended for capital investment purposes for current expenditures. In addition, poor investment policies and mismanagement have contributed to the depletion of these funds. Interest payments, intended to provide the main financial support of the system, have gradually diminished in importance as a budget source for the system. . . .
>
> Because of the lack of adequate resources for the system, bureaucrats are forced into a "formalistic" position. They tend to avoid action which would lead to an exposure of the tenuous financial position of the system. Pensions are delayed, red tape multiplied and those not able to bring pressure on the bureaucracy are likely to spend long hours in line only to be turned away disappointed when they finally reach its head. Unless one is able to cut through the bureaucratic obstacles through some form of personal access, he is likely to have to comply with every minor provision of the law which relates to his case. For some this process means years of waiting to collect a pension.[6]

Often the business of the *cajas* was handled by the deputies' secretaries. Deputy Jorge Sanhueza said that he had one secretary working full-time on matters relating to social security. The other secretary was charged with correspondence and work in the ministerios on behalf of municipalities and groups such as syndicates. Sanhueza claimed that seventy-five percent of the work of his staff went to constituency-related problems, of which approximately fifty-five percent were devoted to personal matters and twenty-five percent

6. Charles Parrish and Jorge Tapia, "Welfare Policy and Administration in Chile," *Journal of Comparative Administration*, 1, no. 4 (February, 1970), 455–76.

to matters brought up by groups and municipalities in the constituency. The rest of the work of the staff was spent on party matters and on legislative activities. Sanhueza's correspondence was made up almost entirely of petitions from individuals. During the week of the interview he had received fourteen letters from individuals dealing mainly with *caja* problems, three letters from municipalities and four letters from a couple of syndicates and *juntas de vecino*. In addition he received five replies from government agencies to *oficios* which he had sent inquiring about various constituency-related problems.

Regidores and alcaldes figured prominently in the groups that come to Santiago to see congressmen. Deputies from the Concepción area and the mining area mentioned that syndicates were the most frequent visitors. Most deputies reported receiving visits from regidores and alcaldes every week, while others said that these visits came once every two weeks. Only two deputies said that they received regidores and alcaldes once a month. However, deputies were quick to point out that they saw regidores more often than that on their weekly trips to *la zona*, when they made a conscious effort to see people in different municipalities.

For an interview with one deputy the author agreed to see him during his *horas de audiencia* (appointment hours). I arrived promptly at the hour agreed upon and found eleven people waiting to see the deputy. Most of them apparently were from Concepción and had made the trip to Santiago to do *trámites*. One said that this was the third time he had come, because the deputy did not get around to seeing him the first time and the second time he had to leave abruptly for a meeting. He was hoping he would have better luck this time. He had been trying for some time to get his son, who was in a coma, transferred from one hospital to another closer to his home.

The first man to see the deputy when he arrived a half an hour later was a syndicate leader from Tejidos Caupolicán, a large textile firm. He was recognized by the deputy and invited into his office. Though it was difficult to hear all of the details of the conversation, it was clear that the man was seeking the deputy's help with some problems his union was having with welfare matters. Godoy promised that he would see the proper authorities on the matter. He then called his secretary to his office from the desk he occupied in the waiting room and told him to try to get an interview set up with the Ministerio del Trabajo for Tuesday or Wednesday for a delegation of workers from Tejidos Caupolicán. The secretary asked whether the interview would be with the minister. The deputy answered yes, but then added that it would actually be better to set it up with the minister's administrative secretary, since he handled those matters anyway and was, moreover, a good friend of the deputy's. The next man that went in was also from the Concepción area. The deputy recognized him and greeted him, and then had his secretary get on the phone to call someone in the Ministerio de Hacienda about "the matter of this gentleman." The secretary called and requested that an appointment be set up with the undersecretary of the Ministerio. When asked what the matter was, the secretary said it concerned a job list from the ministry. Apparently a series of individuals on the list would be offered jobs in the ministry and the deputy was going to see the undersecretary about the possibility that the person in question would be one of those to get the job.

The next person to see the deputy was a man who was concerned about getting a law of benefits passed for pharmacists. The deputy suggested that he see one of his colleagues who had more experience with the matter. At that moment the door opened and another gentleman came, only to be ushered in directly to see the deputy. He was the mayor of a relatively large town and was looking into the paving of some streets. He had come to see whether an appointment with Vialidad had been set up. It so happened that his appointment was only a few minutes away and the deputy left with the mayor before the author had an opportunity to conduct his interview. Three other appointments had to be made before the interview was finally conducted.

Congressmen as National Brokers

The discussion so far has served to demonstrate that congressmen were the key brokers at the national level to whom private citizen and lower level officials continually turned for help. At this point it is necessary to specify more clearly how congressmen exercised their brokerage role on behalf of their constituents. Congressmen had several opportunities and resources which they could put to good use on behalf of their clients. Some of these opportunities and resources derived from the legislative role itself, while others were more informal in nature, and involved more direct access to the bureaucracy.

The Legislative Arena: Particular Laws and Budget Laws. In the legislature itself, congressmen could support their clients in one of two ways. In the first place they could sponsor legislation specifically designed to favor an individual or a municipality. Or, secondly, they could see to it that a budget law was amended in such a way that resources could be earmarked to a particular community or individual.

While the overwhelming majority of small favors for individuals was transacted by approaching the bureaucracy, at times a law was required to satisfy individual demands. Jorge Tapia Valdés has noted that between 1938 and 1958, 55.2 percent of all laws passed in Chile dealt with *asuntos de gracia*, or matters related to pensions and retirement benefits. He notes further that "these laws have been converted into a real panacea for the economic problems of those favored by them. . . . Many times pensions are given to persons . . . that don't need them to escape misery. . . . In fact, however, many of these laws are motivated by the need to correct imperfections of our social security system."[7] In the legislative period 1965–1969, 383 out of 871 bills were private.[8]

Deputies and senators were able to get legislation approved providing constituents with pensions or social security benefits or retirement funds because colleagues were willing to support such legislation in return for support of similar legislation introduced by them. Often the need for these bills was brought to the attention of the deputy or senator by local officials intent on satisfying the demands of their constituents.

In the same way that laws were approved for individuals, senators and congressmen sought to have legislation approved to benefit a particular community. An example of such a law was the one debated in the Chilean Senate in August of 1969. This law was aimed at permitting professional employees of the municipality of Santiago to rise in rank without making it necessary to increase salaries commensurate with the higher rank. Such a provision would make it possible for officials to take over the leadership of various departmental services within the municipality which otherwise would be barred to them by law. In turn the municipality would not have to increase their salaries. When this project was being debated, Senator Luengo from the provinces of Bío-Bío, Malleco and Cautín offered an amendment to add another article to the bill to benefit another municipality in his district. This article "authorized the municipality of Rengo to transfer during the present year and on only one occasion up to E°250,000 from income perceived from Law No. 16,591 into its ordinary budget."[9] According to the senator, the municipality of Rengo was facing a serious financial crisis and was not able to pay its employees. Law 16,591 provided for a special tax on matches, part of which was assigned to the municipality of Rengo for new projects. Clearly the intent of this

7. Jorge Tapia Valdes, *La técnica legislativa*, (Santiago: Editorial Jurídica, 1960), p. 237.

8. Chile, Senado, Oficina de Informaciones, *Boletín Estadístico XXXIII* (n.d.), 15.

9. For a transcript of this debate, see *El Mercurio* (Santiago), August 21, 1969, p. 13.

act was not to provide money for the operating budget of the municipality, but Luengo argued that the financial crisis made it imperative to come to the rescue of this municipality. Some senators objected that the measure had not been discussed in the appropriate commission and thus had not been studied in detail. Another noted that the measure might prejudice a more permanent solution to that municipality's problems. Nevertheless, the measure was approved by a vote of fourteen in favor and one against. Ten other senators abstained, while four others were paired. Though the Nationals did not support the measure presented by a senator from the leftist coalition, they did not oppose it, and abstained.[10]

A very common measure that was usually approved by unanimity with no debate was a law allowing a municipality to borrow funds for local improvements. Congressmen told the author that this was essentially a pro forma matter and usually no objections were raised to the approval of such a law. Neither the Chilean Constitution nor the laws dealing with municipalities required that a law be enacted in order to permit a local government to secure a loan. Nevertheless, the practice developed to have the loan sanctioned by law. This legal formality was said to assure correct investment of municipal funds and proper servicing of the debt. In some cases these laws called for special taxes in order to meet new financial obligations.[11]

These laws were pro forma in the sense that they did not really guarantee that a loan would in fact be secured. In order to obtain a loan a municipality had to approach a bank, usually the Banco del Estado (State Bank), and secure a loan through regular channels. Congressmen usually portrayed the passage of the law itself as a victory for the municipality and evidence that the congressman was hard at work on behalf of his constituents. But if they were really serious about procuring the loan they would have to approach personal contacts within the bank to *tramitar* the loan itself.[12] In some cases the congressman's initiative had to go even further, as the following example will illustrate.[13]

The new mayor of one of the municipalities visited by the author realized when he took office that his municipality had received earlier

10. Ibid.
11. Loans are usually amortized for a ten-year period with a special territorial tax $(20 \times 1,000)$ from which $1 \times 1,000$ is reserved for amortization of the loan. The financial department of the Ministry of Finance asks the Internal Revenue office for an appraisal and the Caja Autónoma de Amortización de la Deuda Pública to take over the amortization of the loan while the actual loan is granted by the Banco del Estado.
12. The reader is referred back to chapter 6 for examples of correspondence dealing with the matter.
13. The following example is drawn from interviews with the mayor, deputy and department head in question.

authorization, by an act of Congress, to obtain a loan, but the money was nowhere to be found. In consultation with his predecessor and "his" deputy he discovered that the municipality had tried without success to obtain a loan, based on this authorization, from the Banco del Estado. However, in reviewing the loan law, the congressman discovered that the law specifically stated that if a loan was not provided by the bank, the government would be required to issue a decree providing the expenditure out of government funds. The previous mayor apparently had not understood or was not aware of this provision, so that the municipality had never pressed for this money. The mayor then made a special trip to Santiago to investigate the matter, and with his deputy went to the Department of Finance. The head of the department told them that it was impossible for the Ministry of Finance to find out whether the loan had or had not been obtained and that it could thus not automatically issue the appropriate decree providing the finances in question. As it turned out, the head of the department promised the mayor that he would get the minister to issue the decree soon, just before the deadline.[14] Clearly, if the mayor had not gone with the deputy to see about this matter, the municipality would have lost E°20,000.

The centenary celebration of municipalities in Chile has often been used as an occasion to obtain a major loan for community improvement, and congressmen have been very willing to support the authorization of substantial funds. Again, obtaining the loan from the bank proved to be a problem, but several congressmen interviewed by the author boasted that they were able to bring about significant changes for several towns in their districts "for the centennial celebrations."

These examples have illustrated how congressmen could obtain legislation favorable to individual constituents and communities. However, such legislation was severely limited in scope and for the most part called for the enactment of authorizations to secure loans and not direct grants from the state. It was during the process of approval of the budgetary law that congressmen could have an important influence.

The Ministry of Finance was the key actor in the early stages of the formation of budgetary policy. With the president of the republic having the final say, the Dirección de Presupuesto of that ministry

14. An example of the language used in senate debates in approving a loan is as follows: "En Facil Despacho, se aprueba, sin debate, el segundo tramite constitucional, un proyecto, eximido del tramite de Comisión, sobre EMPRESTITO PARA LA MUNI-CIPALIDAD DE MOSTAZAL."

prepared the public budget for congressional consideration.[15] The first phase began when the Dirección set the general limits on expenditures which each ministry had to adhere to in preparing its budgets. This limit was calculated, taking into account revenue calculations from the Servicio de Aduana and the Servicio de Impuestos Internos. The criterion for setting these limits was basically incremental. The previous year's authorizations were carefully studied and rough calculations made of the necessary readjustments which were required to cope with inflation and the small margin of resources needed to start new projects. In theory the Office of National Planning (ODEPLAN) set up by the Christian Democrats was supposed to specify national priorities based on general development plans and these priorities were supposed to be translated into specific budgetary recommendations. However, ODEPLAN did not have an important impact. As one analyst in the Dirección de Presupuestos put it, "ODEPLAN has many general theories but without specific studies, and the statistics with which they work are practically null." Except for new agencies that were created to carry out new programs, there was very little room in the planning of the budget for new projects.

At this stage the ministries decided in very broad terms how much they were going to request for each one of their bureaus and departments. Little attention was paid to more detailed projects and programs which might have been of interest to municipalities. When the budget requests were sent back to the minister they were invariably larger than the limits set by the Dirección, and thus the minister of finance had to decide what would be cut. The Dirección was charged with this task, and analysts critically evaluated the sums which were being proposed for subunits of the ministries. Again, except in the case of major projects such as the transfer of the National Airlines from the airport of Los Cerillos to the airport of Pudahuel, at this stage only general sums for each of the bureaus was discussed. Several cabinet meetings were held in which various ministers argued for a restoration of funds. Though at this stage some changes may have been introduced involving "political considerations" in line with general governmental priorities, these changes did not generally perturb the analysts in the

15. The Dirección de Presupuesto is a highly skilled and very professional organization well regarded by administrators in the various ministries. An indication of this comes from a study of forty-eight key people — *cargos de jefatura formal o informal* — in one agency. When asked which external agent had the most influence on the agency, the Dirección de Presupuesto ranked highest. Unfortunately, the authors of the study did not include political elements such as congressmen in their closed question. They were also unclear as to what kind of influence was involved. (Study in progress by Rafael López and Jorge Tapia, Instituto de Administración, Universidad de Chile.)

Dirección because they were not of a magnitude which might affect a "good budgetary system."

The only *parlamentarios* that had influence at the early stages of the formulation of the budget under the Frei administration were those who formed part of the *comisiones tripartitas*. These were special commissions within the Christian Democratic party which dealt with affairs relating to each of the ministries; thus there was a commission for the Ministerio de Obras Públicas, the Ministerio de la Vivienda, the Ministerio de Agricultura, etc. These commissions were made up of representatives from the party and the executive branch, together with Christian Democratic members of the appropriate commission in Congress. These commissions met usually once a week, generally over lunch, and discussed the general subject matter with which the particular ministry was concerned. At times clear divisions emerged among members of these commissions. The members representing the executive branch were usually most concerned with keeping budgetary allocations in perspective with those of other sectors in thinking about the general needs of the nation. Party people, on the other hand, were most concerned with pushing programs which were attuned with party ideology and were most capable of providing the party with new constituencies. Congressmen, finally, were concerned with projects and programs which might have a direct impact on their constituents. These were of course general orientations; a blurring of these divisions of the tripartite commissions might take place at any time over specific issues.

On budgetary matters the tripartite commissions came to general agreement on policy and budgetary recommendations to be forwarded to the executive. Generally, they argued for an increase in funds for the ministry in question, appealing directly to the minister of finance. Since general budgetary allotments were considered at this point, government congressmen could not push for specific projects for their constituents, and as one deputy put it, "The opinion of the executive carries great weight in determining general financial limits." However, individual congressmen or senators with good contact with the president or the minister of finance, either because of a high party post or prior friendship, could be influential in seeing to it that a particular bureau or agency receive a higher allotment. For example, a congressman might push for a greater amount for a program such as *operación sitio*, or for new housing to be handled by different subdivisions of the Ministerio de la Vivienda. By pushing programs that administrators want, especially new programs which are more likely to receive increased funding, an influential congressman could gain credit with these administrators for help in the allocation of funds for a specific project which the congressman had in mind. Analysts in the Dirección de Presupuesto, in charge of specific ministries,[16] told the author that bureau heads from that ministry contacted them and the director of the Dirección in an effort to soften cuts from their budgets. While they claimed that very little was changed as a result of this, they admitted that if the minister ordered a certain reinstatement of funds, it often came as a result of political pressure.

The budget was then sent to Congress for its approval. Under the Constitution the Congress was not allowed to increase the level of expenditures from that suggested by the president. The budget was discussed in the Comisión de Hacienda (Finance Commission), and before its various subcommittees representatives of the Ministerio de Hacienda, Dirección de Presupuesto, and ministers and undersecretaries of the various ministries testified. Occasionally they would argue in response to questions from congressmen that they needed higher authorizations for certain items, to the annoyance of the minister of the interior and "the government," who expected solidarity with the decisions made.

According to functionaries in the Dirección de Presupuesto, the Congress was the place where the budget was "totally distorted." "Congress creates an extraordinary rigidity in the budget law, parcelling it out completely." What Congress did in essence was to take the appropriations for various *direcciones* and specify that funds from that item go to specific projects. Thus, for example, in the general budget of the Dirección de Servicios Sanitarios of the Ministerio de Obras Públicas a provision could be added that a certain percentage of the funds be spent on potable water in commune X, and another could specify that E°10,000 of the appropriation be spent on sewers for commune Y. Ministry people argued against such a "distortion" of the budget law, claiming that it made it impossible to go ahead with their plans and programs.

Congressmen sought support for their individual *iniciativas* from their colleagues. Usually such support was forthcoming and even congressmen from the opposition parties succeeded in getting their *indicaciones* approved. Government party congressmen supported these *indicaciones* for two reasons. On the one hand they got support for their own *iniciativas* and, on the other, they realized that the president would veto each one of the *iniciativas* that he did not concur with, and thus most of them would not be approved. This was the case because overriding of a veto took two-thirds votes in both houses and

16. Each ministry has an analyst who works with four or five aides on the budget of that ministry exclusively.

the government congressmen did not support *indicaciones* of opposition members.

Only on rare occasions did the Congress in the Christian Democratic administration override a presidential veto of an item introduced by one of the members, even if he was of the government party. What government congressmen did to retain their *indicaciones* was to bring influence to bear on the minister of finance so that their particular *indicaciones* were not vetoed. This, then, was the strategy of members of the Christian Democratic group, and only the most influential legislators of the party succeeded in getting the "government" to make an exception and not veto their particular projects. Occasionally the government was forced to veto an *indicación* by a friendly congressman. Thus Renato de la Jara presented an amendment for the extension of the potable water system of the town of Yumbel. He then went to see Minister Zaldivar and got the minister's assurance that his *indicación* would not be vetoed. However, in the Senate this *indicación* was put together with other similar *indicaciones* in one package, and the president vetoed the entire item. De la Jara was upset and went back to see Zaldivar. Zaldivar was very apologetic but insisted that he could not accept all of the other *indicaciones* at the same time.

A prominent Radical congressman was more successful during the Alessandri administration. He boasted to the author that he was able to secure promises from the administration many times not to veto his *indicaciones*. During the Frei administration, however, his *indicaciones* were always vetoed, so that he came to concentrate on an overseer role during that administration.

Whether *indicaciones* were successful or not, congressmen liberally introduced them because it gave them an opportunity to inform municipal leaders and other constituents that they had succeeded in getting Congress to specify in the budgetary law the expenditure of resources for a project dear to their hearts.[17] Later of course the congressmen could blame the administration for vetoing a measure of "obvious local benefit."

Aside from *indicaciones* to the budget law specifying funds to be used or projects to be undertaken in a particular area, there was another form of congressional specification of funds. This was through *leyes especiales* (special laws), laws approved before the budget law and calling for the destination of funds to specific areas or programs. The most important of these was the Ley del Cobre (16,524), which

17. So many amendments are presented to the budgetary law that when the law returns to the Congress after being sent back to the executive the vetoes are larger than the budget bill itself.

required that a certain percentage of the copper revenue be invested in those provinces in which copper is mined.

Sometimes specific laws were enacted for a particular community. As noted earlier, this often took place when a municipality was having an important anniversary, such as the centenary. In the 1968 and 1969 sessions of Congress, a series of *obras* for the municipality of Parral was thus discussed and approved so that it could celebrate its centenary.[18] Some laws assign funds for specific investments in particular municipalities. Examples are Laws 16,447, which destined funds for the installation of potable water service in the municipality of Chanaral, and 16,945, which appropriated funds for streetpaving in the municipality of Pica. These specific laws were unusual, however, and during the Frei regime could only be enacted with executive support.[19]

An illustration of a budgetary item, containing both funds to be allocated through the Ley del Cobre as well as funds to be allocated through amendments sponsored by congressmen and upheld by the executive, is the following extract from the Budget Law of 1969, dealing with the Dirección de Vialidad of the Ministerio de Obras Públicas:

Programa 11: Conservación de Obras Viales
Item 12/02/11.065   Inversión Real   E°166,000,000

To conserve and improve roads, including the continuation and expansion of existing contracts and the execution of new projects and contracts, expropriations, liquidation of old contracts and technical inspection of projects; construction of laboratories and work camps, purchase and acquisition of machinery equipment and materials, transformations and repositions. From this sum the amount of E°12,214,945 will be destined to the conservation, improvement of roads and execution of projects in the provinces of Tarapacá, Antofagasta, Atacama and O'Higgins, in accordance with Article li of Law 16,624.

Charged to this item, preference will be given to the construction of a road between the Población Guacolda and the city of Traiguén, province of Malleco, and immediate preference will be given to the construction of a new bridge in replacement of Puente Largo, and the following sums will be invested in the following projects: E°250,000 in finishing the road from Lago Ranco to Rininahue, E°70,000 in finishing the road from Maullin to Chuyaquen, E°70,000 on the road of the island of Pulaqui, and E°50,000 on the extension of the road from San Agustín to Huelma.

This sum will be available in accordance with the effective returns of the law.

Total program costs: E°166,000,000[20]

18. *Diario de Sesiones del Senado*, pp. 11, 1033.
19. *Diario de Sesiones del Senado*, March 24, 1966 and September 26, 1968.
20. Taken from República de Chile, *Ley de Presupuesto del Ministerio de Obras Públicas y Transportes: para el año 1969* (Santiago: Talleres Gráficos "La Nacion," 1968), p. 67.

The budgetary process thus provided congressmen and senators with a series of opportunities to intervene on behalf of constituents for specific projects. Influential congressmen were able to settle debts with administrators at an early stage in the budgetary process by pushing for more funding for particular agencies and bureaus. During the congressional stage most congressmen succeeded in designating general amounts for specific purposes. In 1969, however, unless they were able to convince the executive not to veto their *indicaciones,* or two-thirds of their colleagues to overrule a veto, many of these amendments were not enacted into law.

Congressmen, including several Christian Democrats, resented the attempts of the Eduardo Frei administration to curtail congressional initiatives for local projects. By enforcing party discipline, Frei was able to use his large majority in the Chamber of Deputies to sustain presidential vetoes of amendments introduced by legislators. Previous administrations had been supported by a coalition of parties, encouraging log-rolling and accommodation, and forcing the President to be responsive to congressional demands. The Christian Democratic administration, from its unique position of strength, went a long way toward undermining the effectiveness of the legislature as the key arena for political accommodation. Following a trend given impetus in the administration of Jorge Alessandri, politics was viewed as illegitimate and a detriment to "rational" planning. Even subsidies for organizations, a favorite source of congressional patronage, were restricted, though they represented only a miniscule portion of the budget.[21]

Even if a congressman succeeded in getting an amendment through requiring an agency to invest a given amount of its budget on a specific project, it still faced serious potential road blocks. Administrators in the ministries did not like to have their hands tied to specific projects required by law and shared the view of the budget analysts and other tecnicos that the rash of *indicaciones* was an aberration to a scientific budgetary process. Administrators could then resort to various tactics to delay or cancel out a particular project. They argued, for example, that all projects require a technical feasibility study befor they could be undertaken and before funds could be spent to implement the project. The phrase "it is under study" was used often as a delaying tactic. Delay of the project, in turn, reduced the chances

21. Planners simply did not realize that by undermining the role of Congress they were undermining an important arena for accommodation in Chilean politics and thus undermining the stability of the regime. For a discussion of the effect which planning had on the Chilean Congress see Arturo Valenzuela and Alexander Wilde, "Presidentialist Politics and The Decline of The Chilean Congress," in Lloyd Musolf and Joel Smith, eds., *Legislatures and Political Development* (forthcoming).

that it could be funded, as inflation diminished the purchasing power of allocated funds or the funds failed to materialize altogether. All the budget law did was specify the minimum funds which could be allotted to a specific agency. If in the execution of the budget there was not enough money to meet the initial projected expenditures, then the budget could be cut down to minimal levels. Thus the budget for a given ministry could be cut back from 600 million to 400 million escudos. In August or September the Servicio de Tesorería of the Ministry of Finance would announce the cuts to be applied to the various public agencies, necessitated by the failure of projected income to meet expectations. Thus, if custom duties had fallen below expectation, some agencies would feel this cut in their operating budgets. This meant that many agencies simply would not have the funds to carry out some projects written into law, at least for the time being. These uncertainties in the budgetary process meant that individual congressmen had to constantly be on the alert to see to it that their particular projects were implemented. If the Dirección de Riegos of the Ministry of Public Works had planned to build five dams, but because of cutbacks could only build four, sponsors of the various projects had to struggle to insure that their particular dam was not eliminated.

This discussion points to the fact that congressmen had to approach bureaus and agencies directly, either to press for the execution of a project which they had successfully written into the budgetary law or to convince administrators to undertake a particular project not so specified out of the agency's funds for that purpose. This chapter will conclude by evaluating the congressman's role as a broker dealing directly with the public agencies of the Chilean government to obtain national resources for investment in particular localities.

Congressmen and Bureaucrats. Each one of the ministries, once the budget was approved, drew up its program in conformity with the law. In the key ministry dealing with local services, the Ministerio de Obras Públicas, planning at this stage for specific projects used to be a rather haphazard process. Local representatives of the ministry (known as *ingenieros zonales*) would report to the various *direcciones* the basic needs of the region over which they have jurisdiction. The line agencies in charge of particular programs would then go about setting priorities with the general approval of the minister. According to the head of the newly created Departamento de Planes de Desarrollo, this procedure invited the intervention of *parlamentarios* in the planning process, each pushing for his particular project.

With the inauguration of the Frei administration this pattern changed. Central planning agencies within the ministry were charged with drawing up general plans which were not as dependent on the needs of the local agency representatives. These plans conformed with national priorities set by the National Planning Office (ODEPLAN). In fact, the planning office in the ministry was referred to by its head as the "ODEPLAN office in the ministry." The bureaus were sent these plans and were expected to follow the general recommendations.[22] "That way planning is not disturbed by politics," as one official put it. The inauguration of program budgeting was also aimed at rationalizing the investment process for the good of developmental schemes.[23]

In practice, however, the various line agencies of the ministry did not follow the plans with any great care. In the Dirección de Obras Sanitarias plans set up by ODEPLAN in response to requirements of the Alliance for Progress were never followed completely. Among other goals these plans called for potable water for all towns of more than 10,000 inhabitants and sewer systems for all those over 5,000, as defined by the 1960 census.

Plans were not strictly adhered to in part because of the great growth of urban areas which made it difficult to follow specific criteria. Expanding large towns need as many services as the smaller zones that have never received such services. The increasing number and variety of needs and the limitation of resources has meant that specific communities, able to muster political pressure, succeeded in playing an important role in the allocation of resources for specific programs and projects. Deputies and senators, then, were in fact able to exert influence at this stage of the budgetary process—that is, in the determination of programs and the setting of priorities for specific activities within the various *direcciones*. Thus, a municipal building could be built by the Dirección de Arquitectura and a sewer system expanded by the Dirección de Obras Sanitarias and a bridge built by the Dirección de Riego because particular communities were able to exert influence.

Planning officers interviewed consistently decried the intervention of politicians and the consequent distortion of their plans. Other bureaucrats were not as prepared to completely condemn this outside intervention. Though stressing that the intervention of politicians did

22. On the history of planning in Chile see Osvaldo Sunkel, "Structural Change Development Strategies and Planning in Chile" (mimeographed, 1969). On ODEPLAN and its weaknesses from a "planner's" perspective see Osvaldo Contreras Strauch, *Antecedentes y perspectivas de la planificación en Chile* (Santiago: Editorial Jurídica, 1971).

23. For an evaluation of this effort see Insora, *Evaluación de la experiencia del presupuesto por programa en Chile* (Santiago: Insora, 1971).

not conform to the best administrative standards, they pointed out that *parlamentarios* could be very useful in bringing to the attention of administrators needs in various areas of the country. The director of the Dirección de Obras Sanitarias of the Ministerio de Obras Públicas, charged with developing potable water and sewer systems much in demand by individual municipalities, went so far as to say: "I think that in the final analysis it is not necessary to have detailed planning, since people make noises about what they need. They know what they need for their towns more than we do." In a situation of very scarce resources many administrators found that they appreciated learning about the problems of different communities across the nation from knowledgeable individuals. Plans, on the other hand, were often elaborated completely in a vacuum, with faulty information and unrealistic goals. If communities were able to make their needs known in an intelligible manner, agencies were often in a better position to make concrete and rational decisions for expenditure of resources. Another high-ranking official whose department also dealt with projects of interest to municipalities told the author: "The congressman is the element of connection (of course, that is not his natural function, but it is without a doubt his real function), and he is important because there has never been in Chile a better mechanism. . . . The congressman is the sounding board of the locality, he gathers and synthesizes problems and sees to it that the law is enforced." Invariably, bureaucrats recognized that some communities might be left out if they did not have effective help from *parlamentarios* in Santiago. But this was perceived as a fact of life, and administrators often repeated in interviews the expression "guagua que no llora no mama" (a baby that does not cry does not feed), or "si no hay piteo no se alimenta" (if there is no whistling it is not fed), indicating that pressure and complaints are expected if something is to be done for local communities.

The magnitude of the requests received from the congressmen can be illustrated by the fact that when the author interviewed the director of the Dirección de Obras Sanitarias of the Ministerio de Obras Públicas, his office had received thirty *oficios* (official memos) from legislators in two days. A full-time staff member was employed just to answer the various communications that came in. In this office the director showed the author two separate charts. One had the original plans and priorities drawn up by the planning office of the Dirección, while the other had actual and projected plans which he had finally decided on. These were based on the needs of his office, and on information he had received from outside — including information given by *parlamentarios*. He freely admitted that one of the main influences in changing the original priorities came from deputies and senators.

Congressmen and senators were infinitely more effective in getting things for their particular communities if they could provide ideas as to how the projects could be carried out at minimum expense. Often this could be done by obtaining funds from the community in question. Various schemes existed whereby a community could contribute a certain percentage of the total cost, either through general funds or by soliciting individual contributions. Several deputies stressed to the author that their success was a product not only of good contacts and influence but the result of hard work and knowledge of the law, which made it possible for them to come up with formulas guaranteed to convince bureaucrats to invest in a certain project.

Thus the Dirección de Servicios Sanitarios of the Ministerio de Vivienda y Urbanismo built extensions to established potable water systems with matching funds given by individuals or communities interested in this service. The agency determined what amount citizens had to pay, and after forty percent of the local funds had been deposited, the technical study on the project was begun. After seventy percent of the funds had been deposited (not including funds spent by the agency), actual work on the project was started. One deputy boasted that he was successful in getting many towns in his *zona* to put forth the money. In one case he even suggested that a poor community hold a festival to raise money for the project from local people and tourists. The money was raised. Another deputy convinced a local municipality to purchase a cheap and good piece of property in front of an old school. With an attractive piece of land already purchased it was much easier to convince the Ministerio de Educación to go ahead with a construction project for a new school. Another *parlamentario* said that he made a practice of studying carefully the budgetary law and expenditures and would invariably find sums of money which would have been lost if not expended. He would then convince the appropriate agency to invest in a project of his liking.

Whether a particular local contribution was prescribed by law or not, bureaucrats acknowledged that the availability of funds made it much easier for them to decide on investments. As one put it, "Our wallet is very open for those that help finance their project. . . . I always go with the community with more money deposited. If the congressman helps obtain financing, I help with grants from the bureau. If municipalities don't contribute, the sissies are not given anything [no se les da ná a los perlas]."

Though the influence of *parlamentarios* was clearly enhanced by their ability to obtain counterpart funds or other resources to entice agencies to invest in a particular community, they also had other resources which they could use to get action. It was noted earlier that certain legislators were able to exert influence at the early stages of consideration of the budget and could consequently accumulate favors from certain agencies to be used at a later date. The most prevalent way of exerting influence on a bureaucrat, however, was to get elements at higher levels to order him to undertake a project. One influential deputy recounted the procedure he used in the following terms:

I always return to the office before going to a ministry to call a functionary and make sure that it is a good time to go see him. I begin at the lower levels, with the bureau heads. They, after all, are charged with the details and must see to it that projects are met. I treat them cordially, and generally they perform well. But of course, once the matter has been stated, I talk with the people higher up, with the minister or the under-secretary so that he can also see to it that things go well. If I don't know the minister well, then I ask Renán Fuentealba [an influential senator, and president of the Christian Democratic party] to place a couple of calls about the matter.

Clearly, then, congressmen from the government party had a much better chance of obtaining resources from the ministries. They were more likely to have good contacts with government appointees and a much better chance of receiving favorable action from the minister or the undersecretary. One opposition deputy told the author: "One can accomplish much as a congressman from the government. When we were the government with Alessandri, I extracted a whole bunch of things for my region. Now that I am an opposition congressman, I serve another function—the function of auditing the government. It must be stopped when it gets carried away [hay que pararle el carro cuando se le pasa la mano]."

Opposition legislators who were in office for many years nevertheless retained a good deal of influence with civil servants with whom they had worked earlier. Some had influence by the fact that they had cooperated in some way with the government in legislative matters in which the government needed their support. In some cases opposition legislators had certain departments or agencies where they could receive a favorable hearing. Thus, when the Christian Democrats came into office they encountered some resistance to their community development plans in the key Ministerio de Obras Públicas. Since civil service laws made it impossible to change that ministry drastically, some of the functions of Obras Públicas were taken over by the new Ministry of Housing and Urbanism set up by the Christian Democrats. Thus the Ministry of Housing had a Dirección de Servicios Sanitarios which in reality performed the same functions as the Dirección de Servicios Sanitarios in the Ministerio de Obras Públicas. Ostensibly the first of these was charged with extension of existing services, while the latter was charged with new services. In practice their functions overlapped, and opposition elements found a more favorable hearing for their projects in the agency of the Ministerio de Obras Públicas.[24]

Opposition deputies and bureaucrats agreed that the legislator from the government party, with his easier access to the top officials in an agency, did not have to bring as much community pressure to bear on an agency as the opposition legislator. The latter were much more likely to show up in a ministry with a huge delegation of people from a particular commune to stress the legitimacy and urgency of their demands. An opposition deputy put it this way: "It is better if the deputy arrives at the Banco del Estado or a ministry with all his regidores to make his presence known—they pay more attention to you."

Socialist and Communist deputies appeared to have the least influence in the public administration during the Frei administration. More than others they would resort to the device of mobilizing a whole community to put pressure on the government to get a project approved. The usual tactic was to stage large demonstrations or marches of community people to dramatize the demands. This was especially effective in Santiago, where the media were quick to pick up the demonstrations and the government was more directly challenged to respond.

So far this chapter has suggested that the direct influence which legislators had on bureaucrats was mainly a function of their ability to represent sensibly the needs of constituents as well as of their ability to exert pressure on superiors to have a particular topic enacted. A more direct method of pressure was probably still important in Chile: that is, government legislators appeared to have some influence over the hiring and promotion of civil servants in the Chilean administration. Through party and government contacts, friends and clients could obtain jobs mainly at lower levels but also at important intermediary levels. Patronage was particularly important in new agencies created to carry out new projects in conformity with government policy.

Since most political influence was aimed at the level of *dirección* it is necessary to realize that it was precisely at this level that people aspired to higher bureaucracy positions, such as appointment to be

24. The rivalry between these two agencies was very intense, even though the Ministerio de Obras Públicas agency was considerably larger, with 5,000 to 6,000 employees in the field, mainly in maintenance capacities. The Ministry of Housing counterpart had only 150 employees. They both claimed that the other was on its way out (interviews with the directors and key staff members of both agencies).

undersecretary or minister. Thus the director of Vialidad may very well have aspired to become undersecretary of the Ministerio de Obras Públicas. Senators or deputies with influence in the government party or with good contacts with a particular minister could be of great help in promotions. In the Frei administration, the *comisiones tripartitas* sometimes became involved in appointments. A Christian Democratic congressman of the *comisión tripartita* dealing with a particular ministry would suggest a particular individual to be appointed head of an important *dirección* and, conversely, could have sought to have someone removed from a particular post. Deputies were reticent to bring this up specifically, but the implication was understood by everyone. One influential deputy told the author when asked, "How do you approach a functionary in a particular ministry?" that "I believe that it is a good policy to be very cordial with the functionaries and always maintain good relations. I, for one, never imply that I would or would not support a functionary for a higher post, and they never ask me to. We both know that when the opportunity arises I will remember them as competent civil servants."

Deputies were asked by the author whether they thought that in Chilean public administration personal advancement was due principally to dedication to work, integrity and competence. The overwhelming majority thought that "unfortunately the political element is most important in Chile," and that advancement is due mostly to political influences of friendship. "it is a vice in Chile," remarked one deputy. "Pull [la cuña] is the most important thing in Chile," remarked another.

Administrators interviewed also admitted that *parlamentarios* could either make it easy or more difficult for advancement, underscoring, however, that the key influence was the minister and the government itself (the president and his entourage). While little empirical data on this matter exists, one study conducted at the Institute of Administration of the University of Chile (INSORA) in CORVI (Corporación de la Vivienda), one of the corporations associated with the Ministry of Housing (MINVU), confirms these findings.[25] A sample of 230 functionaries in the agency was asked to weight the influence of certain outside agencies and actors on the hiring of personnel. Table 6.2 shows in descending order which organizations and individuals had the most influence. *Parlamentarios* were rated second only to the Junta in their influence on the hiring

25. I am grateful to Rafael López Pintor for this information. For the best study on Chilean bureaucracy see his "Development Administration in Chile: Normative and Behavioral Constraints to Performance" (Ph.D. dissertation, University of North Carolina at Chapel Hill, 1972).

of personnel in CORVI. The fact that they were rated higher than *jefes de oficina provinciales, intendentes* and *personal técnico* is particularly revealing.

How important patronage considerations were in the influence which parlamentarios exerted over the bureaucracy is difficult to assess without further study. What is clear, however, is that they were successful in getting projects for their particular localities out of the national government. It should be stressed, however, that the Chilean budgetary process was incremental and that in any given year the resources available for new projects were quite limited. Indeed, if too many demands came in they could not all be met, even if important politicos were pressing for them. However, it is precisely this scarcity of resources which contributed to maintenance of a system allowing for direct intervention by politicians. Because there were not enough resources to go around, some criterion had to be used for assigning priorities. The criterion used in investments in Chilean communes for improvement of community infrastructure was primarily political.

TABLE 6.2. Rank order of agencies and individuals perceived by MINVU functionaries as being most important in the hiring of personnel.

Agency or individual	Rank	Weight
La Junta (agency executive committee)	1	72
Parlamentarios	2	54
Jefes sub-dept. (heads of bureaus)	3	50
Jefes de oficinas provinciales (heads of provincial offices)	4	40
Intendentes and alcaldes	5	35
Personal técnico de CORVI (technical personnel of CORVI)	6	30
Beneficiarios en general (clients in general)	7	
Usted mismo (you yourself)	8	
Contratistas privados (private contractors)	9	
Cajas de previsión (welfare agencies)	10	

7. Vertical Brokerage Networks in Chilean Politics

From the northern-most city of Arica, to the city of Punta Arenas more than 2,600 miles south, Chilean communities divided sharply at election time on the choice of candidates for local office. Yet Chilean municipalities had few resources and an increasingly reduced jurisdiction over local matters. This paradox, of a keen struggle to attain an office with seemingly unimportant functions, could not be resolved simply by holding that the local office served as an important stepping stone in a national political career. Though local officials from provincial capitals were often recruited to become candidates for deputies, the vast majority of municipal councilors stood little chance of climbing up the political ladder. Field research in a sample of Chilean municipalities revealed that while the formal functions of municipalities were indeed weak, local officials performed two basic functions which consumed their every effort. In the first place they were instrumental in satisfying a host of particular demands for their followers, either with personal, municipal, or national resources obtained from the center. And, despite the poverty of municipal coffers, local officials, particularly the mayor, performed a critical service in "extracting" necessary projects and programs from the agencies of the national government. In performing both of these functions, local officials acted as brokers between individuals, or the community as a whole, and the vast, seemingly impersonal, bureaucracy. Their task, however, would have been impossible without the aid of other brokers located in a strategic place in the national political arena: the legislature. Congressmen, as national brokers, either generated projects for constituents through the legislature itself, or more often, by interceding on behalf of local clients before bureaucrats. Bureaucrats were conscious of the support they could receive for their agency in the legislature, or the help an influential congressman could provide in the all important quest for a promotion. At the same time, many government functionaries realized that legislators provided key information that often was more reliable in making investments than plans based on dubious statistical sources. Congressmen could also be very helpful in proposing ways in which an investment could be made in a particular community at the lowest possible cost, with maximum political benefit for the agency.

Though partisan disputes, so prevalent at election time, tended to disappear after the election, in the face of the dominant individualistic transactions characteristic of both local politics and center-local linkages, it was the political party networks which provided the key channels between local officials and their national brokers. Favors and projects emanating in the center and following downward to the locality were only part of the reciprocal exchange along these vertical networks. In return for the efforts of their national counterparts, local officials promised to deliver those crucial votes congressmen needed for political survival.

The orientation of local politics toward these vertical hierarchical relationships discouraged collective action in the municipality. There was little incentive to structure agreements on common activities if results could be obtained by mobilizing contacts in the center. Individual and, at times, factional rivalries often resulted from this set of political arrangements. Some communities, however, minimized sharp rivalries by structuring log-rolling arrangements designed to channel resources from the center. The lack of collective action at the local level no doubt also helps to explain the relative absence of organized groups in the community designed to pressure local government. Individuals preferred to obtain benefits through more personal contacts since those contacts were much more productive in obtaining benefits. Groups who sought more general benefits, in turn structured their own, largely personalistic contacts to the center.

How can this pattern of political arrangements be characterized? And, how can we understand the place of this system of relations emanating from local communities within the general context of Chilean politics? Both of these questions are of central importance and will be treated in turn.

At first glance local politics and center-local linkages in Chile would seem to conform to a patron-client model of politics. Drawing on the work of Carl Landé, James Scott has summarized some of the basic distinctions between patron-client forms of association and associations of a more categorical nature, either traditional (ethnic groups) or modern (interest groups or class associations).

1. Members' Goals: Clients have particularistic goals which depend on their personal ties to the leader, whereas categorical group members have common goals that derive from shared characteristics which distinguish them from members of other such groups.
2. Autonomy of Leadership: A patron has wide autonomy in making alliances and policy decisions as long as he provides for the basic material welfare of his clients, whereas the leader of a categorical group must generally respect the *collective* interests of the group he leads.
3. Stability of Group: A patron-client cluster, being based on particularistic vertical links, is highly dependent on the leader's skills and tends to flourish or disintegrate depending on the resources of the leader and the satisfaction of individual client demands. A categorical group, by contrast, is rooted more firmly in horizontally shared qualities and is thus less de-

pendent for its survival on the quality of its leadership and more durable in its pursuit of broader, collective (often policy) interests.
4. Composition of Group: Patron-client clusters, because of the way they are created, are likely to be more heterogeneous in class composition than categorical groups which are based on some distinctive quality which members share. By definition, patron-client pyramids join people of different status rankings while categorical groups *may or may not* be homogeneous in status.
5. Corporateness of Group: In a real sense a patron-client cluster is not a group at all but rather an "action-set" that exists because of the vertical links to a common leader — links which the leader may activate in whole or in part. Followers are commonly not linked directly to one another and may, in fact, be unknown to each other. An organized categorical group, by contrast, is likely to have horizontal links that join members together so that it is possible to talk of a group existence independent of the leader.[1]

As Chapter 4 noted, there are few "horizontal" groups in Chilean local politics. Local politics is characterized by particularistic goals and leaders are not generally subject to collective interests as such. Local brokers also tend to deal with a clientele of diverse class composition more akin to an "action-set" than an identifiable group with an existence independent of the leader. The Chilean pattern shares many of the features of patron-client politics.

And yet, Scott notes in the above distinctions between two broad types of political organization that "by definition, patron-client pyramids join people of different rankings while categorical groups *may or may not* be homogeneous in status." Robert Kaufman, in evaluating the work of Scott, Landé, and John Duncan Powell, underscores this point by noting that "almost everyone agrees that the relationship [between patron and client] should be defined as 'asymmetrical.'"[2] He argues further that scholars tend to disagree more on "the degree of voluntarism associated with the relationship and the degree to which customary or legal transactions enter into clientelistic transactions."[3] These restrictions placed by scholars in the field on what should be understood as a patron-client system raise serious

1. James C. Scott, "Patron-Client Politics and Political Change in Southeast Asia," *The American Political Science Review*, 66, no. 1 (March, 1972), 91–113. For Landé's expanded distinctions between the two types see his "Networks and Groups in Southeast Asia: Some Observations on the Group Theory of Politics," *The American Political Science Review*, 67, no. 1 (March, 1973), 103–27.
2. Robert R. Kaufman, "The Patron-Client Concept and Macro-Politics: Prospects and Problems," *Comparative Studies in Society and History*, 16, no. 3 (June, 1974), 285, n. 3.
3. Ibid. The work of Landé includes *Leaders, Factions, and Parties: The Structure of Philippine Politics* (New Haven: Yale University Southeast Asia Studies Monograph no. 6, 1964) and the article cited in note 1, this chapter. For Powell's work see his *Political Mobilization of the Venezuelan Peasant* (Cambridge: Harvard University Press, 1971) and "Peasant Society and Clientelistic Politics," *The American Political Science Review*, 64, no. 2 (June, 1970), 411–25.

questions about the general applicability of that model to the Chilean case. The transactions which occurred in Chile between the local municipal officials were based almost exclusively on a voluntary selection process. Community residents had a choice of several community leaders they could turn to and were free in determining who they should vote for. Favors on the part of a particular leader implied reciprocity around election time—but in no way guaranteed it. The same could be said for the relationship between mayors or regidores and congressmen. Each could terminate a relationship depending on the political calculations of the moment. Furthermore, and more importantly, the transactions conducted at various levels of the vertical "pyramid" in the Chilean case were not exclusively between individuals of different social statuses. In fact, in Chile many regidores and mayors shared a similar status with an important segment of the community—the small shop keepers, the butchers, the auctioneers, the medium sized landowners, the school teachers, etc. Many constituents, such as "campesinos," were of "lower status," but this was in no way an essential characteristic of the relationship. Likewise, the relationship between congressmen and municipal officers, while often involving somewhat unequal statuses, was not uniformly so. Local officials and their national counterparts can be much more appropriately characterized as political brokers who owed their continuation in office to their ability to deliver goods and services from one end of the pyramid for votes on the other. Scott, in fact, notes that there is a clear distinction between such brokers or middlemen and the classic patron of the patron-client dyad, in which the patron maintained his position not only because of his ability to deliver goods but because of his ability to command "respect and affection."[4] Though a Chilean regidor might have enjoyed prestige in his community, it was due to his attainment of political office, and not because of any "traditional" status. The peasant who wanted a local official to grace his wedding ceremony was not restricted to one regidor in particular, but, in a pinch, could turn to several regidores in the community to add prestige to his ceremony.

It would be easy to forget these basic restrictions on the use of patron-client terminology and apply concepts from that literature to a system such as the Chilean one. However, that practice carries real risks. It ignores the roots of the concepts in the anthropological literature and stretches them so much that they lose their analytical usefulness in identifying classic patron-client phenomena.[5]

4. Scott, "Patron-Client Politics," p. 95–96.
5. See the excellent critique by Robert R. Kaufman of studies that have attempted to stretch the "patron-client" concept too far, in Kaufman, "The Patron-Client Concept and Macro Politics."

But if local politics and center-local linkages as described in this study were not patron-client in the pure sense of the term, neither can they be understood as being class or interest based. Scott's various criteria for categoric politics as described above simply do not apply to the Chilean system. How can this system be differentiated from the others?

Very simply, Chilean politics were broker politics. Vertical networks of brokerage clusters extended from all of the nation's communities to the center. Local brokers interacted with their followers and the national broker, who in turn interacted with the local broker and government bureaucrats and ministers. This system can be best distinguished from others not by focusing on the status of actors or whether their transactions were culturally determined, but by distinguishing between two critical variables: the *goals* of the transaction and the *nature* of the transaction. For the sake of simplicity transactions can be said to have either *particularistic* or *categoric* goals; while the transactions themselves can be understood to be either *individualistic* or *collective* in nature.

Particularistic goals are those which are sought to satisfy the needs of an individual or his immediate family. They include items such as the obtention of a job permit, social security papers, a piece of land, a judicial pardon and similar favors which in Chile were often referred to as *gauchás chicas. Categoric* goals, on the other hand, were designed to meet the needs and demands of a group or groups of individuals. Examples include a new pension plan for a labor union, legal recognition for a church, a new bridge for a village or a new steel plant for the nation.[6] A classic patron-client system would focus exclusively on obtaining particularistic goals, whereas a political system based on interest group politics would be oriented primarily to the obtention of broader categoric goals or policies.[7]

Particularistic goals are, in turn, processed through *individualistic* transactions. These involve the mobilization of either a patron or a broker's own resources or the resources obtained through face to face contact with a higher level intermediary or patron. For the most part, individualistic transactions are conducted on the executive or implementing side of the policy process. Categoric goals, by contrast, are the result of transactions involving *collective* bargaining and accommo-

6. This does not mean that individuals within groups may not involve themselves in the organization primarily for personal benefits. This is of little consequence to the argument at hand. Categoric goals resulting from the same transaction go to several individuals which are identified as group members, by contrast with particularistic goals which benefit an individual and his family. On the problem of motivations for group participation see Mancur Olson, *The Logic of Collective Action*, rev. ed. (New York: Schocken Books, 1971).

7. See the third distinction "Stability of Group" drawn by Scott quoted above.

dation between individuals, or more often, functional organizations such as interest groups and political parties. Unlike individualistic transactions which are structured upwards along various brokerage clusters in a vertical hierarchy, collective transactions involve horizontal interaction between relatively coequal groups and institutions usually at the same level of the policy process. Collective transactions are thus typically located at the legislative stage and involve programmatic and ideological considerations.

Brokerage politics of the variety described in this book can be distinguished from patron-client politics in that they involve *both* particularistic and categoric goals. And yet, unlike an "ideal type" interest group or class based system, the categoric goals, as well as the particularistic ones, were satisfied through *individualistic* transactions. Thus, a mayor could obtain a social security check for a widow with the help of a diputado in the morning, "extract" a new sewer system for the community at noon, and arrange to have a bill introduced giving legal recognition to the fire department in the afternoon. The activity of the morning led to a purely particularistic action to satisfy a personal demand, while the later activities resulted in categoric goals to benefit the community and satisfy the firemen. All of the transactions, however, were of the *individualistic* variety.[8]

The distinctions between the *goals* and the *nature* of transactions are presented in the following table which summarizes how the brokerage model can be differentiated from patron-client and interest group models.

As table 7.1 shows, the patron-client model would fit exclusively in cell 1. Its transactions are purely individualistic and the goals particularistic. The interest-group model, by contrast, is primarily located in cell 4. The goal is the generation of categoric policies, processed through collective transactions. The brokerage model, by contrast bridges more cells than the others, and is primarily located in the top two cells. Particularistic as well as categoric goals are sought through individualistic transactions.

Under certain conditions cell 3 can be said to conform to the brokerage model; under others to the interest-group model. The brokerage model applies when a local broker through an individualistic transaction approaches a legislator for a private bill which is then generated collectively by the legislature. This is different from the private bill generated by an interest-group model where a col-

8. Again, in making these distinctions we are not concerned with the motives of the actors. One mayor may be motivated by a search for prestige and see all of his actions as contributing to that goal. Another may be genuinely concerned about the effect that poor community water may have on the community's children. The author encountered both kinds.

lective agreement is reached to adopt a private measure without individualistic pressures. Such cases are rare and would involve items
such as the granting of a life-long pension to a presidential widow who
did not seek the support.

Brokerage politics was a fundamental characteristic of Chilean
politics and can be differentiated from patron-client political associations and interest or class association. However, at this point it is
necessary to stress emphatically that brokerage politics in Chile was
not the only, nor even the dominant political pattern. Collective transactions with categoric policy ends have been extremely important in
that country for generations. Classes and interest groups have confronted one another with ever increasing force, mediated and controlled by the country's strong ideological parties, since the turn of the
century. Interest group politics thus paralleled and were intermeshed
with the more individualistic pattern of political interaction. For
analytical purposes it is possible to argue that the former predominated in the *center arena,* whereas the latter was more characteristic
of the *local arena.*

The politics of the *center arena* were located predominantly in
Santiago where most of the power was concentrated, and most of the
decisions made. Programmatic considerations and ideological motivations were paramount as parties sought to shape public policy to conform with their platforms and program objectives. Political parties

Table 7.1. Nature and goals of transactions as aids in distinguishing between patron-client, interest, and brokerage
political patterns.

Nature of transaction	Goal of transaction	
	Particular	Categoric
Individualistic (primarily executive stage)	#1 *Policy example:* job social security judicial pardon *Type of system:* Patron-Client Brokerage	#2 *Policy example:* bridge hospital *Type of system:* Brokerage
Collective (primarily legislative stage)	#3 *Policy example:* Bill of attainder Municipal loan *Type of system:* Brokerage Interest	#4 *Policy example:* steel mill rural union *Type of system* Interest

dominated most of the key institutions, from labor federations and employer associations to government ministries and agencies. The legislature was the key institution for the aggregation of interests and the adoption of *fundamental* policy, but the executive, dominated by one party or a coalition of parties set the basic agenda.

The key actors of this subsystem were party elites, most of whom were recruited into leadership positions through party youth and university movements, though the Communist party typically turned more often to labor unions for elite recruitment. A few prominent party officials who held key positions either as legislators or as government administrators devoted themselves almost entirely to programmatic and ideological considerations. In fact, in the legislature, parties had recognized specialists on subjects such as constitutional law, economics, land reform and copper policy. Top leaders like Salvador Allende or Eduardo Frei, though elected to the Senate, paid little attention to particularistic matters and concentrated on broader political strategy for their respective party organizations. By contrast, other leaders, including most congressmen elected to office in the "provinces," concerned themselves not only with programmatic and ideological matters but with playing key brokerage roles on behalf of constituents. Unlike the top political leadership, these elements provided the basic political ties between the *center arena* and the *local arena*.

During the Frei years parties sought to mobilize sectors previously excluded from active participation in societal benefits. These groups included primarily peasants and marginal urban inhabitants. Mobilization efforts contributed to greater competition between Chile's highly ideological political forces, more and more concerned with achieving political supremacy, and less and less concerned with conforming to the traditional bargaining style. Competition became confrontation during the Allende years as a greater number of issues became the subject of partisan disputes. These issues ranged from trivial ones to the fundamental one of introducing radical changes in the political, economic and social system. The radicalization of the political process, and the inability of center forces to reach a consensus ultimately opened the door for a violent reaction, and the breakdown of Chile's constitutional regime. This is not the place to analyze in depth the institutional and the political dynamics which characterized the center arena or the factors which led to the demise of Chilean democracy.[9] Suffice it to say that the great issues in Chilean

9. For a study that accomplishes both purposes see the author's *The Breakdown of Democracy in Chile* (Baltimore: The Johns Hopkins University Press, 1977). An

politics including nationalization of industries, land reform, political participation, and industrial relations were fought out between parties and interests in a collective decision-making process, involving clear programmatic and ideological alternatives.

By contrast, in the local arena individualistic transactions with particularistic ends continued to predominate. As this book has noted in examining peripheral municipalities and tracing the political linkages which extended from the locality to the center, programmatic and ideological considerations were not paramount. Collective decisions of importance were not arrived at in municipal council meetings, as resources were extracted through individualistic brokerage connections by individual local officials. With the exception of a few local officials in provincial capitals, the vast majority of local officials did not rise into national politics. Most local officials aspired to become mayors, and remained active in the local political environment. Parties were the key linkages between the local and center arenas, but there was relatively little recruitment from one to the other.

In very small towns and peripheral areas municipal government was the primary locus of this local political arena. Other organizations were scant, and municipal officials served as key brokers not only for individuals but also for the few and weakly organized groups. However, in small towns with a specialized or dominant industry, such as a large saw mill, mine, sugar refinery, or in larger towns with a more differentiated social and economic structure, other organizations diminished the importance of municipal government as the sole locus of local politics. This study has not systematically examined labor and peasant unions or lower level employer and merchant associations. However, enough evidence emerged from the study of local governments to suggest that while union leaders often worked through the municipal officer as a contact with the center, they just as often approached national brokers on their own. The brokers they approached were for the most part the same ones—diputados and senators, though contact with them was, in turn, often made with the help of national officers of the syndicates in question.

It should be stressed that for the most part the transactions structured outside of the local government channels were also individualistic. Though categoric goals were at times sought, a large number of particularistic favors were secured for individual members of the organizations in question. Often union leaders, like mayors, carried with them in their trips to the capital several requests for particular

abridged version entitled "Il Crollo di la Democrazia in Chile," appeared in the *Rivista Italiana di Scienza Politica*, 5, no. 1 (April, 1975), 83–129.

favors for specific union followers. Thus, countless vertical networks, parallel to those emanating from local governments, linked communities from all reaches of the country to the political center. Like local government networks, they developed as a response to the marked centralization of the political system, the scarcity of resources and the primacy of competitive political parties as basic linkage networks.

And yet, it would be a serious error to ignore the fact that in very recent years, newer local organizations such as peasant unions and squatter settlements increasingly took matters in their own hands, relying less and less on the important center contact. Land takeovers during the Frei administration, which were sharply accelerated in the Allende period, are a good case in point.[10] The Movement of the Revolutionary Left (MIR) communities, organized primarily in large cities, were also made possible by a significant increase in collective local action.[11] Sometimes these developments were encouraged by government bureaucrats who penetrated the local arena rather than responding only to the inquiries generated by the brokerage chain. But these phenomena did not become dominant features of Chilean politics.[12]

It should be stressed again at this point that the distinction between the center and local arenas is an analytic one. A strong case can be made for the argument that the more peripheral and the smaller the community, the greater the likelihood of finding a dearth of programmatic and ideological politics. Nevertheless, even in such communities certain features of the center arena were present at least at certain times. This was principally the case because linkages between the two arenas were channeled through the political parties. While parties at the lower level mobilized clienteles primarily through particularistic means and served as networks for processing individual transactions, their highly ideological character could not help but add an ideological and organizational dimension to local politics if not to local government per se. This was the case, as noted in chapter 4, with national elections which mobilized people even in the most rural areas along ideological appeals. Though local brokers attempted

10. See Brian Loveman, "The Transformation of the Chilean Countryside," in Arturo Valenzuela and J. Samuel Valenzuela (eds.), *Chile: Politics and Society* (New Brunswick: Transaction Books, 1976).
11. See for example the preliminary reports of the study on "Reivindicación Urbana y Lucha Politica: Los Campamentos de Pobladores en Santiago de Chile," in *Revista Latinoamericana de Estudios Urbano Regionales (Eure)*, 2, no. 6 (November, 1972), 55–81. See also the studies by Rosemond Cheetham, et al., *Pobladores: del legalismo a la justica popular*, 2 vols. (Santiago: CIDU, 1972).
12. This was the case with INDAP, the agricultural reform agency charged with leadership development. See Loveman, "The Transformation of the Chilean Countryside."

to deliver their "clienteles" to satisfy previous commitments, this was not always possible. Unlike local elections which often were conducted on a face to face basis, national elections involved many more rallies, concentrations and meetings.

During the Allende years this more or less latent ideological dimension of the national party system became increasingly manifest even in the most remote locality. Confrontations originating in Santiago had a way of filtering down. The exclusion of parties of the center and right from access to patronage from the bureaucracy further reenforced, if not a collective style of action, a sharp confrontational style at the local level. Particularistic transactions continued to be crucial in obtaining resources for individuals and for general community progress, but obtaining resources for any purpose took a back seat to the increasingly violent political struggle which permeated the country and finally resulted in military intervention.[13]

The existence of two arenas, a local and center one, with different though at times overlapping features, was a fundamental element of Chilean politics. It has important implications for understanding Chilean politics, but also for understanding party politics elsewhere. Thus, scholars who have described politics in countries where parties revolve around individualistic transactions and particularistic goals have often argued that such orientations lead to diffuse and unideological political parties. For example, John Duncan Powell has argued that "one of the limitations of clientelist politics is the strain it places on coherent ideologies. This may manifest itself in several important ways. Ideological parties may find it so difficult to reconcile discrepancies in ideas and reality that they will be either unable to build a clientelist base to begin with, or to maintain one if they do. Therefore, other more pragmatic parties may outdo them in competition for the peasant vote."[14] Likewise Landé has argued that Philli-

13. When the author returned to eight of the 14 municipalities he had studied in 1969 he was able to talk at some length with many former local officials, primarily of the Christian Democratic party. Political struggles over national issues became much more commonplace during the Allende years. In several communities land seizures by campesinos and farm expropriations by the government were the subject of sharp, often violent, disputes structured primarily along party lines. The 1973 election of congressional members, structured in two large slates—government versus opposition, marked the total polarization of most communities. Linkage networks to the center continued to be the key form of political transaction to obtain goods and services, but the political struggle involving increased popular mobilization became the dominant feature of the system by mid-1973. Opposition regidores claimed that this situation was aggravated by the chronic shortages of the period and by the fact that government regidores were charged in many places with distributing goods. The inability of opposition elements to obtain access to food and basic commodities was the source of great bitterness.

14. Powell, "Peasant Society," p. 422.

pine parties with their particularistic orientations could not develop strong ideological orientations.[15] The Chilean case, however, provides an example of a political system where predominantly particularistic orientations coexisted with predominantly ideological programmatic ones. This dual system was linked by party networks bridging both arenas. Though performance of individualistic transactions was often viewed as distasteful, it is clear that in Chile a particularistic style of politics did not undermine ideological parties or lead to the emergence of more "pragmatic" party organizations. Parties pursued their ideological programs and goals at one level, while continuing to rely on "clientelistic-like" transactions in mobilizing the vote and accommodating supporters.

How can we explain this apparently deviant case? Though in depth systematic and comparative study would be necessary to fully resolve the issue, it seems that in large part the problem has to do with the implicit assumptions behind the clientelistic model used by the scholars in question.

In borrowing the classic patron-client concept, they have also borrowed the underlying assumption that clientelistic relations are maintained through the shared beliefs and orientations peculiar to "traditional" societies. Though often patron-client concepts are stretched to include higher level brokerage roles, the cultural explanation for clientelistic phenomena is retained. Because of traditional cultural features, clientelistic politics are consequently said to involve "expressive" or "affective" as opposed to "instrumental" or "rational" orientations and behavior.[16] Such cultural orientations would thus exclude, by definition, programmatic and ideological orientations as well as collective action. It follows that where programmatic considerations do emerge, these have to result from cultural change

15. See his *Leaders, Factions and Parties*, pp. 69, 107. A similar argument can be found in Nicholson's review of factional politics. See Norman K. Nicholson, "The Factional Model and the Study of Politics," *Comparative Political Studies*, 5, no. 3 (October, 1972), 301. Likewise, Sidney Tarrow points to the "clientelistic" features of the Italian south as evidence for the lack of ideological politics in that area. He leads the reader to conclude that if the Italian north were also characterized by clientelistic politics, Italy would not have ideological parties. See Sidney Tarrow, *Peasant Communism in Southern Italy* (New Haven: Yale University Press, 1967), ch. 10.

16. See chapter 3 for the distinction between "expressive" and "instrumental" in the literature on political culture. The hypothesis advanced by Payne to explain why politicians seek office despite their lack of program orientation is based on cultural explanations. The answer is that Colombian society encourages politicians to seek "status." Rene Lemarchand and Keith Legg refer explicitly to patron-client ties as being affective – whereas "formal organizations" have more "rationality." See their "Political Clientelism and Development: A Preliminary Analysis," *Comparative Politics*, 4, no. 2 (January, 1972), 153. Lemarchand and Legg argue that the patron-client concept can also apply to the transactions between a congressman and a local official.

either within the society at large or within a subgroup of the society— leading to a clash between the modern and traditional sectors. Or, if clientelistic politics remains in less traditional settings it would have to result from the maintenance of traditional cultural beliefs. As Powell notes, "where the political culture is a carrier of patron-client patterns of behavior, the disintegration of peasant clientelist politics does not mark the demise of the generic pattern. To the contrary, urban-based clientelist politics may proliferate."[17]

If scholars, such as Powell, had restricted their cultural explanations to the traditional "patron-client" dyad, there would be little difficulty in coming to terms with the Chilean case. The problem, however, is that they describe phenomena very similar to the individualistic transactions and particularistic goals found in Chile in the same cultural terms and as features of "traditional" politics. These patterns of behavior are said to stand "in sharp contrast to the relationship between citizen and representative, or even party member and party leader, in modern systems of political transactions."[18] In sum, then, the importance of cultural explanations for clientelistic phenomena, and the sharp distinction which is drawn between "modern" and "traditional" politics, precludes a fusion of two patterns of politics without noting a basic conflict between the two or the "transitional" nature of the relationships.

By distinguishing between the *nature* of transactions and the *goals* of transactions in order to draw the contrast between brokerage politics and other varieties of politics this author consciously avoided the cultural assumptions of the patron-client literature. This is so because the evidence emerging from this study suggests that the reason why clientelistic-like networks predominated in Chilean local arena was not because of shared patterns of say "expressive" versus "instrumental" orientations, but because of certain structural features of the system. The scarcity of resources, the centralization of the polity and the presence of parties as networks to the center reenforced individualistic as opposed to collective action at the local level. There simply was no incentive at the local level for collective action around programmatic goals when local resources were so scarce. The only resources available were the resources in the center. And yet, even there there was not enough to go around. Over time, a pattern of brokerage relations developed to permit local officials to "extract" resources from the center through individualistic transactions. Though these patterns go back to the turn of the century, they are reenforced by highly instrumental goals on both sides. National brokers seek votes,

17. Powell, "Peasant Society and Clientelist Politics," p. 423.
18. Ibid., p. 424.

bureaucrats seek political support, local leaders seek projects and favors, and constituents need particularistic rewards for basic survival. These findings, relying on a macrosociological approach, suggest that it is not the shared attitudes of individuals which reenforce a particular pattern of political behavior affecting the nature of transactions and the shape of institutions. Rather, it is the scarcity of resources, the structure of local politics, and the nature of center-local linkages which reenforce, say, particularistic versus categoric goals, and individualistic versus collective transactions. This approach helps to explain why Chile was characterized by a dual political system, in which "clientelistic" type politics coincided with "ideological" politics. As one moves from the local arena to the center arena, one does not move from one culture to another, nor does one find more "modern attitudes"; one simply finds different structures and issues of the political game. It also helps to explain, as chapter 4 noted, why some communities had more bitter factional disputes than others. Some were not more modern—or possessed of different norms—but were simply able to structure more successfully local political patterns to fit in with the vertical brokerage networks necessary for local progress.[19]

But, it is not sufficient to say that scarcity and centralization reenforce a dual pattern of political transactions. Cultural explanations can be criticized as "reductionist" because they tend to beg the basic question as to why a particular pattern of relationships developed.[20] It is not sufficient to substitute "structural" explanations if an analysis is not provided suggesting how those structural features developed. Of necessity this involves turning to an examination of the evolution of Chilean politics over time.

To this end, the last part of the book will turn away from the analysis of contemporary local politics and consider the evolution of center-local linkages in Chile over time. How did vertical brokerage networks appear? Why were local communities unable to generate sufficient resources? Why was the system centralized? What accounts for the emergence of political parties as the key linkage mechanisms between the local and center arenas?

19. It should be stressed that this conclusion contrasts with Tarrow's conclusion for Italy. For Tarrow a dual system of ideological politics and clientelistic politics exist because the society is divided into traditional and modern sectors. In Chile the dual political system existed with a basically homogenous society, and was due to structural not cultural factors. This analysis raises the possibility that the dual system in Italy was not due so much to cultural features as to structural characteristics revolving around center-local linkages. A systematic comparison between northern and southern Italy would be necessary to follow up this hypothesis. See Tarrow, *Peasant Communism*.

20. See Amitai Etzioni's discussion of the "atomistic approach" in his *The Active Society* (New York: The Free Press), ch. 4.

Part III

8. Center-Local Relations in Chile Over Time: The Emergence of Vertical Linkages

The Consolidation of an Oligarchical Democracy In Chile: A Deviant Case

In sharp contrast to most of its neighbors in Latin America, Chile was able to establish a viable national political authority at an early date. From the middle 1830s onward, national political elites gradually fashioned a set of institutions and rules for governing the society and resolving the problem of succession to the principal positions of power. From that date, almost every president was elected to office and stepped down at the end of his constitutional term to make way for a duly elected successor. Though often the electoral process was not impartial and incumbent presidents and political factions had great influence over the selection of congressional and presidential candidates, the fact is that with the exception of the civil conflict of 1891, and the turbulent late 1920s, the use of force did not significantly disrupt the institutional order until the breakdown of Chile's regime in 1973.

The problem of establishing legitimate political authority was the principle legacy of the bloody wars for independence in all of the former Spanish colonies. The Spanish colonial empire had been governed by a classic patrimonial system of authority relations. By avoiding the creation of a rigid hierarchy of authority and refusing to endow political structures with functional specificity, the king was able to deal directly with political subordinates at every level and act as the final authority and arbiter of the system.[1]

Though many factors have been advanced as causes of the War of Independence, historians agree that the final demise of the system came when the legitimate centralized authority disappeared following

1. For a good introduction to the Spanish colonial system see C. H. Haring, *The Spanish Empire in America* (New York: Harcourt, Brace and World, 1963). An excellent description of the Spanish colonial system, employing Max Weber's concept of patrimonialism to describe its major characteristics, is Richard N. Morse, "The Heritage of Latin America," in *The Founding of New Societies*, ed. Louis Hartz (New York: Harcourt, Brace and World, 1964), pp. 123–77. Other treatments include Magali Sarfatti, *Spanish Bureaucratic-Patrimonialism in America* (Berkeley: Institute of International Studies, Politics of Modernization Series no. 8); and John Phelan, *The Kingdom of Quito in the Seventeenth Century* (Madison, Wisconsin: The University of Wisconsin Press, 1967), ch. 7.

the Napoleonic invasions of the Iberic peninsula.[2] With the removal of the king, latent political divisions and conflicts came to the surface. War broke out as Spanish authorities battled different elements either seeking independence or claiming to represent the legitimate authority of the crown.

In Chile, as in the rest of Latin America, the wars for independence were actually civil wars between differing constellations of factions and groups with different motivations and interests. Though the war did not affect the social stratification system, it virtually shattered the political framework which the country had had from the days of the conquest. From independence to the decade of the 1830s the Chilean political system, like those of other Latin American countries, was characterized by disorganization and anarchy. There were no acceptable and stable national political structures capable of undertaking the basic tasks of government. Nor were there any peaceful rules to determine the circulation of elites. Factions or groups, with enough armed might to impose their will, served as government until they were replaced by other more powerful factions or until their own coalitions disintegrated.[3] Chile, during this period can be thought of as a praetorian society where social forces were codeterminous with political forces and all struggles became political struggles unmediated by political structures or rules.[4] The legacy of a violent civil war for independence thus made it difficult to inaugurate a stable representative regime.

The standard interpretation for Chile's deviation from this pattern holds that Diego Portales, a Valparaiso businessman who served as minister after an important civil war in 1830, was able to successfully use strongman tactics to inaugurate stable and conservative presidential rule. Fredrick Pike, for one, notes that there is little disagreement that Portales was the "guiding spirit in molding the Chilean nation."[5] Echoing this theme, John Johnson notes that "Portales used

2. A good summary of the many arguments can be found in R. A. Humphreys and John Lynch, eds., *The Origins of the Latin American Revolutions, 1808–1826* (New York: Alfred A. Knopf, 1965). For the importance of the Napoleonic invasions in the final collapse of the empire see p. 5.

3. The first Chilean congress, opened in 1811, was overthrown two months later by a military force. Two more coups occurred that same year. Chile was then reconquered by a Spanish force which reinstituted control over the country for an additional three years. After the war, Bernardo O'Higgins served as dictator for three years. His overthrow led to a succession of regimes from 1822 to 1830. For a good account in English of these events see Luis Galdames, *History of Chile* (Chapel Hill: University of North Carolina Press, 1941).

4. The term praetorianism is used in Samuel Huntington's sense. See Huntington, *Political Order*, ch. 4.

5. Fredrick Pike, *Chile and the United States 1880–1962* (South Bend, Ind.; University of Notre Dame Press, 1963), p. 11.

demotions and executions to remove liberal oriented officers and other 'undesirables' from the military and brought the institution under civilian control . . . ; barracks revolts and coup d'etats, practically standard practice elsewhere in Latin America, were ended."[6] Richard Morse, in assessing Portales' contribution, has argued that his genius lay in his ability to recreate the patrimonial authority.[7] More recently Francisco Jose Moreno has maintained that the colonial legacy left Chile with an "authoritistic" political culture and Portales' quasi-dictatorial rule made it possible for governmental institutions to become congruent with popular political attitudes.[8]

There is no doubt that Portales was a very skillful politician able to bring together disparate factions into a relatively strong governmental coalition under the leadership of President Joaquín Prieto. Under Portales' guidance and that of another minister, Manuel Rengifo, vigorous economic policies were pursued aimed at improving the fiscal condition of the government and expanding international trade. At the same time a constituent assembly drafted a document setting up a representative system of government with separate legislative and executive branches. Unlike previous documents which called for a loose federation, this one set down the guidelines for strong presidential leadership. It is crucial, however, not to confuse the adoption of a document with its acceptance, the establishment of a system of government with its consolidation.[9] Without denying the important role which Portales played in establishing the Chilean system, an examination of the historical record raises serious questions about the view that holds that Portales consolidated lasting authority structures.[10]

6. John Johnson, *The Military and Society in Latin America* (Stanford: Stanford University Press, 1964), p. 24.

7. Morse, p. 163.

8. Francisco José Moreno, *Legitimacy and Stability in Latin America: A Study of Chilean Political Culture* (New York: New York University Press, 1969). Moreno's thesis is quite far-fetched, for he essentially claims that the "authoritistic" political culture is still a feature of Chilean society. Thus whenever there is disorder—it is due to a departure from authoritarian rule congruent with the culture. Not only is there a serious lack of documentation of the thesis—it is a notoriously circular argument.

9. In analyzing the development of democratic procedures Dankwart Rustow notes the importance of distinguishing between the "decisional phase," when the shape of the system is decided upon—and the "habituation phase" when it becomes accepted. See his "Transitions to Democracy," *Comparative Politics*, 2, no. 3 (April, 1970), 337–64.

10. The literature on the Portales period is very extensive. The reader is referred to the following works as particularly useful ones: Ramón Sotomayor Valdés, *Historia de Chile bajo el gobierno del jeneral D. Joaquín Prieto* (Santiago: Fondo Histórico Presidente Joaquín Prieto, 1962, 3rd ed.); Francisco Antonio Encina, *Portales* (Santiago: Editorial Nascimiento, 1964), 2 vols.; Diego Barros Arana, *Un decenio de la historia de Chile* (Santiago: Imprenta Universitaria, 1906), 2 vols.; Aurelio Diaz Meza, *El Advenimiento de Portales* (Santiago: Ediciones Ercilla, 1932). A classic study of the economy and economic policies during the period is Daniel Martner, *Historia de Chile:*

It is difficult to fully accept the standard interpretation for two fundamental reasons. In the first place, Portales was actually in office for a total of only three years, serving first from 1830 to 1831 and coming back to the government in 1835. During his absence he lived in Valparaiso and devoted himself mainly to private matters. There is no record that he had any direct influence on the drafting of the 1833 Constitution which set up Chile's presidential system of government.[11] In the second place, Portales was assassinated in June, 1837, only about a year and a half after he rejoined the government as minister of war and minister of the interior. His assassination came at a time when there was widespread dissension and unrest across the land. Plots and conspiracies, which had subsided after 1833, once again reappeared. Portales' intention to pursue a war against the Peru-Bolivia Confederation under General Santa Cruz contributed further to open hostility from many quarters. The minister was actually murdered by mutinous army officers whom he thought supported the government. Anarchy, which had followed the independence movement, once again threatened to tear the country apart. Chilean political elites had little sense of common solidarity or community and did not share common notions about the legitimacy of the new political structures and rules.

Ironically, however, through one of those strange quirks of fate which history occasionally provides, Portales in death may have contributed more to the stability of the regime he had sought to mold than Portales in life. His assassination proved to be an important step in convincing Chilean elites that they should risk a war against General Santa Cruz and the combined forces of Peru and Bolivia. The violent death of one of the country's most prominent leaders was widely condemned, not only for the severity of the measure, but also because "friends and enemies of the government thought . . . that

---

Historia económica (Santiago: Balcells and Co., 1929), vol. 1. Among the best general works useful in understanding the period and which for the most part praise Portales are the following: Alberto Edwards Vives, *La Fronda aristocrática* (Santiago: Editorial Ercilla, 1936); and Luis Galdames, *History of Chile* (Chapel Hill: University of North Carolina Press, 1941). Critical assessments of Portales come both from liberal and Marxist historians who condemn the 19th century Chilean state as serving in an autocratic fashion the interests of the landed aristocracy. Among liberal historians see Ricardo Donoso, *Desarollo político y social de Chile desde la constitución de 1833* (Santiago: Imprenta Universitaria, 1942), and his *Las ideas políticas en Chile* (Santiago: Editorial Universitaria S.A., 1967, 2nd ed.). Among Marxists see Julio Cesar Jobet, *Ensayo crítico del desarollo económico y social de Chile* (Santiago: Editorial Universitaria, 1955). Both critics and admirers of Portales agree that he was responsible for establishing the institutional structure of 19th century Chile.

11. In an excellent though uneven collection of essays on Portales, Jay Kinsbruner makes these points persuasively. See his *Diego Portales: Interpretative Essays on the Man and Times* (The Hague: Martinus Nijhoff, 1967).

the mutiny and assassination were products of the intrigues and gold of Santa Cruz. . . . The disappearance of Portales had cooled off the hatred of many of his most bitter enemies."[12] This alleged intervention in Chilean domestic affairs outraged Chileans from different factions and contributed to a growing movement of support for the previously unpopular military effort. At the same time it gave a new lease on life to the government headed by President Joaquín Prieto. He moved swiftly to take advantage of the political moratorium which the war effort provided. Officers and soldiers who had been dismissed for antigovernment activities were invited back into the armed forces to strengthen the Chilean expeditionary contingent.[13]

In broader terms, the war against the Peru-Bolivia confederation had the effect of bringing together for the first time disparate elements of the Chilean elites. Previous wars, including the War of Independence, were civil conflicts with a profoundly divisive effect on the new nation. For once Chilean elites were joining in combat against a common foe. And, even more significantly, their effort was rewarded by a very clear victory after several difficult battles fought in the heart of enemy territory. Defeat would probably have contributed to a further disintegration of the Chilean polity; victory contributed to a new found unity which would serve as a base for future stability.[14]

For months after the conclusion of the war a festive air reigned in the country as citizens celebrated the valor of their new heroes. Common songs and national symbols emerged for the first time which did not evoke conflicting or partisan reactions. Theatre groups and puppet shows, some of which lasted for years, reenacted scenes of battle.[15] Perhaps one of the most important events was a victory ball held at the presidential palace. It was attended by political opponents and rivals who had not been seen together at a joint function in years.[16] Pride in victory was also enhanced by the praise which the Chileans received for their victory in Europe, where Chile began to be singled out as the most powerful country in the South American continent. The political effects of this pride are summed up by Encina who noted that "the great majority of the country forgot the origins of the Prieto government."[17]

12. Francisco Antonio Encina, *Historia de Chile* (Santiago: Editorial Nascimiento, 1941–42) vol. 9, p. 312.

13. Barros Arana, vol. 2, p. 39.

14. Encina subscribes to this view when he says that defeat would have sent leaders, government and order tumbling to earth. See vol. 9, p. 483.

15. Barros Arana, vol. 1, p. 55.

16. Ibid., pp. 54, 219.

17. Encina, vol. 9, p. 493.

Scholars who have turned their attention to the process of political development and change have noted that the path to the modern world is smoother when the problem of national identity is resolved before the onset of other problems such as the establishment of a viable central authority or the incorporation of the masses into full citizenship. A feeling of national unity facilitates the development of legitimate political institutions for governing the nation and makes it easier at a later date to incorporate new groups into the political process.

The war against the Peru-Bolivia Confederation resulted in the establishment of a new government with widespread support. It was headed by a military hero who embodied in a very tangible way the new sense of unity. Manuel Bulnes, the victorious general, was selected president of the Republic with the support of the vast majority of the politically relevant Chilean populace. It was the first peaceful transition to the highest office of the land.[18]

Bulnes' legitimacy, however, was a product of his great prestige as a military hero and not a product of his election to the presidency itself. As such, Bulnes might have been able to take advantage of his highly personal style of legitimacy and disregarded constitutional precepts to concentrate all authority in his own person. In spite of the elite unity which prevailed at the moment such a course might well have weakened rather than strengthened the procedures for public contestation envisioned in the 1833 Constitution. For, as Max Weber has indicated, charismatic authority is by definition highly unstable; unless the leader is constantly able to prove to his followers that he possesses great virtue, he may be quickly discredited. When the highly personal legitimacy disappears, the system as a whole may disintegrate. A charismatic leader must attempt to routinize his authority or, in essence, attempt to establish rational-legal forms of authority in place of personal ones.[19]

Bulnes, however, shunned the role of charismatic leader, refusing to follow the path of Manuel Rozas in Argentina, who from 1828 until

18. His selection to be a candidate for the presidency was fortuitous in more ways than one. Bulnes, like his predecessor Prieto, was a native of Concepción, the major regional center of the country which had produced several armed challenges to central authority in the past. Furthermore, he was the nephew of the outgoing president, thus making the transition easier. He was the undisputed leader of the most powerful armed group in the country—the expeditionary army. Finally, he married the daughter of his only rival in the presidential race—a "liberal" who earlier had agreed to stay in the presidential race and not make an alliance with a small group of conservative opponents to the Bulnes candidacy. See Encina, vol. 12, p. 112, and Barros Arana's account of the election in vol. 1, pp. 173-85.

19. See H. H. Gerth and C. Wright Mills (eds.) *From Max Weber: Essays in Sociology* (New York: Oxford University Press, 1958), pp. 248-49.

1852 exercised personal rule of a rather despotic nature over the people of the sister republic. During the ten years of his administration, he deliberately supported the development of the weak political institutions and rules embodied in the Constitution of 1833. According to this interpretation, then, it was General Manuel Bulnes, from his unique position of strength, that provided the guiding spirit in consolidating strong presidential activity. Five factors were important in this process.

In the first place, Bulnes was a conciliator willing to bring men from different factions into the government. These men were for the most part moderates within their respective groupings and willing to compromise and work with others. The first cabinet, to last almost his entire first term in office, clearly reflects this policy. It was headed by a respected moderate of liberal persuasion and included an opponent in the recent presidential race, a general who had not supported his candidacy, and a couple of men identified with more conservative groups. Later, cabinets also included men from various elite factions. The president's authority was supreme in the matter of appointing and dismissing the cabinet; but he chose to give the cabinet and individual ministers considerable influence in the development and implementation of policy.[20] Though the ministers differed somewhat on the extent to which the government should control pockets of opposition, they all shared a commitment to commercial progress and the consolidation of government institutions. They would consequently agree to efforts to expand the government bureaucracy and to state intervention in economic policies. They also would agree on the supremacy of the state over the church in temporal affairs much to the dismay of the clergy and some of its conservative allies. From the nucleus of ministerial and congressional politics emerged the political parties and factions which would in later years dominate the political scene. Many individuals, including several future presidents, began their political careers during the Bulnes era.[21] The roots were set for

20. Though the goal at the time was to set up rational-legal authority, Bulnes' authority in the earlier years probably resembled more closely the authority of personal rulership. That is, it was not based on charismatic appeals or qualities nor was his authority the same kind of national authority of the patrimonial empire; but, rather, it was based on strong leadership — in which the leader controls important resources such as the power of appointment and other payoffs. On the distinction in Max Weber between personal rulership and other styles of authority, see the excellent article by Guenther Roth, "Personal Rulership, Patrimonialism, and Empire-Building in the New States," *World Politics*, 20, no. 2 (January, 1968), pp. 194–206.

21. For a detailed discussion of all of Bulnes' cabinets and their activities and policies, see Barros Arana, vol. 2. A fascinating essay suggesting the importance of the "politics of moderation" during the Bulnes period to future political developments, is Alberto Edwards' introduction to Antonio Varas, *Correspondencia sobre la candidatura presidencial de Don Manuel Montt* (Santiago: Imprenta Universitaria, 1921).

the development of a distinctive political class—which in turn would contribute to increasing the power of the state, often at the expense of some of the dominant economic interests in the country.

The most important feature of the Bulnes decade is that the president, while retaining a central control over the government, supported the development of differentiated governmental structures. In particular, he abided by constitutional precepts and encouraged the development of the elective legislature and a relatively independent judiciary. Though the Congress served mainly to ratify cabinet legislation, it soon became an important forum for the articulation of elite demands and the discussion of key issues. As an example, in Bulnes' second term, the Congress discussed at great length a measure introduced by a young deputy that would have abolished entailed estates, one of the cornerstones of the landed aristocracy.[22] Throughout the decade, several laws originating in the legislature were enacted into law—though in all cases they met with cabinet approval.[23]

As early as November 3, 1841, the legislature, presaging future events, began to show real signs of independence. On that date, the Senate unanimously adopted a resolution suspending consideration of tax and budget laws until the administration agreed to consider legislation requiring budgets to conform to specific standards. This incident, and a later more serious one in which Congress again delayed approval of appropriations measures, were resolved through compromise.

That the legislature itself had some legitimacy is evidenced by the fact that cabinets went out of their way to influence the electoral process in order to insure a majority favorable to the government. But, despite the interference of the minister of the interior in the electoral process, opposition elements gained a few political positions in the legislature. Thus, in the election of 1849 where the government intervened vigorously in the electoral process, a few prominent opposition elements were elected. More significantly, during the Bulnes presidency, opposition emerged in another manner.[24] In 1849, Bulnes dismissed a ministry which had apparently lost significant support because, among other factors, of allegations of corruption. The new ministry that came into office faced a large opposition in the Congress because most legislators had been elected thanks to contacts and

22. Though the measure failed, it was brought up again under the presidency of Bulnes' successor, Manuel Montt, and enacted into law in 1852. The enactment of such a provision illustrates the fact that the traditional landed aristocracy did not dominate the politics of the period as fully as some observers imply.

23. For a discussion of the role of the legislatures, see Barros Arana, vol. 1, pp. 166–72.

24. See Varas, p. xx, and Barros Arana, vol. 2, pp. 279–82.

support from members of the departing ministry.[25] Opposition thus emerged not because of a great struggle between the in's and the out's but because of shifting alliances. As the years went by, this procedure would help to reenforce the rules of the game and the legitimacy of a "loyal" opposition.

Two incidents illustrate in very concrete terms the support which the president gave to this institutionalization process. During his second term, the minister of the interior brought a suit against the editor of a newspaper because the latter attacked the government for intervening in the congressional elections. A lower court convicted the editor, but the Supreme Court later overruled the lower court's decision. The minister was furious at this action and was determined to attack the court directly to obtain a favorable ruling. Though the president had supported his cabinet in its electoral policy, he refused to endorse an attack on the Supreme Court. The incident instead contributed in part to the dismissal of the cabinet.[26]

The second incident is extremely important. The Constitution specified that the president of the republic could serve only two five-year terms. Manuel Bulnes clearly had the support and the power to continue in office if he so desired. Nevertheless, he chose to step down. Furthermore, he maintained a position of neutrality over the choice of his successor, suggesting that a convention be held to select a candidate from the government coalition.[27]

When the electoral results went in favor of Manuel Montt, the defeated candidate from the southern region of the country with the support of some liberal families in Santiago led an insurrection against the government.

Bulnes personally led government militia forces to combat and defeat the insurgents.[28] At the end of his term, Bulnes stepped down from office in favor of his elected successor and resorted to arms in support of the institutions he had upheld. The closing remarks of his last speech to the Congress are instructive of the man:

The attractions of power have never fascinated me. I have gladly given up this heavy charge of responsibility and cares. . . . The sacred trust of the con-

25. The dismissal of the Ministry headed by Don Manuel Camilo Vial, a conservative from the "filopólita" faction is discussed in Barros Arana, vol. 2, pp. 289–94.

26. Barros Arana, vol. 2, pp. 289–94.

27. On the neutrality of Bulnes, see Barros Arana, vol. 2, pp. 440, 553. On the idea of a convention, see Varas, pp. xxxiv–xxxvii. There is some controversy on how neutral Bulnes was. Barros Arana notes that Bulnes probably supported that Montt candidacy because his choice of a new cabinet presumably favored Montt. Edwards, on the other hand, argues that the head of the new cabinet was proposed by members of the resigning cabinet who did not favor the Montt candidacy. See Varas, p. xi. Whatever the case may be, Bulnes in public remained neutral.

28. For Encina's account, see vol. 8, p. 155.

stitution, which you confided in me, has passed to other hands, pure, intact, more deserving than ever of your veneration and love.[29]

Thirdly, the gradual process of setting up civilian political institutions was accompanied by a concerted and deliberate effort to curb the potential threat of armed elements. Though a military man, once Bulnes assumed the presidency, he neglected his former role and embarked on a program to reduce the size and resources of the armed forces. Thus by 1840, the army, which had had 5,400 men in the expeditionary force to Peru, had been reduced to 2,200 men.[30] Military equipment and ships were sold at public auction to increase government revenues.[31]

An examination of the reports of the minister of war to the Chilean Congress during the entire Bulnes period shows increasing military frustration over cutbacks and general neglect. Reforms which the army asked for to professionalize the institution were not enacted; when economies were made, the army was the first to suffer; salaries for officers were maintained too low; and the national guard was allowed to expand challenging the institutional integrity of the armed forces.[32] It is clear that the government was not in any way interested in expanding the potential of the army and that it sought to create the militia as a counterforce. Thus in 1845, while the army had a total of 2,044 men, the national guard had been increased in size to 56,829 men.[33] Clearly the guard was an important source of patronage for chief executives and cabinets. As such, they constituted a loyal force that could serve as an effective deterrent to the regular army. The guard also was a readily accessible pool of voters for government candidates — and in a very limited electorate, eligible militia constituted a rather sizable percentage of the total suffrage.[34]

29. Chile, *Documentos Parlamentarios. Correspondientes al segundo quinquenio de la administración Bulnes, 1846–1850.* (Santiago: Imprenta del Ferrocarril, 1858), vol. 3, p. 800.

30. See Jesus Galves F., "El ejército Chileno," *Revista de Cultura Militar* (28 de Mayo de 1943), p. 83, for the first figure and Encina, vol. 9, p. 554 for the second. According to Carlos Graes, this was a smaller figure than the 2,700 figure which the army had in 1837. See his "La supuesta preparación de Chile para la guerra del Pacífico," *Boletín de la Academia Chilena de la Historia*, no. 5 (1935), p. 113.

31. Encina, ibid.

32. See Chile. *Documentos Parlamentarios: Discursos de apertura en las sesiones del Congreso i memorias ministeriales* (Santiago: Imprenta del Ferrocarril), vols. 2, 3, 4 and 9. A year by year summary of some of the demands and complaints from the ministers of war can be found in Arturo Valenzuela, "The Chilean Political System and the Armed Forces, 1830–1924" (Columbia University Master's Essay, 1967), ch. 3.

33. *Chile, Documentos Parlamentarios: Discursos . . .* , vol. 2, pp. 412–13.

34. On the vote of the national guard, see Barros Arana, vol. 2, p. 458. Later in the century as more opposition developed to the government elites, the availability of the guard for electoral purposes would become more important.

It would not be until the year 1879 with the War of the Pacific that the army would be increased in strength, and military men would have to wait until the 1890s for some of the institutional reforms which were first suggested during Bulnes' presidency. Manuel Bulnes was clearly proud of his role in this regard as evidenced by his farewell message to the nation at the end of his second term:

Turn your attention to two points which I believe are crucial, for they reveal the fidelity of the government to the spirit of republican institutions. . . . The forces of the permanent army were limited in 1842 to 2,216 men; and I leave a total of 2,226 men; an insignificant difference, quite disproportionate, without a doubt, to the development of all the other social elements in this period. On the contrary, the national militia has multiplied extensively; armed citizens in the defense of the nation and the law amount to nearly 70,000 armed men.[35]

A fourth development which helped to legitimize governmental authority was the dramatic progress of the nation's economy. Government policies, originated by Portales and especially by Manuel Rengifo who served as minister of finance in both the Prieto and Bulnes administrations, helped to stabilize the country's public finances. External debts were repaid or renegotiated, the internal debt was reduced, and the governmental budget was rationalized. At the same time, an effort was made to spur external commerce by improving dock facilities and opening up new ports. Regulations favoring imports and exports in Chilean bottoms encouraged the development of a merchant marine.[36] Spurred in part by these and other government measures, Chilean exports of both mineral and agricultural products increased significantly. As table 8.1 shows, exports went up almost five times from 1844, the first year in which data is available, to 1864. The import trade grew at a similar pace, though on the whole the Chilean economy registered a favorable balance of trade throughout most of the 19th century.[37]

The table also shows the percentages of exports represented by the mining and the agricultural sectors. In general, from the 1840s to the War of the Pacific, agricultural imports represented about 25 percent of the total while mining exports varied from about 50 to as high as 70 percent. The mining sector, first with silver and then with copper, became one of the most dynamic sectors of the economy, earning the

35. *Chile, Documentos Parlamentarios: Discursos* . . . , vol. 3, p. 795.
36. For a detailed discussion of economic policy in the period, see Daniel Martner, *Historia de Chile*, vol. 1.
37. As Pinto notes, the currency remained relatively stable throughout the period. Between the 1850s and the 1860s, the exchange varied between 43 and 46 pennies to the Chilean peso. See Anibal Pinto, *Chile un caso de desarollo frustrado* (Santiago: Editorial Universitaria, 1958), p. 15.

Table 8.1. Chilean exports and imports and agricultural and mining exports in selected years.

Year	Imports	Exports	Agricultural exports	Percent of total exports	Mining exports	Percent of total exports
1844	8,596,674	6,087,023	897,025	14.7	3,618,987	59.4
1849	10,722,840	10,603,447	1,780,349	16.7	6,607,048	62.3
1854	17,428,299	14,527,156	3,336,356	22.9	9,610,538	66.1
1859	18,395,654	19,559,254	4,111,357	21.0	13,735,968	70.2
1864	18,867,365	27,242,853	6,260,352	22.9	19,722,169	72.3
1869	27,232,218	27,725,778	7,451,234	26.8	18,067,018	65.1
1873	37,928,427		12,565,145	32.3	18,140,980	46.7

Source: República de Chile, *Estadística Comercial Correspondiente al año de 1875.* (Valparaiso: Imprenta del Universo de G. Helfmann, 1876), pp. 570 and 573; and ibid. 1875 (Valparaiso: Imprenta del Mercurio de Torneroy-Letelier, 1874), p. lxxxii.

bulk of the foreign exchange. The dynamism of the Chilean economy contributed to the fact that Chilean issues brought higher prices on the London market than those of any other Latin American country.[38]

Economic success was paralleled by vigorous cultural activity as educational institutions, including the University of Chile, were created. The intellectual movement of 1842, attracting intellectuals from all over Latin America, added further prestige to the government.[39] Undoubtedly, the favorable economic picture contributed to a feeling among Chilean elites that the government was effective.[40] Effectiveness, in turn, can contribute over time to reenforcing the legitimacy of government institutions. At the same time in these early years, the favorable economic climate provided channels for advancement, success, and upward mobility outside of the military and the government, minimizing the struggle for governmental position among the ambitious elements of society.[41]

In the fifth place, beginning with the Bulnes period, the government was able to extend increasingly its authority over the nation. This consolidation of national authority implied a greater centralization of the political system. This chapter will expand this last point, analyzing over time the evolving center-local relationships in Chile in order to isolate the origins of the system described earlier.

The Struggle between Presidential and Local Interests

As the 19th century progressed, political elites in charge of the Chilean central government attempted to increase further the extrac-

38. Ibid.
39. For a discussion of this movement, see Galdames, pp. 274–80.
40. See the discussion of this matter in Juan Linz, "La Caduta dei regimi democratici." *Rivista Italiana di Scienza Politica* Anno V, no. 1 (April 1975), 7–43. Linz distinguishes between efficiency, or the capacity to formulate policies that are satisfactory to the common unity and effectiveness, or the capacity to actually implement policies once decided. Progress in the economic sphere in Chile at this time was probably due not so much to government policies as to generally favorable economic conditions. Nevertheless, the government could benefit from the satisfactory progress. Seymour Martin Lipset has also noted that effectiveness in the economic sphere may help to reenforce the legitimacy of a regime over a period of time. See his *Political Man* (New York: Doubleday, 1960), p. 70.
41. See the thesis of Merle Kling in his "Toward a Theory of Power and Political Instability in Latin America," *Western Political Quarterly*, 9, no. 7 (March, 1956), 21–35. Kling argues that instability in most of Latin America is the result of the "contradictions between the realities of a colonial economy and the political requirements of legal sovereignty." The route to wealth is foreclosed to most elements in society and thus the only channel still available for social mobility is through the governmental apparatus. The struggle for control of politics—as a means of gaining wealth—contributes to the unstable nature of Latin American politics.

tive, regulatory, and distributive capabilities of the state. Resources were sought from the society in the form of taxes and duties. At the same time, the government sought to redistribute these resources by instituting a variety of programs such as large-scale public works projects. Much of the impetus for government expansion in the mid 1850s derived from the revenues which the Chilean state obtained from the booming external trade. Customs duties, applied primarily to the import business which kept close pace with the fortunes of the export trade, provided the principal source of income.[42] From 1830 to 1860, fiscal income increased seven times, an average increase of about 6.2 percent per year. Expenditures on education alone quadrupled in the period 1845–1860.[43] State revenues enabled the construction of the second railroad system in Latin America as well as numerous other public works projects.[44] Major public works projects such as the railroad involved a multitude of decisions of a political nature which could dramatically affect the lives of citizens across the country.

An increase in the government's extractive and distributive capability was accompanied by a gradual but significant expansion of government political authority over the society. By 1860, the national government bureaucracy had expanded to the point where 2,525 individuals worked for the state.[45] More importantly, government institutions and structures extended downward into local communities.

The Constitution of 1833 had provided for considerable executive control over local governments, but, for many years, municipalities operated only in the departmental capitals and in the towns of Caldera and Viña del Mar.[46] Localities were for the most part autonomous and independent of national authority. In 1854, however, in an effort to extend executive control into the local arena, the first municipal law was adopted. Under its provisions, executive appointees would not only dominate the local policy making process but would also have effective control over electoral registration and voting.[47]

42. Throughout most of the 19th century, custom duties represented around 60 percent of all ordinary income. Ordinary income, in turn, accounted for approximately 90 percent of all government revenues. See Carlos Humud T., *El Sector público chileno entre 1830 y 1930.* (Santiago: Facultad de Ciencias Económicas, Universidad de Chile, Memoria, 1969), cited in Jorje Leiva *El sector externo, los grupos sociales y las políticas económicas en Chile 1830–1940* (Santiago: Centro de Estudios Socio-Económicos, 1970, mimeographed) p. 9.
43. Humud T., cited in Leiva.
44. For material on government economic activities in this period, consult Daniel Martner, *Historia de Chile: Historia Económica*, vol. 1.
45. Humud T., cited in Leiva, p. 27.
46. Alejandro Silva Bascuñán, *Tratado de derecho constitucional* (Santiago: Editorial Jurídica de Chile, 1963), vol. 3, p. 467.
47. According to the law, the governor appointed by the president would be the presiding officer and a full voting member in all the municipalities under his juris-

Executive control over registration and voting was reenforced by the large number of electors under direct government influence. Not only did local officials have many clients willing to support presidential candidates in return for patronage or favors, but the executive could count on the votes of members of the armed forces, public employees, and workers on government sponsored projects. Opponents of the government claimed that over half of the very limited electorate around midcentury fell into this category. For instance, José Victorino Lastarria, a prominent liberal, argued that:

According to the 1862 electoral census there were registered to vote the following: (1) 5,535 agriculturers, of which at least four fifths are citizens that due to their moral condition are under the influence of agents of the government. (2) 3,734 *artisans who are, like the agriculturers, enrolled in the national guard, and therefore under the direction, and even under the pressure of the agents of the executive.* . . . (3) 1,850 public employees, and 1,110 private employees, the latter being mainly employed by the Municipalities that usually register their dependents and servants as private employees. To this group of citizens must be added 337 army officers and 55 naval officers. . . . All of these add up to the enormous sum of 12,600 voting citizens, that form the electoral base of the government, especially in the countryside and in the numerous small centers of urban population.[48]

It must be underscored that attacks on the control of suffrage did not come only from the liberal side of the political spectrum. One of the most prominent individuals opposing presidential intervention in suffrage was Abdón Cifuentes, the longtime spokesman and orator of the Conservative party. He notes that:

---

diction. In case of a tie, his vote would count double. The governor was also charged with executing all agreements and making all municipal appointments. Any complaints on the election or qualifications of municipal officials could be appealed only to the Council of State, a body that served at the pleasure of the president. The law was to last over thirty years and provided the basic legal mechanism through which the executive maintained close control over the Chilean locality. See Jorge Gustavo Silva, ed., *La Nueva Era de las municipalidades en Chile* (Santiago: Boyle y Pellegrini Ltda., 1931) p. 36. For an excellent comparative treatment of this municipal law with the one that was adopted in 1891, see the thesis by Luis Moya Figueroa, *Estudio comparativo de la lei de Municipalidades de 22 de Diciembre de 1891* (Santiago: Imprenta Mejía, 1901). The Chilean Constitution of 1833 can be found in Luis Valencia Avaría, *Anales de la república* (Santiago: Imprenta Universitaria, 1951), vol. 1, pp. 160–217.

48. Camara de Diputados, Sesión Ordinaria del 7 de Octubre de 1869 Santiago de Chile, p. 462, cited by Julio Samuel Valenzuela in his "Determinants of Suffrage Expansion in Chile: The 1874 Electoral Law" (seminar paper, Columbia University, 1972). Valenzuela has calculated that this means that 57 percent of all registered voters were controlled by the government. While he thinks the figure is probably somewhat high, it nevertheless reflects the broad control which the government had over the electorate. The quote also suggests that many of the rural workers supported the government not because of the support of rural elites but because these workers had been recruited into the national guard. Patterns of mass and elite support for government and opposition in this period need to be systematically studied. Much of the data for such a study is readily available in statistical annuals of the period.

Electoral power was entrusted to the municipalities who were dependent on the executive and its docile instruments. They named officials of the tables charged with qualifying citizens who were eligible to vote—that is, the officials that formed the electoral registers; and they were also the ones that named the officials of the polling tables. Intendants and governors, direct agents of the executive and dominators of the municipalities, were in the final analysis those who named the officials to one or another table, the ones who denied opponents with a thousand excuses first registration, and then to those who had managed to register, their freedom to vote. Since the government owned both the municipalities and the police, it was impossible to defeat it in an election. If an opposition element managed to win, it was due to chance or negligence or to simple condescension on the part of the government, as it happened to me, when I was deputy for Rancagua for the first time in the year '67.[49]

The strong and sometimes violent disputes between the government and the opposition, centering primarily on the struggle over suffrage, has been interpreted by many scholars as a struggle between a state serving conservative landed interests on the one hand and a rising liberal bourgeoisie based on mining on the other.[50] The quotes from both a prominent liberal and a prominent conservative spokesman raise some questions about this view. The fact is that in Chile an industrial or commercial bourgeoisie did not emerge in the 19th century to challenge the interest of the landowning sectors. It will be recalled that, while agriculture was the dominant economic pursuit, mining from the very beginning of the 19th century was the principal export, accounting for the lion's share of foreign exchange. A dynamic mining sector did not really pose a threat, however, to the agricultural sector. Landowners were already heavily involved in the export trade with agricultural products accounting for about a fourth of all exports. Issues of protectionism or the break up of landed estates to create new markets were largely irrelevant in the heavily export oriented economy of the 19th century. As Claudio Véliz notes, the Chilean economy stood on three different legs—mining, agriculture, and export import commerce—all oriented to international trade, all with coincident interests.[51] A study of the *Boletines* of the National Society of Agriculture, formed in 1838, found that in the period from

49. Abdón Cifuentes, *Memorias* (Santiago: Editorial Nascimiento, 1936), 106–7. For a detailed and fascinating account of how another election was "stolen" from him, see pp. 122–29.

50. For example, see Julio Heise Gonzalez, *150 años de evolución institucional* (Santiago: Editorial Andrés Bello, 1960), pp. 62–64. Julio Cesar Jobet, *Ensayo crítico del desarollo económico social de Chile* (Santiago: Editorial Universitaria, 1955), p. 40; and Hernán Ramirez Necochea, *Historia del movimiento obrero* (Santiago: Editorial Austral, 1956), pp. 76–77. All are cited in J. Samuel Valenzuela, "Determinants," p. 17–19.

51. Claudio Veliz, "La Mesa de Tres Patas," *Desarollo Económico*, vol. 3, nos. 1–2 (April–September, 1963), pp. 173–230.

1840 to 1870 quotes such as the following were very common: "The miners have been in this country the most constant promoters and protectors of agriculture. This is not only true because of the great impulse which capital formed in mining has given agriculture, but also because the mining capitalist has at the same time greater intelligence in the mechanical arts which he has been able to apply with great advantage to the cultivation of the land."[52] Samuel Valenzuela notes that the coincidence of interests among the dominant sectors in Chile was probably also due to the fact that the principal figures in one sector also had strong interests in others. Prominent figures who made great fortunes in mining became owners of large tracks of land and also invested in commerce. Though one can distinguish differences in social background and economic interests, as Valenzuela notes, it is an exaggeration to argue that these constituted a basis for class based conflict between a hegemonic "landed oligarchy" and a rising "bourgeoisie."[53]

Conflict among Chilean elites was not based primarily on economic differences between distinct and contradictory sectors. Rather, conflict revolved primarily around ideological questions such as the role of the church in society and political questions such as patronage and control over government resources. As the presidency expanded and encroached upon local notables, the latter sought greater autonomy and control over their own destiny. A fundamental center-periphery conflict arose.

As in Europe, the expansion of the secular state at the expense of the church became a key issue. As early as the 1850s, a direct confrontation took place between the president and the Bishop of Santiago over the question of *patronato*—whether the chief executive should have the right to appoint the clergy. Many previous supporters of the government left it over this issue and formed the Conservative party in 1856. The Conservative party, backed by local notables wary of central control, found itself in opposition along with ideological liberals, seeking further liberalization of suffrage and wider freedoms of participation and expression. Despite their many disagreements, they actually joined together in a common opposition movement to

52. Armand Mattelart, Carmen Castillo, Leonardo Castillo, *La ideología de la dominación en una sociedad dependiente* (Buenos Aires: Ediciones Signos, 1970), p. 73, cited in Valenzuela, "Determinants," p. 31.
53. Valenzuela bases his assertions not only on evidence from the *Boletines* of the agriculture society, but also on an analysis of social background data of important figures in the Chilean economic and social elite. The Conservative party included in its ranks families not only with landed wealth but also with investments in mining and in commerce. The same was true of the Liberal party. The Radicals, while recruiting individuals of lesser status, combined among its ranks miners and merchants in the north and agriculturalists in the Concepción region. See pp. 62–63.

the government. In turn, liberals who frowned on this "fusion" formed the Radical party, also in opposition.

Thus, by midcentury, opposition political factions were coming together to work for mutually beneficial objectives in spite of serious personal and policy differences. This reenforced the norms of cooperation and give and take which had characterized the Bulnes presidency. As a strategy, they sought control of the legislature in an attempt to erode the political strength of the group of individuals who, in control of executive authority, were bent on expanding the influence and power of the secular state.[54]

In 1858, a serious civil disturbance broke out in the country which was eventually controlled by the administration. At the root of the issue was fear among opposition elements that the president would try to impose its successor. A compromise was finally worked out and the official candidate withdrawn with all parties, those in the government and those in the opposition, supporting the candidacy of Jose Joaquin Perez. The new president then realized the strength of the opposition and set up a cabinet with elements of the opposition Liberal and Conservative fusion. The result of this decision was to split the executive from the legislative since the legislature was dominated by elements favorable to the outgoing cabinet.

The phenomena of opposition elements coming into the government at the behest of the president had occurred earlier in the Bulnes presidency, and it would occur again in later years. Though it was difficult for opposition elements to gain influence in the government through suffrage because of the overwhelming executive influence over the process, it was possible for opposition elements to show their political capabilities and gain entrance into the government by virtue of their potential rather than actual threat to executive authority. Alberto Edwards has noted the irony of this political game in which an opposition group "to win at the ballot boxes must first of all, take charge of the ministry of government. . . ."[55] Once again, the president was the key actor in this process. Though the final arbiter of the system, he could not survive without the support of what Edwards called the "active political forces"; "without them, presidential power could not survive by its own virtue."[56] Political success for any

54. The emergence of an independent executive power not closely tied to dominant economic groups was recognized as a possibility by Karl Marx in his *Eighteenth Brumaire*. Max Weber notes the importance of the rise of individuals dedicated to politics as a profession. See his essay "Politics as a Vocation," in Gerth and Mills, pp. 77–128.
55. Edwards, *Fronda*, p. 93.
56. Ibid., pp. 101–102.

group then did not mean defeating the government but capturing its favor.[57] However, as a group captured the favor of the government and entered the cabinet, it had to face opposition majorities in the legislature selected by previous cabinets. In turn, this led to an increasingly assertative role on the part of the legislature which would gradually contribute to the erosion of presidential authority. With switching majorities, Congress was able in 1861 to restrict the president to one term and set up a permanent electoral registration system. In 1869, the armed forces were barred from the voting booths.

When the shaky coalition of Liberals and Conservatives in the government broke down by 1872 and the Conservatives left the government, the cabinet of government Liberals once again faced a hostile parliamentary majority. The opposition majority, made up primarily of Conservatives, Radicals, and left Liberals, would press for the passage of one of the most significant pieces of legislation in the nation's history: the expansion of the electorate. Except for a retention of literacy requirements, the 1874 suffrage law virtually provided the statutory basis for universal suffrage.[58] The law was not the creation of Liberals seeking to curb the excesses of an authoritarian state in the hands of Conservatives but of a coalition seeking to curb the power of the presidency.[59] As in several European countries, the coalition included Conservatives who believed that a freer suffrage system would be to their advantage because of the control which local notables had over the political behavior of elements of the lower class.[60]

The adoption of the suffrage law, opposed by the government, resulted in a threefold increase in suffrage from 49,047 in 1872 to 148,737 in 1878. "The 1878 figure represents close to 30% of all males over 25 years of age in the Republic and more than 90% of all those eli-

57. Valenzuela, "Determinants," p. 64.

58. Control of elections was placed in the hands of the largest taxpayers of local communities. The election of deputies was to be done by cumulative voting, enabling the representation of minorities in Congress. In addition, secret voting procedures were instituted and all property qualifications were abolished. Literacy requirements, however, were retained, and, so that the Constitution would not have to be changed, the law read that "it is presumed that those that can read have the proper income." For a discussion of these reforms and especially that of November 12, 1874, see Encina, vol. 15, pp. 327–30 and pp. 74–79; Joselin de la Maza G., *Apuntes para un estudio sobre la organización local en Chile* (Santiago: Imprenta Claret, 1917), pp. 121–23; Jorge Luis Castro A., *El sistema electoral chileno* (Santiago: Editorial Nascimiento, 1941), p. 22.

59. J. Samuel Valenzuela documents the role of Conservatives in pressing the law. See ch. 4 of "Determinants."

60. See Stein Rokkan, "Mass Suffrage, Secret Voting and Political Participation," *Archives Européennes de Sociologie*, 2 (1961), 132–52.

gible to vote."[61] Furthermore, it had the effect of giving landowners for the first time a control over a majority of the suffrage.[62]

However, the 1874 suffrage law was not sufficient to curb the influence with the executive exercised over the electoral process. The basic structure of local government remained unchanged, and the agents of the executive retained a dominant influence over local governments and the electoral process, if not over the electorate.[63] Intervention in suffrage, however, became much more difficult and violent acts became more prevalent. Encina notes that "this series of reforms, on the one hand, reflect the efforts to consolidate electoral freedom, and, on the other, by posing obstacles to executive intervention, they diminished his electoral power, forcing presidents to turn to violence when they tried to block minority intervention, as happened in 1882 and 1885, with the resulting disparagement of the traditional regime."[64] In 1886 alone, violence surrounding the electoral process left a total of 45 dead and 160 injured in Santiago alone.[65]

The continued intervention in the electoral process and the control which executives continued to exercise over the power and resources of the central government led to further moves supported by local interests to restrict presidential authority. In 1887, a second municipal law was adopted providing for an elected mayor to oversee local administration. However, the law did not satisfy the adversaries of executive authority. They wanted a law which would effectively give control over the suffrage system to local communities, removing it entirely from the hands of executive officials.[66]

In 1888 a mixed commission (of both houses of Congress) was charged with drawing up new legislation and, significantly, with preparing a law on municipal autonomy and a law on electoral reform. This commission worked on the project for approximately three months, and it reached the Chamber of Deputies in June, 1889, for consideration.[67] The atmosphere in the country had worsened considerably. President Balmaceda was accused of having selected his minister of the interior as an "official" candidate, and opposition elements feared that he would go to extremes in order to have him

61. Valenzuela, "Determinants," pp. 2–3

62. Ibid., p. 79.

63. For testimony of this, see José Miguel 2° Irarrázaval, *El Municipio Autónomo* (Santiago: Imprenta Cervantes, 1902), p. 31.

64. Encina, vol. 15, p. 502.

65. Ibid., vol. 20, p. 29.

66. Luis Moya Figueroa, *Estudio Comparativo*, p. 41, and Gustavo Silva, *Nueva Era de las Municipalidades*, p. 36.

67. See Chile, *Boletín de las Sesiones de la Camara de Diputados de 1890* (Santiago: Imprenta Nacional, 1890).

elected.[68] Four parties, known as the *cuadrilatero*, and including the independents, Nationals, doctrinaire Liberals and Radicals, opposed the president. Debates in Congress reflected the tension of the times and the fact that municipal autonomy and electoral reform were one and the same issue, aimed at curbing the centralized authority of the president. Thus, in the session of June 12, 1890, Deputy Julio Zegers of the Conservative party made the following speech:

These and other evils, offspring all of the official intervention in elections, are the causes of the instability to which the nation is heading. Congress has, then, the responsibility to place, once and for all, unbreachable barriers to intervention and citizens must trust that it will do so, exercising, one by one and with serenity, the faculties which the Constitution of the State has placed in its hands for this purpose.

It is no longer a partisan cause or issue; it is a national cause, of the suffrage of the rights of citizens, the sovereignty of institutions, and the best proof of this is the attitude assumed by the parliamentary parties in voting a censure of the presidential Cabinet.

Evidence of this is also the unbreakable resolution sustained by the Congress to pass an election law and a law of municipalities to reestablish the vitality of electoral jurisprudence and debilitate the administrative impotence which has caused so many evils and threatens with even worse evils.[69]

Members of other parties were not quite as convinced as the Conservative party leaders, who were primarily responsible for drafting the law (especially Irarrázaval, the acknowledged author), of the merits of decentralization, but went along with the proposed legislation as a way of providing a decided defeat for presidential intervention in elections. Enrique MacIver, one of the most prominent leaders of the Radical party, remarked, "It is not so much good administration of local interests that is sought as the curtailment of the powers of the president of the Republic, and with this the removal of powerful means of influence in popular elections."[70]

Indeed, Liberals supporting the government argued strongly that the legislation should be opposed by Liberals because it might favor the Conservatives. They held that the law's provision for small municipal units and for the creation of popular assemblies would enable local oligarchs, landowners and elements of the clergy to take over local administration and the electoral process.[71]

68. Encina, *Historia de Chile*, vol. 20, p. 36.
69. *Sesiones de la Camara de Diputados*, June 12, 1890, p. 69.
70. Encina, *Historia de Chile*, vol. 29, p. 230.
71. See, for example, the arguments of Ricardo Letelier, *Sesiones de la Camara de Diputados*, June 12, 1890, p. 77. Encina also notes that some Liberals feared that autonomy would reduce their political power. See *Historia de Chile*, vol. 29, p. 205. It is interesting to note that even local communities, where there was strong sentiment in favor of Balmaceda, favored adoption of the Municipal Reform Law which the ad-

The legislation in question was not approved in 1890. The crisis of the regime had gone beyond the point of return. When the Congress censured the Balmaceda ministry, the president refused to accept the resignation of his ministers. .The Congress then retaliated by refusing to enact the budgetary law. In turn the president promulgated the budget by decree. This "unconstitutional act" and the unwillingness of either side to compromise finally plunged the nation into civil war. The Congress, backed by the navy and by widespread support across the nation,[72] was able to defeat the president backed by elements of the army.[73] Municipal autonomy was finally approved after the bitter fratricidal battle on December 22, 1891. The law and the Civil War of 1891 were the culmination of a long struggle between the central authority of the executive on the one hand and the Congress and coalitions of local notables on the other. With the defeat of the executive, the strong presidential system was altered, inaugurating a new chapter in Chilean history in which the locality and the Congress would become the main focuses of political power.[74]

---

ministration was reluctant to approve. This was the case in the town of Angol in Malleco province, where the local paper, El Colono, editorialized as follows on April 14, 1890: "We are hopeful that once the law is adopted establishing municipal autonomy . . . each province and locality will be able to create the resources necessary to have a well-organized police force . . . and it will not be long before each honest man will be able to devote himself without hesitation to his work, and can live safely, and sleep safely in his home." The editorial of the same paper on June 16, 1890 makes it clear that they were partial to the president and not Congress.

72. Encina, Historia de Chile, vol. 20, p. 50.

73. There are three major trends in the literature on the conflict. The first group of works are partisan treatments defending the president (e.g., J. Bañados Espinosa, Balmaceda, su gobierno y la revolución de 1891, 2 vols., Paris: n.p., 1894) or the Congress (e.g., Joaquín Rodriguez Bravo, Balmaceda y el conflicto entre el congreso y el ejecutivo, 2 vols.; Santiago: n.p., 1921 and 1926). These works emphasize ideological differences and personal differences between major actors. The second group of works stresses more the institutional cleavages which developed between the two institutions, particularly over the problem of electoral intervention. In this group one finds historical treatments such as Francisco Encina, Historia de Chile; Domingo Amunátegui Solar, La Democracia en Chile: Teatro Político 1810–1910 (Santiago: Universidad de Chile, 1946); etc. The third interpretation is that of Hernán Ramirez Necochea, La Guerra Civil de 1891: Antecedentes Económicos (Santiago: n.p., 1951). He argues that foreign nitrate interests were being hurt by Balmaceda and that in alliance with local elements which were bought off they overthrew the president. A good article on the historiography of the civil war is Harold Blakemore, "The Chilean Revolution of 1891 and Its Historiography," Hispanic American Historical Review (August, 1964).

74. From this analysis it is apparent that Peter Cleaves' assertion that the municipal law was adopted by Congress to "help it maintain its recently gained hegemony" is erroneous. It was the end result of a struggle which went on throughout the entire nineteenth century. See Developmental Processes in Chilean Local Government (Berkeley: Institute of International Studies, University of California, 1969), p. 9.

The Chilean "Parliamentary Republic" and the Emergence of Political Parties as Linkages between the Center and the Locality

During the period known as the Parliamentary Republic (1891–1925) the character of Chilean politics was drastically altered as the center of gravity of the political system shifted away from the presidential palace to the local town hall. The new Autonomous Commune Law provided Chilean local governments with considerable independence from the power of the national executive. While presidential officials could still preside over municipal sessions, they no longer enjoyed voting privileges. If presidential officials vetoed local resolutions as detrimental to the public order, local elected officials could now appeal to the courts for a reversal of that action. The *primer alcalde* (first mayor) of the municipality, elected by his fellow councilors, became the chief executive of the local government, with authority to execute all decisions and make all necessary appointments.

The most radical innovation of the law was the creation of the Asambleas de Electores (Assemblies of Electors). These assemblies, made up of all eligible voters within the commune, were charged with electing the municipal officials as well as with approving the municipal budget, municipal taxation and municipal loans. In addition, they had to approve all municipal agreements and ordinances sanctioning fines.[75]

The most significant aspect of the new political arrangement consisted in the fact that autonomous municipal governments gained control of the electoral process. They were charged with registering voters, naming the polling officials, and administering the elections proper. Control over suffrage gave local governments a powerful tool, and before long deputies and senators were forced to institute alliances and to bargain with local elites in order to obtain the necessary votes to gain or remain in office. This gradual establishment of ties between local notables and individuals and factions at the center had a profound and longlasting impact on the Chilean political system as it led to the formation for the first time of political parties with roots outside of parliamentary factions.

The shift of political influence from the center to the locality and the emergence of political party organizations, while democratizing Chilean politics, did not result in an "ideal" democracy where citi-

75. A good comparative discussion of the 1891 law and the laws of 1854 and 1887 is Luis Moya Figueroa, *Estudio comparativo de la Lei de Municipalidades de 22 de Diciembre de 1891.* The best and most comprehensive analysis of the 1891 law is Agustín Correa Bravo, *Comentario y Concordancia de la Ley de Organización y Atribuciones de las Municipalidades* (3rd ed., Santiago: Librería Tornero, 1914).

zens freely chose their representatives only on the merit of the issues. Though the violence surrounding elections disappeared, graft and electoral fraud became central features of the system. Encina noted the nature of this shift when he says that "with the demise of the official party the frauds and assaults perpetrated by intendants, governors, judges, sub-delegates and police commanders ceased, and in their place arose those of the parties and electoral *caciques.*"[76] Local notables, and later brokers of lower- and middle-class background, controlled the nation's municipalities and became the key local links in a system in which votes, accepted as the main political currency, were bought and traded.[77] Local officials could either mobilize their own followers and supporters to vote for the candidate of their choice, or, if this strategy failed, they could attempt to change the electoral records to reflect the desired outcome. The latter practice, referred to as *cohecho* or *el tutti*, became a widespread practice in the smaller rural communities, while direct bribery and mobilization of supporters became the more common pattern in the nation's urban areas.[78] By 1900 the expenditure of vast amounts of money in order to secure seats in the national legislature had become a universal phenomenon. Thus the prestigious newspaper *El Ferrocarril* commented editorially on March 7, 1900, shortly after an election:

As has become increasingly apparent in recent years, and as it was repeated in still larger scale during Sunday's election, venality plays a role that is as improper as it is decisive in electoral results; so much so that, at the rate we are going, legislative and municipal posts, in the vast majority, are obtained solely through the influence of the largest possible sum of money which can be spent to assure the triumph of the candidacies.[79]

76. Encina, *Historia de Chile*, vol. 20, p. 341.

77. It must be noted that national politicians, while instituting alliances with local notables and brokers, were a distinct group. Evidence from biographical information shows that in 1912, at the height of the Parliamentary Republic, seventy-four percent of all deputies in the Chamber had university education, while only nine percent had only a primary education. That these people were clearly a highly educated elite is shown by the fact that according to the 1907 census, fifty-eight percent of Chilean males were illiterate. Furthermore, in 1912 only one percent of the small population of individuals studying at all levels of the educational system were in university training. A further characteristic of the parliamentary elite is that of the university-trained deputies, seventy-six percent were lawyers in 1912. (In 1920 only .2 percent of all Chilean males were lawyers.) This evidence suggests that local notables and local party brokers did not achieve national office in this period, but rather served primarily a brokerage function for a special group of individuals with university training and more particularly with legal training. Biographical material was obtained from Alejandro Valderrama, *Albúm Político* (Santiago: n.p., 1915). Census material was obtained from the Dirección General de Estadísticas, *Censo de Población de la República de Chile: Levantado el 15 de diciembre de 1920* (Santiago: Soc. Imp. y Litografía Universo, 1925).

78. See Manuel Rivas Vicuña, *Historia Política y Parlamentaria de Chile* (Santiago: Ediciones de la Biblioteca Nacional, 1964), vol. 1, pp. 84, 263.

79. Cited by Domingo Amunátegui Solar, *La Democracia en Chile*, p. 313.

In the same vein Abraham König, an eminent commentator of the period, noted that "Congress is not the faithful expression of the free vote of the electors. Many of its members have triumphed through frauds, falsifications, and illicit influences, and the majority through bribery. . . . Many congressmen spend money and time to be elected, not to serve their party or their country, but themselves, and they take advantage of their situation to prosper and do business."[80]

While the success of a national politician could be measured in part by his ability to pay for individual votes at election time, his success was also contingent upon his ability to deliver goods and favors to local brokers for the benefit of the latter's proteges and the progress of the community.[81] Arranging employment in the growing public bureaucracy is an example of the kind of favor that a deputy or senator could provide his clientele. Manuel Rivas Vicuña, a prestigious legislator and minister, noted that during the "Parliamentary Republic" the civil service fell increasingly under the control of party interests. "The small functionary was losing the character of servant of the state to become agent of a party or a *caudillo.*[82] Congressmen insisted that prefects and other officials of the Department of the Interior be appointed only after consultation with them. The magazine *La Política,* for example, reported one incident of a congressman from La Serena who made a strong and vehement protest because a prefect not of his choosing was appointed to La Serena.[83] On May 18, 1911, the same magazine reported editorially its feeling that in Chile "the parties have abandoned their doctrines, their ideals, to play politics with public offices. In one of those rare phenomena which reveal societies in decay, the great struggles of thought have been replaced by struggles of the stomach."[84]

Figures on the growth of the public bureaucracy during the parliamentary republic are vivid testimony to the increasing importance of political patronage. While in 1880 the number of employees of the central government amounted to 3,048 or 500 more than in 1860, by 1900 that figure had quadrupled to 13,119. By 1919, the bureaucracy had doubled again to 27,479.[85]

Of greater significance than a legislator's role in providing for employment was his role in providing local brokers with resources from the public treasury for local projects and services. Indeed, pork-

80. Abraham Konig, "Necesidad de reformar el sistema de elección presidencial," *Revista Chilena de Historia y Geografía,* 50 (2nd semester, 1924), 31.
81. Paul S. Reinsch, "Parliamentary Government in Chile," *American Political Science Review,* 3 (November, 1909), 528.
82. Rivas Vicuña, *Historia política y parlamentaria,* vol. 1, p. 202.
83. *La Política,* 1 (July 27, 1911), 27.
84. *La Política,* 1 (May 18, 1911), 27.
85. Humud T., cited in Leiva, 27.

barrel legislation and log-rolling to obtain it became the central activities of the Chilean political system. Since Congress had absolute
control over the budgetary process, innumerable additions to the
budgetary law were constantly made by both senators and deputies
seeking specific funds for particular projects. Thus the budget passed
by Congress was invariably higher than the budget originally submitted by the president. Ministers who in earlier times paid attention to the demands made by prefects and governors for regional
development were now forced to make accommodations with legislators' demands for specific public works programs.[86] During much
of the Parliamentary Republic the Comisión Mista, with members
from both chambers, was the key focus for much of the bargaining
over budgetary matters. Political parties and factions tried to gain
representation on the committee so as to improve their chances of
obtaining services and public works projects for constituents.[87] Individual legislators at different times during the Parliamentary Republic were able to present amendments to the budget law, even
when articles were not debated by the entire chamber due to lack of
time. Numerous amendments were thus automatically approved in
the final vote.[88]

In sum, elections during the period revolved around the ability of
national politicians to obtain money and projects for their districts.
Eliodoro Yañez argued, an election "is in most cases a battle of personal interests and money. The candidate begins by cajoling popular
passions and exciting in each important elector interest in fighting
with the coffers of the state; a subsidy or pecuniary aid, a job or a

86. Reinsch, "Parliamentary Government," p. 529.
87. Rivas Vicuña, *Historia política y parlamentaria*, vol. 1, pp. 74–75; see also the
debate on amendments to the budget law in *Boletín de las Sesiones Extraordinarias
de la Camara de Diputados en 1906* (Santiago: Imprenta Nacional, 1906), 1207–8.
88. This was especially the case between 1903 and 1906. Several times the legislature limited the ability of members to present amendments when articles were not
debated. Nevertheless, during most of the Parliamentary Republic the legislators were
able to offer amendments providing for expenditures exceeding those recommended
by the executive. The result of this practice was an increasing deficit and a prolongation
of the discussion on the budget act. Sometimes it was not until March or even August
that the budget was finally approved, rather than going into effect on January 1 as required. In 1906 the budget deficit amounted to twenty-five million pesos. For an interesting discussion of the process of budgetary approval, consult the *Boletín de
Sesiones de 1906* for the parliamentary debates of the seventeenth, eighteenth and
nineteenth of December (pp. 1181, 1199–1209, 1241–53, 1276–82). Delay of approval
of the budget is mentioned as one of the factors which contributed to the constitutional
reform of 1925 in Facultad de Derecho de la Universidad de Chile, *La Constitución
de 1925 y la Facultad de Ciencias jurídicas y sociales*, Colección Estudios jurídicos
y sociales, no. 16 (Santiago: Editorial Jurídica de Chile, 1951).

promotion, a road or a bridge, the purchase of his home for a school from one or the installation of a public service to benefit another."[89]

This practice of relying on the center to provide resources for local community development meant that it was unnecessary for the newly "autonomous" local governments to tax their own communities. This was a profoundly important development for it prevented municipalities from becoming self-reliant. Indeed, the Municipal Law of 1891 had envisioned financial as well as political autonomy for the nation's communes. It provided that property taxes, personal taxes, taxes on tobacco and alcoholic beverages, and taxes and licenses of industries and professions be turned over to the municipality.[90] The income for the national budget was to rely almost entirely on customs duties and income from the exportation of nitrates, which came to account for seventy percent of national expenditures.[91] The tremendous wealth from the nitrate fields made it possible for citizens as well as local governments to rely less and less on direct taxation to run the government. According to Julio Philippi, this was a conscious policy pursued by Chilean elites, including President Balmaceda, who had argued that "equal distribution of public jobs and the suppression of direct and sub-alternate taxation . . . has constituted the foundation of the economic policy to which I have been conforming in a gradual and constant fashion."[92]

In an important article dealing with trends in taxation during the early years of the Parliamentary Republic, Alberto Edwards documented this virtual elimination of taxes on wealth with the advent of the great nitrate boom. He also showed, however, that the elimination of taxes on wealth did not lead to an elimination of regressive forms of taxation. Indeed, such taxes were increased proportionally because the political costs of such measures were less at the time than income taxation, which affected the wealthier strata of society.[93] The following table presents Edwards' findings on the evolution of taxation other than customs or export taxes:

89. Speech by Eliodoro Yañez, senator from Valdivia, July 29, 1912, reprinted in Partido Liberal, *La Reforma Electoral ante el Senado* (Santiago: Imprenta Universitaria, 1912), p. 8.

90. Correa, *Ley de Organización y Atribuciones de la Municipalidades*, pp. 589–96.

91. See Horacio Manriquez Riviera, "Contribuciones Municipales," Santiago, 1901, p. 10; Julio Philippi, "La Nueva Ley de Contribuciones," *Revista de Gobierno Local*, 1 (June, 1916), 9–10.

92. Cited by Jorge Gustavo Silva, *Nueva Era de las Municipalidades en Chile*, p. 10.

93. Alberto Edwards, "Nuestro Régimen Tributario en los ultimos 40 Años," *Revista Chilena*, 1 (April, 1917), 345. Philippi also notes that taxation ceased to be in proportion to ability to pay. See "Nueva Ley de Contribuciones," p. 15.

Table 8.2. Distribution of taxation in several categories in selected years from 1880 to 1913.

Year	Tax on wealth	Tax on consumption	Stamps	Public service
1880	18.0%	77.9%	2.4%	1.7%
1883	16.2	79.1	2.4	2.3
1886	16.9	77.7	2.4	3.0
1889	8.0	86.5	2.5	3.0
1892	5.1	89.5	2.4	3.0
1895	0.0	93.2	2.1	4.7
1913	1.2	90.3	3.4	5.1

Source: Alberto Edwards, "Nuestro régimen tributario en los ultimos 40 años," *Revista Chilena*, 1 (April, 1917), 337–56.

As table 8.2 shows, the advent of the Parliamentary Republic coincided with a sharp drop in direct taxation and a concomitant rise in sales taxes, while taxes on public services and stamps remained about the same. This trend continued well into the Parliamentary Republic.[94]

What about local governments? Evidence from the period indicates that local communities were unwilling to impose taxation. One author notes that the new taxation system which was introduced by the Law of 1891 was "generally much less onerous for landowners than the three which it replaced."[95] Municipalities found that it was not politically feasible to enforce the laws requiring them to collect revenues. Not only were the locally-appointed commissions inclined to underassess property to reduce the tax rate, but in most cases taxes were simply not collected.[96] Municipal expenditures by the local

94. Edwards does note, however, that by 1915 the country began to experience serious financial difficulties as government capabilities exceeded government demands. In 1915 taxes on wealth had to be increased as high as 27.3 percent, while taxes on consumption were raised to 62.4 percent. However, while an income tax was introduced, it did not hit the wealthier citizens very hard, as it was confined primarily to public servants. Indeed, in 1916 property taxes were halved. ("Nuestro Regimen Tributario," p. 348.) Both Edwards and Philippi, in another article entitled "La Reforma del Sistema Tributario Fiscal," *Revista Chilena*, año 2, vol. 5 (August, 1910), 5–18, cautioned against over-reliance on nitrate income as potentially disastrous for the country. Their advice was not heeded until it was too late, and Chile experienced increasing economic as well as political difficulties toward the end of the Parliamentary Republic.

95. Manriquez Rivera, "Contribuciones Municipales," p. 11. It should be noted that prior to the Law of 1891, government revenue was obtained from three sources (not including customs and export taxes): the Tax on Agriculture (laws of June 18, 1874, September 2, 1880, and September 5, 1883), the Tax for Rural Police (law of July 28, 1881), and the Tax for Nightwatchmen and Lighting (law of October 23, 1835).

96. Silvestre Ochagavía Hurtado, *Dos causas de la ineficiencia de nuestro sistema comunal* (Santiago: Imprenta Cervantes, 1920), pp. 20–21; Manriquez Rivera, "Contribuciones Municipales," p. 19; Philippi, "Nueva Ley de Contribuciones," p. 14.

governments themselves consequently remained very low. This was especially true of the majority of smaller municipalities across the country. Alberto Edwards again shows that, at the height of the Parliamentary Republic, the vast majority of small municipalities had extremely low per capita expenditures, while the larger ones had higher per capita expenditures. The data in table 8.3 report his findings. According to Edwards, per capita expenditures in Chilean municipalities at the time were considerably lower than expenditures in European and Argentinian cities.[97]

It is clear that the political system of Chile at the time made it unnecessary for the local communities of the country to become financially autonomous. It was much more to the advantage of local brokers to bargain with legislators at the center to obtain resources, than to risk the loss of local influence by attempting to make the local community self-sufficient. And, as long as the national government had plenty of resources and as long as the system was primarily one of log-rolling, local communities clearly benefited by the arrangement.[98] The tradition of turning to the center via national brokers was

Table 8.3. Per capita expenditures in municipalities of differing size in the Parliamentary Republic.

Population of head town of communes	Number of municipalities	Per capita municipal expenditures
Over 100,000	2	$20.28
From 20,000 to 100,000	6	18.30
From 5,000 to 20,000	20	5.23
Less than 5,000	36	3.32
Rural municipalities	224	4.11

97. See "Datos y observaciones sobre finanzas municipales de Chile," *Revista de Gobierno Local*, vol. 2 (May, 1917).

98. Though article xxxiv, sec. 4 of the Municipal Law prescribes that the legislature provide the municipalities with some funds for their services, this was never enacted on an across-the-board basis, municipalities preferring during the early years to obtain specific projects from the government, thus over-burdening the budget. (See Correa, *Ley de Organización y Atribuciones de las Municipalidades*, p. 283). Only when the national budget came into difficulty and there was a move to municipal reform did a cry come out that the legislature provide municipalities with more funds. By this time, however, the national government was in such straits that much of the burden was passed on to the municipality rather than vice-versa. As the *Revista de Gobierno Local* noted editorially in September, 1920, "these funds [from the central government] have never been granted to the municipalities . . . [and instead] the procedure has been developed of assigning municipalities tasks that do not correspond to them, which with grave repercussions to those functions which they are supposed to exercise, deprive them of their always scarce resources" (vol. 44, p. 452). As an example the maga-

thus reinforced by the availability of ample resources in the center. This was a curious development because local notables and their party allies had fought for so long for genuine local autonomy. With the demise of executive authority, not only were local governments to control suffrage, they were also to maximize their own extractive and distributive capabilities. Ironically, precisely because they gained control of suffrage and direct access to the central coffers of the state, they had no incentive to institute the taxes required by the municipal law, which would have given them "truer" autonomy. The roots of the center-local linkages described earlier in this book can be clearly traced to these developments at the turn of the century.

The need to distribute national resources to local communities meant that political factions in the legislature had to structure alliances in order to service constituents. However, alliances were also the product of the tremendous expense involved in conducting elections. Since campaigning became very expensive, legislative elites formed complex coalitions to improve their electoral chances at the lowest possible monetary cost. These *pactos electorales* were made possible in part by the adoption of cumulative voting procedures shortly before the Civil War, on August 20, 1890.[99] By means of these pacts various factions would agree to support each other in constituencies where one faction was strongest and thus avoid direct confrontation. Arrangements were also made with influential persons in local government so that two opponents could be guaranteed victory by placing their names on the same list in order to avoid competition.[100] Often these local agreements cut across party lines so that in one community a Radical might make a pact with a Conservative, and in another a Radical might make a pact with a Liberal. However, grand alliances were made at the national level. In 1912, for example, the Nationals left their alliance with the Conservatives and joined the Liberals. A new set of electoral agreements had to be worked out because in many constituencies National candidates were opposing Liberals with the backing of Conservatives and Liberal Democrats. With the shift in alliances the Nationals lost the backing of Conservatives and Liberal Democrats who would put up their own candidates in constituencies where the Nationals were strong. Under the

zine cited the recent Ley de Caminos, "imposing on the municipality the contribution equal to one-third of the property tax." (See also Hector Vigil, "Como disminuyeron las rentas municipales en Chile," *Revista de Gobierno Local*, 45 [October, 1920], 542–50). Municipalities were burdened with other services which the central government could not undertake. Thus, for example, while electoral administration was taken away from the municipalities, they still had to pay for it.

99. Domingo Amunátegui Solar, *La Democracia en Chile*, p. 287.
100. Rivas Vicuña, *Historia política y parlamentaria*, 2, 275.

new agreement Nationals would support Liberals in constituencies where the Liberals were strong, and the Liberals would reciprocate. The magazine *La Política* bitterly attacked the practice of creating such alliances in the following editorial: "The Santiago oligarchs, to avoid expenditures and confident of the meekness of the populace and of its naivete, and taking advantage of their own positions as heads of parties to deceive and betray their own correligionists, agreed to sign the distribution of senatorships, taking special care to assign themselves the safest ones and without doing battle."[101]

The result of these political pacts for electoral advantage and governmental resources was marked instability in the Chilean "parliamentary" system. Parliamentary majorities came and went as legislative factions in both houses sought to maximize their electoral fortunes or sought to obtain a maximum of benefits for constituents from the national treasury. No doubt, cabinet instability was also due to the desire of many congressional figures to hold a cabinet post—both for the prestige and the resources which such a position commanded. A detailed analysis of the biographies of all deputies in the Congress of 1912 reveals that fifty-two percent of all deputies had served or would serve in the position of minister at least once in their legislative careers.[102] Since a ministry would fall if it experienced an unfavorable vote in either house of Congress, the likelihood of failure was much greater than in an essentially unicameral regime. Likewise, the president or minister of the interior's inability to call an election in the face of an unfavorable vote or a vote of censure provided few restraints on the actions of passing parliamentary majorities.[103] In the 34-year period from 1891 to 1925, Chile experienced 93 complete cabinet changes and 12 partial changes. Not counting the first cabinet appointed by each new president, 489 ministerial positions were vacated and filled. The average cabinet remained in office for only 133 days.[104] These figures contrast sharply with the period before

101. *La Política*, 28 (February, 1912), 19.
102. Biographical information was obtained from Alejandro Valderrama, *Album Político* (Santiago: n.p., 1915). Information was cross-checked with the listing of deputies in Luis Valencia, ed., *Anales de la República* (Santiago: Imprenta Universitaria, 1951), vol. 2.
103. The Chilean political system of the period was consequently not a parliamentary system in the strict sense of the word. Congress could censure ministries—and they had to respond to congressional majorities. The president was more than a ceremonial figure—and yet he did not have the authority to dissolve parliament.
104. During the period the following vacancies took place: 69 in Interior, 56 in Foreign Relations, 67 in Justice, 66 in Finance, 81 in War and 77 in Industry. Of course, the number of positions that opened up does not coincide with the number of individuals who occupied ministerial positions since many occupied different posts at different times. In total 305 different individuals served as minister during the "Parliamentary Republic." Twenty-eight men served as minister more than four times.

1891. As table 8.4 shows, during the "Presidential Republic," 31 ministerial changes took place over a period almost twice as long.

President Federico Errázuriz Echaurren experienced nine cabinets during his term. Among these, one was made up of separatist liberals, two of government Liberals, Liberal Democrats and Conservatives, and one of Liberal Democrats and Liberals. In Pedro Montt's presidency, of the nine cabinets formed, four were made up of the diametrically opposed Radicals and Conservatives.[105] Yanez, in criticizing this system, noted that "The Congress has a tendency amongst us to no longer be the deliberate assembly of the nation where the general interest and not local interests must prevail, and it converts the people's representatives into agents of those interests to assure themselves reelection or to satisfy personal ambitions. This is the cause of the frequency with which one sees Chambers that sustain

Table 8.4. Number of cabinets in the presidential and parliamentary republics.

President	Years	Number of cabinets
Presidential republic		
Prieto	1831–1841	4
Bulnes	1841–1851	5
Montt	1851–1861	4
Perez	1861–1871	6
Errazuriz	1871–1876	5
Pinto	1876–1881	6
Santa Maria	1881–1885	5
Balmaceda	1886–1891	13
Total	59 years	48 cabinets
Parliamentary republic		
Montt	1891–1896	9
Echaurren	1896–1901	11
Riesco	1901–1906	15
Montt	1906–1910	10
Barros Luco	1910–1915	13
Sanfuentes	1915–1920	13
Alessandri	1920–1925	18
Total	34 years	79 cabinets

Source: Calculated from lists of ministers and cabinets in Luis Valencia Avaria, *Anales de la República* (Santiago: Imprenta Universitaria, 1951), vol. 1.

These figures were calculated from the compilation of ministers in Avaría's *Anales de la Republica*, vol. 1, pp. 354–400.
105. Rivas Vicuña, *Historia política y parlamentaria*, vol. 2, pp. 281–85.

or overthrow Ministries because of the honors, services or favors which members obtain."[106]

Parenthetically, it seems ironic that, while the Chilean Parliamentary Republic was highly unstable at the cabinet level, the transfer of the center of political gravity from the center to the local arena meant greater stability in representation patterns. Stable relationships between national politicians and local brokers meant that deputies in the parliamentary period were more likely to serve their time in office as representatives from only one district. By contrast, deputies in the presidential period were more likely to be transferred from constituency to constituency, depending on presidential strategies for the electoral campaign. These facts can be noted in table 8.5, which compares two Chambers of Deputies in the presidential period with two Chambers of Deputies in the parliamentary period.[107]

Despite the efforts of political elites, complex alliances did not succeed in reducing substantially the costs of political campaigning, nor did they halt the process of institutionalization of the party system. For one thing, citizens were not very pleased when local bosses

Table 8.5. Constituency service of a sample of deputies from the presidential and the parliamentary periods.

Type of constituency service	Total N	1876–1882		1912–1921	
		N	percent	N	percent
Deputies serving in predominantly *one* constituency	36	9	47	27	77
Deputies serving in separate constituencies	18	10	53	8	23
Total deputies serving several Congresses	54	19	100	35	100
Total deputies serving one Congress	19	7		12	
Total deputies in sample	73	26		47	

106. Eliodoro Yanez, speech reprinted in *Reforma Electoral ante el Senado*, p. 9.

107. A random sample of all deputies in each Congress was selected. Deputies serving predominantly in one Congress are those who served at least sixty-five percent of the time in their career as representatives from a single constituency. Two other indices of "localism," taking into consideration birth place of deputies and service in local office, also showed that the "parliamentary" Congresses were more local than the "presidential" ones. For a complete discussion of the sampling procedure and the sources used, see Appendix II.

agreed to fix an election or candidates agreed not to run against each other. Encina quotes Luis Galdames, who notes that "there were cases of insurrection in several villages against the best-known resident electoral agents, whose homes were stoned by the mob because political parties had made agreements there to avoid the battle. Since this meant having to vote for only one list, electors were left free to vote with or without pay."[108] Independent candidates also made it difficult for the regular parties to adhere to electoral strategies which called for a minimum of expenditures, because many of them spent lavishly to secure a seat in the legislature.[109]

While parties were willing to institute temporary alliances, they did not relax in their effort to win the support of local brokers and citizens in different regions of the country in order to solidify their electoral fortunes. Indeed, the instability of the alliances made it necessary for political factions to consolidate widebased support. As a consequence, parties gradually established networks of local contacts and even party organizations in municipalities across the country. As early as 1909, Augusto Vicuña Subercaseaux, secretary of a new municipal reform movement, complained that municipalities had indeed been taken over by party organizations:

Many municipal candidates are not selected because they deserve the general confidence. . . but because they are useful elements for the party and the candidate for senator or deputy who has them on his list. Once in office these municipal officials, those same councilors, and even those with most dispassionate spirits, feel themselves contaminated with the spirit of party; majorities and minorities spy on each other, and battle for the first mayoralty.[110]

The patron-client origin of party networks and the prevalence of diverse alliances cutting across class lines and geographical regions meant that different parties did not represent significantly different cross sections of society. The basis of support of a given party was not a political class or an occupational group but a community with a clientele cutting across class and occupational lines. Some parties would be stronger than others in differing areas of the country but not until many years later did parties begin to represent significantly different social groups.

The above generalizations are supported by a detailed electoral analysis of the 1920 Chilean elections making use of aggregate statistics. Table 8.6 presents the results of multiple regression analysis for all 300 Chilean communes with party strength as the dependent

108. Quoted in *Historia de Chile*, vol. 20, p. 355.
109. *La Política*, 24 (January, 1912), 27.
110. Cited by Jorge Gustavo Silva in *Nueva Era de las Municipalidades*, p. 37.

variable and three socioeconomic variables as independent variables in the 1920 congressional and municipal elections. The independent variables are percentage of the urban population, percentage of the population literature, and percentage of the population which is urban and male.

As the table reveals, none of the parties drew its strength primarily from urban areas or from areas of high literacy. The only significant associations related to urbanism are the negative ones of the Conservative and the Democrat parties and the positive one of the Socialist party. Negative associations with literacy are found with the Conservative party and the Liberal Alliance, while the Radical party is rather strongly associated with areas of higher literacy. In general, however, the chart reveals that the socioeconomic variables don't explain much of the variance in party vote. Thus the highest significant coefficient of determination is the one with the Socialist party which reveals that urbanization and literacy explain only twenty-eight percent of the variance in party vote.[111]

Table 8.6. Correlation between three socioeconomic variables and party vote in the 1921 congressional and municipal elections by commune.

Party	Congressional election				Municipal election			
	Urb Mal	Rur Mal	Lit/21	R^2	Urb Mal	Rur Mal	Lit/21	R^2
Conservative	−.18°	.14°	−.13°	.08	−.18°	.17°	−.19°	.09
Democratic	.35°	−.30°	.23°	.18	.36°	−.29°	.28°	.21
Liberal Alliance	−.01	.02	−.05	.02	−.07	.05	−.14°	.06
Liberal Unionist	−.11	.13°	−.18°	.08	−.04	.05	−.10	.02
Liberal Democrat Alliance	−.07	.08	.09	.03	.10	−.09	.12°	.02
Nationalist	−.02	.01	−.11	.02	−.03	.03	−.10	.03
Radical	.04	−.06	.15°	.09	.01	−.02	.19°	.15
Socialist	.06	.01	.44°	.28	.05	.01	.41°	.29

°Significance = .05 (N = 317).
Ur Mal = % of population urban male.
Rur Mal = % of population rural male.
Lit/21 = % of population male, literate, over 21.

Note: technically, significance tests are not necessary since the study deals with the entire universe of Chilean communes and not with a sample. However, significance tests can be of utility in identifying the strengths of various associations.

Source: Calculated from data in Chile, Oficina Central de Estadísticas, *Censo Electoral* (Santiago: Sociedad Imprenta y Litografía Universo, 1922), and Chile, Dirección General de Estadística, *Censo de Población de la República de Chile: Levantado el 15 de Diciembre de 1920* (Santiago: Sociedad Imprenta y Litografía Universo, 1925).

111. The validity of the data can be appreciated in the high negative correlation between the percentage of the population living in urban areas and percentage living in rural areas.

The findings in table 8.6—which must be interpreted with caution because of the general and ambiguous character of the independent variables—can be complemented by table 8.7, which provides a fuller set of independent variables. In table 8.7 the vote for all Chilean parties in the Congressional election of 1920 is examined in relationship to the occupational make up of all 79 Chilean departments. All active adult Chileans have been divided into one of 14 occupational groups.

Although the table reveals many interesting differences, the most striking fact is that the only significant association between occupational categories and party vote can be found in the small Socialist party. Forty-six percent of the variance in Socialist vote is explained by occupational variables—mainly by population in transportation. This effectively meant that socialists drew a large portion of their support from railroad workers and construction workers engaged in building bridges and roads. The table also shows support for socialists among miners—and exhibits a negative correlation between socialist vote and the percentage of workers in agriculture. Bearing in mind that many of the other associations are not significant at the .05 level,

Table 8.7. Correlations between the percentage of the vote received by Chilean parties in the 1921 congressional election and various occupational categories for all departments.

	Conservative		Democrats		Liberal Alliance		Liberal Union	
	r	b	r	b	r	b	r	b
Fishing & Hunting	−130	−.413	228	.139	−075	−.022	−148	−.189
Agriculture	162	.128	−122	.139	154	.129	157	−.522
Mining	−122	−.153	025	−.023	−177	−.079	−188	−.508
Industry	−106	−.055	179	.104	073	.621	−117	−.171
Transportation	−140	.042	163	.022	−129	.284	−170	−.259
Commerce	−113	−.089	131	.107	−047	−.063	−063	−.078
Liberal Professions	−053	.144	091	.142	−087	.171	−155	.068
Medical	−104	−.052	141	−.478	−106	−.443	−136	−.410
Fine Arts	−067	.126	152	.249	−190	−.266	−073	.332
Education	018	.093	060	−.005	−090	−.036	−084	−.124
Religious	−023	−.027	−078	−.161	−025	.112	071	.211
Public Service	−082	−.077	−014	−.226	−214	−.263	−006	−.091
Armed Forces	−117	.121	218	.034	−091	−133	−069	.305
Domestic Service	−090	−.143	116	.035	013	.067	−079	−.070
	R = .254	R² = .064	R = .348	R² = .121	R = .447	R² = .200	R = .39	R² = .152
	N = 79 Departments							

Source: Calculated from data in Chile, Oficina Central de Estadisticas, *Censo Electoral* (Santiago: Sociedad Imprenta y Litografia Universo, 1922) and Chile, Direccion General de Estadistica. *Censo de Poblacion de la*

an examination of simple coefficients reveals that the agriculture occupation is positively associated with the Conservative, Liberal Alliance, Liberal Union, Liberal Democratic Alliance, and National parties, and negatively associated with the Democrats, Liberal Democrats, Radicals, and Socialists. The latter parties constituted the more leftist Liberal Alliance—while the former parties were members of the more conservative National Union. By contrast industry is positively associated only with Democrats, Radicals, Socialists, Liberal Alliance and Liberal Democrats. Though these correlations are suggestive, the overall weakness of associations between occupational categories and support for Chilean parties, with the exception of the socialists, is the key result of this analysis. With some minor variations Chilean parties at the time appealed to similar clienteles.

Secondary sources suggest that the principal variation between parties was in *geographical* strength. The Conservatives, for example, drew most of their support from rural areas in the center of the nation where landlords were famous for taking their followers to the polls after teaching them how to write in order to meet the literacy requirement.[112] The Radicals, who worked most vigorously to establish political support across the nation, made strong headway in northern mining communities while gaining support from southern landlords

Table 8.7. (cont.)

Liberal Demo-cratic Alliance		National		Radicals		Socialists	
r	b	r	b	r	b	r	b
214	.656	024	.256	−016	−.184	011	−.116
087	−.059	206	−.279	−242	.376	−459	−.075
−085	−.110	−178	−.226	271	.412	504	.102
−014	.375	−183	−.048	057	−.393	184	−.041
−071	−.341	−209	−.288	245	.185	522	.859
−063	−.072	−165	−.215	128	.265	118	−.126
−078	.091	−152	−.125	208	−.115	166	−.084
−086	−.466	−153	−.213	157	.383	104	−.102
−038	.171	−202	−.100	280	.148	406	.031
−011	−.051	−052	−.034	195	.271	−135	−.182
−049	.071	−028	.051	−028	−.260	−032	.123
−062	.185	−050	.412	249	.017	263	−.141
−055	−.330	−110	−.061	059	−.023	071	−.211
−060	−.050	007	.037	065	.102	−070	.134
R = .449	R² = .201	R = .366	R² = .134	R = .477	R² = 228	R = .677	R² = .458

Republic de Chile: Levantado el 15 de diciembre de 1920 (Santiago: Soc. Imp. y Litografia Universo, 1925).

112. Rivas Vicuña, vol. 1, pp. 168–73.

and agricultural interests.[113] The Liberals also drew support all over the country, drawing heavily on personalistic ties with local notables.[114] Only the smaller parties such as the Socialists and the Democrats tended to be localized. With strength mainly in urban areas—they drew on emerging worker interests—though it should be recalled that table 8.7 shows that the correlation of Democrats with industry and transportation was not high.

Cross class and heterogeneous support of the parties did not mean however that some did not succeed in establishing relatively stable support. The Radicals in particular by the 1920 election were the largest single party with relatively stable local organizations and contacts. Radicals skillfully made use of political pacts to strengthen their local organizations. According to Rivas Vicuña, the Radicals would make a pact with a Liberal party, supporting that party's candidate for deputy, in return for liberal support for radical candidates to municipal office. Gradually Radicals gained control of a sizeable number of municipal seats—and were then in a good position to bargain with other candidates now that they controlled the locality. They could then gain support of other party's senatorial candidate for Radical candidates for deputy—in return for aid from municipal officials.[115] Simple correlations between the vote of one party in a

Table 8.8. Correlation between votes for the same party in the municipal election of 1921 and the congressional election of 1921.

	Congressional election							
Municipal election	Soc.	Dem.	Rad.	Cons.	Nat.	Lib.Al.	Lib.Un.	Lib.Dem.Al.
Socialist	.903							
Democratic		.711						
Radical			.633					
Conservative				.514				
National					.478			
Liberal Alliance						.354		
Liberal Unionist							.272	
Liberal Democratic Alliance								.072
N = 317 Communes								

Source: Calculated from data in Chile, Oficina Central de Estadísticas, *Censo Electoral* (Santiago: Sociedad Imprenta y Litografía Universo, 1922).

113. Ibid.
114. Ibid., p. 144. Examination of electoral turnout and party vote in different regions of the country support these conclusions.
115. Ibid., p. 115.

congressional election with the vote for the same party in a local election provides some empirical evidence of stability of voting patterns. As table 8.8 shows, the Socialist party has the largest stability with a correlation of .903 followed by the Democrats with a correlation of .711. The liberal parties had the lowest correlations—a further indication of their greater proclivity to engage in political pacts.[116] An examination of the correlations of the vote between the congressional election and the presidential election are also instructive of the relative stability of the vote at the time. The National Union vote in the presidential election correlated most heavily with the congressional vote of parties participating in the National Union coalition and negatively with parties in the Liberal Alliance. By examining the correlation coefficients a perfect prediction can be made of which parties supported which coalition.

In a perfect example of what Robert Merton called the "unanticipated consequences of purposeful social action" the original goal of local notables to break linkages to the center and create autonomous communities resulted in the structuring of alternative networks and the continued reliance of the locality on resources from the center. For concrete and structural reasons, and not because of cultural characteristics, a distinct pattern of center-local linkages emerged. Party networks replaced executive officials as the key linkages between local governments and the national government. The great wealth derived from nitrate exports encouraged localities to continue extracting resources from the center rather than structuring independent local communities. Though at first local notables constituted the fulcrum of the political system, they gradually lost their political prominence, but retained their dependence. The instability and immobility of the "Parliamentary Republic" led, in a time of crisis, to the decline of the legislature-locality axis and the reemergence of strong presidential leadership.

The parties, however, would remain as the key linkage networks of the Chilean system and the principle legacy of the parliamentary period. Their importance cannot be minimized. The vertical nature of party structures meant that Chilean parties succeeded in cutting across actual and potential social cleavages, serving as mechanisms for political accommodation and control. Only in the isolated northern nitrate fields and among transient transport workers did a significant antisystem movement develop and even it would be channeled, in

116. By the same token it should be noted that the highest negative correlation between any two parties in the same election was −.57 between Radicals and Conservatives. This suggests that they tend to compete less in the same areas than other combinations of parties.

time, primarily into electoral politics. In Maurice Duverger's terms, parties were generally created from within the system and not from "without," minimizing potential challenges to the regime.[117]

It is also very important to stress that the party system in Chile emerged before the creation of an elaborate public bureaucracy. This meant that linkages designed to channel the articulation of individual and community interests and distribute governmental resources were structured through party organizations. When bureaucratic agencies replaced the legislature as the key dispensers of public goods, parties continued to act as the key brokers of the system, thus reenforcing the viability of a representative government. Where, as in Brazil, the bureaucracy emerged before the structuring of strong party networks as the fundamental linkage mechanism between center and locality, informal and officially sponsored networks with direct access to the bureaucracy became norm. Under such circumstances an authoritarian regime was much more likely to emerge.[118]

Reaction Against Democratization: The Municipal Reform Movement and its Aftermath

It must be stressed at this point, however, that the creation of parties to incorporate nonelite elements into the ongoing system and to structure linkages from center to locality was not a smooth process. From the point of view of the Santiago elite and local notables across the country the extension of the party system had a serious fault: the elite began to loose its grasp over the country's polity. As traditional patrons lost control over the electoral system, as money became an important tool of campaigns, and as alliances were structured to maximize electoral strategies, party cadres with lower- and middle-class elements came to play an increasingly important political role. In particular, local brokers of more humble origin gained control of local party organizations and key municipalities. Chilean elites may have succeeded in creating political structures designed at coopting lower- and middle-class elements into the ongoing system. But this democratization had its price — it meant that they lost a significant measure of direct control over the political system.

Loss of control in turn led to strong antiparty and antipolitics reactions from the Chilean upper class. Though the party system would

117. Maurice Duverger, *Political Parties*, (New York: John Wiley, 1963).
118. For Brazil see Phillippe Schmitter, *Interest Conflict and Political Change in Brazil* (Stanford: Stanford University Press, 1971), and Douglas Chalmers "Political Groups and Authority in Brazil," in Riordan Roett, ed., *Brazil in The Seventies* (Nashville: Vanderbilt University Press, 1972).

dominate and shape Chilean politics, this antipolitics tradition would continue to play an important role, and indeed become dominant in times of crises. Like the party system, it was a principle legacy of the Parliamentary Republic.

One of the most dramatic examples of concern over democratization and the increasing influence of parties was the important municipal reform movement founded in Santiago in 1908.[119] The principal aim of this movement was to break the influence of parties as linkages between the municipality and the central government, fostering "neutral" local administration. Underlying the movement was a strong feeling that the masses were not prepared for political participation and leadership.

The history of the municipal reform movement vividly confirms the fact that the Chilean upper class had lost a great deal of influence over the political system. With a membership composed of the most illustrious names in Santiago, the Junta de Reforma Municipal took years to make progress on its demands. In fact, a year after its founding in July 1908, the Junta had failed to obtain any response to its demands that reforms be instituted to curtail the influence of municipal leaders. It was forced to resort to a mass demonstration in the center of Santiago to dramatize the seriousness of its demands. El Mercurio reported that over 6,000 people marched to the presidential palace demanding municipal reform. And yet, despite these efforts, the council's activities continued to fall on deaf ears.[120] Even after two more years of lobbying, the Junta Municipal could not gain support for its proposals. On June 11, 1911, 100 of the most prominent members of the capital elite signed a petition demanding the prompt adoption of a law incorporating their program. Since this again proved fruitless, another mass meeting was called in August of 1911. This time El Mercurio estimated that over 10,000 persons were mobilized in support of municipal reform, and another delegation was commissioned to see the president.

The most important meeting took place on Christmas Day of 1911. In a "grandiosa assamblea de notables" as El Mercurio put it, the elite once again sought to mobilize support for municipal reform. In that session, advocates of municipal reform made it quite clear that previous attempts, over the years, to obtain reforms were doomed to failure because the Congress itself was unwilling and incapable of accepting their demands. Legislators owed their political positions

119. It is rather striking how this episode is rarely mentioned by historians. There is no reference to it, for example in Fredrick Pike's Chile and the United States.

120. This and the following newspaper accounts are reprinted in Junta de Reforma Municipal, El libro de reforma municipal (Santiago: Imprenta Barcelona, 1913).

to local leaders in Chilean municipalities, and they simply could not challenge that authority. Alberto Mackenna Subercaseaux, president of the movement, summarized the key sentiments:

The Junta de Reforma Municipal has convened the most prestigious neighbors of Santiago, the youth centers of the various political parties and members of the Federacion de Estudiantes to unite with them in order to carry out a last supreme effort with the object of saving the capital from the band of malefactors who threaten to fall on them, if the Congress does not issue in a short time special laws to protect electoral rights and enable the entry of good social elements into the municipality. If the National Congress in the present period does not approve the various reform laws for which the Junta over which I have the honor of presiding has fought for four years, the future situation of Santiago will be a personal threat to each of its inhabitants. . . . The combined and energetic action of the neighbors will finally make itself felt on the highest authorities and on the legislative bodies who have observed until today the municipal problem with complete disdain. . . . The Junta de Reforma has touched all the means at its disposal, sponsoring a propaganda campaign which has managed to agitate public opinion in the whole country . . . and yet in spite of our unheard-of efforts, nothing positive has been accomplished and we have confronted at each step underhanded resistance from those who do not dare to reveal themselves but are positive obstacles. . . . Santiago is today an embarrassment for civilization and the mockery of South America, because a few gentlemen have in their power the political machine and must have it run by the lowest instruments.[121]

Again, in February of 1912, another mass demonstration was organized. This time the newspaper *La Unión* reported that the attendance was 15,000 persons and that many workers had been mobilized in support of the reform movement.[122] In the same month, the organization put out another declaration addressed to the Voting Neighbors of Santiago:

The refusal of the National Congress to dictate the electoral and municipal reform laws and the resistance of the heads of the political parties to designating people of recognized honorableness to serve in municipal positions show us with complete clarity that the rejection of such just and honorable petitions is the natural result of the domination of the Congress by those unhealthy elements of all parties who supplant the popular vote with uncalled-for electoral machinations. The Congress is responsible today for the fact that in the election of next March 3 the same or similar municipal officials will be elected by virtue of falsifications.[123]

It seems quite clear that the most prestigeous citizens of Santiago were not able to pressure the legislature or the parties to adopt their demands. The "aristocracy" simply did not control the political system as fully as standard interpretations imply. Certainly, the aristo-

121. Ibid., pp. 90–92.
122. Ibid., p. 128.
123. Ibid., p. 158.

crats which Fredrick Pike or Federico Gil describe in their works would not have had any difficulty in extracting from the legislature those measures which they felt to be in their interest. But, in fact national elites no longer controlled all levels of Chilean politics. Political bosses and electoral brokers from the more popular sectors had achieved a significant measure of control over the electoral process.

Finally, in March of 1912, almost four years after its founding, the municipal reform movement's efforts met with a measure of success. Significantly, it was through the courts rather than the legislature that the "better" citizens of Santiago were able to undermine the political strength of local municipal leaders. On that date, local elections were declared void and several local leaders were jailed on charges of corruption.[124] At the same time, spurred in part by judicial action, a special multi-party committee in the Chamber of Deputies recommended that the supervision of elections be taken away from municipal officials and returned to a committee composed of a community's largest taxpayers.[125]

But, it was not until 1914, after further debates on the issue, that several key "reform" measures were adopted. In February of that year, a law was passed calling for the complete renewal of electoral records every nine years — a measure designed to insure that suffrage levels be maintained at "reasonable" levels. At the same time, the administration of suffrage was turned over to a Committee of the Largest Taxpayers. In December of 1914 another law completely eliminated the assemblies of electors, which had functioned as town meetings, and also replaced them with committees composed of the 50 largest taxpayers of each community.[126] The effect of these meas-

124. Ibid., pp. 193–95.
125. Rivas Vicuña, vol. 2, pp. 292–93.
126. For discussions of these laws, see Amunátegui Solar, *La Democracia en Chile*, p. 348; Mesa Torres, *2nd Congreso de Gobierno Local*, p. 663; and Gustavo Silva, *Nueva Era de las Municipalidades*, p. 38. A compilation of all reforms is included in an appendix to Correa, *Ley de Organización y Atribuciones de las Municipalidades*. It must be noted that the reform of 1914 sought to strengthen the municipality by providing the mayor with authority to enforce payment of fines.
One of the major difficulties of the Chilean municipalities under the Law of 1891, which did not help in carrying out local responsibilities, was the fact that the ordinances and municipal agreements would not be enforced directly by the municipality. Moises Lazo de la Vega has noted that with the Código Penal of 1874, municipalities lost the ability to enforce their own laws directly, having to turn rather to the courts for enforcement, "converting local administration in Chile from that time on into an unending and sterile lawsuit, as a result of which the authority of the municipality disappeared as it was converted into a simple litigant." The municipality, though autonomous from the executive with the Law of 1891, remained subject to the courts. Lazo de la Vega, in seeking an explanation for this discrepancy in the law which had sought to give the municipalities much broader powers than they were apparently given, studied the

ures was dramatic. It ended and indeed reversed the democratization trend which had begun in 1891 and was impelled by the expansion of the party system. Voting turnout was reduced substantially. Whereas in 1912 the number of registered voters had been 598,000, in 1915 the number was reduced to 185,000. Valid votes were cut in half during the same period. Not until the middle 1950s would the proportion of the population registered to vote and the population which actually voted in a congressional election match the figure recorded in 1912. Indeed, until the 1940s the percentage of the population registered to vote after 1912 barely exceeded the figure of 1879.[127]

It is interesting to note that the political leadership of most of the parties finally agreed to the restriction of participation. The Radicals, for example, were convinced that their strength derived primarily from middle-class professional elements and, in fact, were concerned that the right had too much control over lower-class elements especially at the communal level. Indeed, only the Conservative party exhibited considerable hesitation over the idea of abolishing the Assembly of Electors; and it was the Conservative party which adamantly and successfully argued that the control of the electoral system remain at the communal level. The Conservative party stood to gain by turning over the electoral administration to the largest taxpayers as opposed to departmental or provincial officials.[128] All political factions had resorted to the mobilization of lower groups and they all seemed to realize that they would gain by restricting mobilization before it got further out of hand. Even the progressive leader, future President Arturo Alessandri, very early in his career expressed serious misgivings over the trend toward greater democratization. In a congressional speech in July of 1905 he noted that:

We have given universal suffrage to a people who was not prepared to exercise this right and this highest of functions of a free and sovereign people. We have been embarrassed by seeing it converted and degenerated into the

sessions of the commissions of the Parliament and the discussion on the floor concerning the bill. He notes that no clue is found to why this weakness of local government was retained: ". . . [I]t seems, then, that the system of constitutional organization established under the political code was repudiated without anyone's considering the far-reaching consequences of this innovation." He concludes that this occurred "because the Spanish penal code was taken literally during the time in which Spain had a highly centralized system." (Moises Lazo de la Vega, speech before the First Congress of Local Government, reprinted in Gustavo Silva, *Nueva Era de las Municipalidades*, pp. 58–70.)

127. Early figures are from Oficina Central de Estadística, *Censo Electoral de 1921* (Santiago: Sociedad Imprenta y Litografía Universo, Santiago, 1922). Later figures are from The Dirección del Registro Electoral. Data was gathered by the author with Rafael Lopez Pintor for an ongoing project on "Political Participation and Political Stability in Chile."

128. Rivas Vicuña discusses the positions of the parties on this issue at some length. See vol. 1, pp. 292–93, 398, 460–64.

ugliest electoral market. We must restrict popular suffrage to contain the excesses of unrestrained electoral graft which is corroding and destroying us.[129]

That the restriction of suffrage continued to be a strong preoccupation of the political elite can be seen toward the end of the Parliamentary Republic when the presidents of the Chamber of Deputies and of the Senate, controlled by opposing coalitions, agreed to restrict registration before the crucial elections of 1923. They agreed that, even though the law restricted registration to only thirty percent of those eligible, the actual number to be registered would be kept much lower.[130] Pacts to restrict suffrage were also agreed upon at the lower level. Thus in the Department of Osorno, the parties agreed to register seventy citizens daily during a short period. Of these, four had to be Balmacedistas, four Liberals, six Democrats owing allegiance to Don Canelario Rozas, three Democrats owing allegiance to don Adolfo Marquez, three Communists, one Conservative, and all the rest Radicals.[131]

Critics of Chilean parties and municipalities won a small victory with the reforms of 1914. However, despite reduced levels of participation, these reforms did not go far enough in the eyes of many Chileans. It became evident very soon that the predominant role of parties in the political process, as basic organizers and mobilizers of the electorate, had not been significantly altered. They continued to function as the key linkage networks between the local and the parliamentary arenas. At the same time, the legislature continued to be the central locus of a political system which was responding too slowly to the pace of socioeconomic change. Chile's quasi-parliamentary regime seemed ill-equipped to respond with decisive policies and vigorous leadership to labor unrest and economic depression. Time-consuming political crises revolving around electoral pacts and ministerial musical chairs continued to be the main preoccupation of political elites.

The reforms of 1914 were consequently only the beginning in a long effort to restructure Chilean political life, which would inevitably involve a frontal attack on the party system and the local legislature axis on which it was based. In 1918, for example, a commission from the Chamber of Deputies travelled to several foreign countries in order to gather material for a study of proposed funda-

129. It is not clear whether this is an exact quote or a paraphrase. The source is Ricardo Donoso, *Alessandri* . . . , p. 96.
130. See the congressional debate of 31 December 1923, in Camara de Diputados, *Sesiones Extraordinarias*, 1923, p. 945.
131. Ibid., *Sesiones Ordinarias*, 1924, July 31, p. 913.

mental institutional reforms.[132] And in 1920, an energetic and forceful candidate sought the presidency of the Republic on a platform advocating basic constitutional changes. Apathy or alienation continued to be widespread, however, for despite the dynamic nature of the campaign, less than fifty percent of the voters turned out at the polls.[133]

After winning the election by a small margin, Arturo Alessandri continued to press for constitutional reforms and concretely for more executive authority. In 1921 this became the main thrust of his presidential address, and in 1922 he set up a commission to produce a working draft of a new document for a constitutional convention.[134]

Progress towards this objective proceeded at a slow pace, however, and new interests became increasingly impatient. The most important of these "new" interests were the younger elements within the armed forces. Trained by Prussian military officers brought to Chile at the beginning of the Parliamentary Republic, these younger officers became increasingly disillusioned with prevailing political practices. They were concerned with the inaction of government in coping with the social and economic crisis and critical of party politics. But even more significantly, they themselves faced a considerable disparity between what they had learned in the academies about their own role and what they faced in Chilean society upon graduating. Not only were the armed forces seriously lacking in the necessary material and organization, but promotion through the ranks was often a function of political contact rather than merit.

The crisis of the regime finally reached a climax on September 24, 1924, when, for the first time in almost 100 years, military men acting substantially on their own succeeded in staging a successful military coup. The action came after the Congress voted pay increases for its own members, while failing to take action on a military pay raise. The atmosphere of political crisis, combined with the frustrations of younger officers, led to the resignation of the chief executive and the shutdown of the legislature.[135]

Though the officers stayed in power for only a few weeks, the fact

132. Facultad de Derecho de la Universidad de Chile, *Constitución de 1925*, p. 31.
133. Chile, Oficina Central de Estadística, *Censo Electoral de 1921*. The low interest in the election certainly calls into question the usual interpretation of this election as a dual between middle-class and traditional elements. See, for example, John J. Johnson, *Political Change in Latin America: The Emergence of the Middle Sectors* (Stanford: Stanford University Press, 1958); Pike, *Chile and the United States*, p. 173; Gil, *Political System of Chile*, p. 56. Rather than being understood as a pivotal election, it can be understood as the last presidential election of the Parliamentary Republic, held in an atmosphere of widespread dissatisfaction with the traditional system. The real change was to come a few years later.
134. Facultad de Derecho, *Constitución de 1925*, pp. 32–37.
135. The best book on the military in the period in question is Carlos Saez Morales, *Recuerdos de un soldado: el ejército y la política* (Santiago: Editorial Ercilla, 1933–34).

that they were able to stage a coup illustrated the extent of deterioration in Chilean institutions. Soon after Alessandri resumed office, a constitutional convention met and a new constitution was drawn up. This document returned to the executive much of the authority which the legislature had exercised for several decades. With respect to municipalities, the convention felt that municipal governments had to be supervised, but did not choose to institute sharp centralization as the formula for such supervision. Instead, it created provincial assemblies which would be formed by the municipalities of a given region and would be charged with advising the intendant as well as with supervision of municipalities.[136] The effect on municipalities was to be more indirect. By limiting the power of the legislature, lower-level brokers closely tied to the Congress saw their influence diminished.

The main attack on Chilean parties and on local governments, however, was yet to come. After continued political instability and two more presidential resignations, Carlos Ibañez del Campo, a military man who had come to prominence in the 1924 coup, was elected president of the Republic in the year 1926. The principal objective of the new president, elected as a "non-political" candidate, was to finally erase all traces of parties and introduce "neutral" administration into Chilean political life. Many of the acts of his administration revealed the influence of the earlier municipal reform movement as well as the influence of the 1924 officer's movement.

One of the first acts of the Ibañez administration was to suspend all elected municipal governments in Chile, appointing instead local bodies known as *juntas de vecinos*. The criterion for the new appointments, according to a circular sent out to all intendants and governors, was to "designate as members of the juntas those elements which, by their correctness, honesty, activity, preparation and public spirit, are a certain guarantee of progressive and honorable municipal administration, where communal monies would be spent with economy, intelligence and opportunity."[137]

And yet, once again the conscious effort to reduce the role of political parties in the nation's affairs did not meet full success. An example of the government's continued concern to stamp out "politics" at the local level can be seen in an official bulletin, issued on June 17, 1927, which stated: "If the partisan acts which have been denounced before the government are not discontinued, we will proceed immediately to dissolve the juntas and replace them with mayors who will respond solely to the executive's control."[138]

136. It is consequently not correct to note that the Constitution of 1925 destroyed local autonomy, as Federico Gil notes. See *Political System of Chile*, p. 132.
137. Gustavo Silva, *Nueva Era de las Municipalidades*, p. 100.
138. Ibid., p. 101.

In August of 1927, Ibañez appointed a high-level commission to study in detail the municipal reform law in order to make recommendations that would insure "neutral" administration.[139] Several important measures were subsequently undertaken. In the first place, with the enactment of Decree 1,860 of April 13, 1928, all municipal budgets were required to be submitted to the Ministry of the Interior for review and approval. This was followed by a detailed set of regulations for making up the municipal budget, with very restricted criteria for individual expenditures. This Reglamento de Contabilidad de Presupuesto, enacted through Decree 2,953 of June 15, 1928, was aimed at facilitating "objective" scrutiny of the financial state of all municipalities.[140] In the words of a mammoth and deluxe publication issued to celebrate Ibañez' initiative on behalf of a "new era" for Chilean municipalities, this ruling "extended to all of the communes of the Republic the benefit of a scientific and uniform budgetary schedule and regularized the handling of municipal resources."[141] In 1931 new provisions governing municipal taxation were adopted. The government also set up a Department of Municipalities within the Ministry of the Interior. This department was later to subsidize the publication of a magazine called the Boletín Municipal de la República, to communicate with local governments and provide various types of consulting and information services.[142]

The Ibañez administration thus went a long way to curb municipal autonomy, bring local governments under the influence of national agencies, and define in strict terms the scope of municipal action. A good way to summarize the intentions of Ibañez' government is to quote at some length from two sources. The first comes from an editorial in the Boletín Municipal de la República, which appeared after his downfall but continued to reflect his municipal policies. It says, "When, in still recent times, Municipalities were deprived of their intervention in electoral books, the zeal for politics and bitter electoral battles was so enmeshed in the spirit of our people that it has been necessary to engage in a long process of elimination to guide them exclusively to their proper role."[143] The second quotation comes from the official volume prepared to celebrate Ibañez' role in fostering the "new era" of municipalities. It reads as follows:

The presidential period of His Excellency Senor Ibañez will leave many aspects worthy of remembrance, but above all he will be remembered with

139. Ibid., p. 112.
140. Gustavo Silva, Nueva Era de las Municipalidades, p. 67.
141. Ibid., p. 133. This volume of close to 1,000 pages is full of photographs of all Chilean municipalities and praise for the actions of Carlos Ibañez.
142. The magazine was founded by Decree Law 249 in the year 1932. The Biblioteca del Congreso has the issues from vol. 3, no. 30 to vol. 15, no. 161.
143. Boletín Municipal de la Republica, 3 (March, 1933), 42.

reference to local government. The purification of public administration, the impressive development of fiscal works and the reforms of our legislation would be enough to fill the aspirations of a president and insure that his name be perpetuated by the voice of history, but if none of that had been undertaken by the present government, the memory of it would be tied in an immortal fashion to Municipal Power. . . . The positions of Mayor today are, thanks to that impartiality of judgment, in the hands of the most representative people in the various communes, and almost always they are the farthest away from the partisan nuclei.[144]

During the administration of Carlos Ibañez the parliamentary period clearly came to an end. The executive rather than the legislature became in fact the dominant force in Chilean politics, though they both would be increasingly limited by the growing bureaucracy which received a strong impetus in the Ibañez government.

However, while Ibañez may have contributed significantly to the reassertion of executive power and inaugurated strict governmental restrictions of local governments, he did not succeed in his goal of eliminating party politics from Chilean life. Throughout his entire administration he struggled with the ever-present vestiges of partisan activity. When he was finally overthrown in 1931, the political party organizations which had emerged during the Parliamentary Republic quickly sprang back to life. On April 6, 1935, municipal elections were held, once again, for the first time since 1924. Shortly before that election, the *Boletín Municipal de la República,* which had been established to help purge partisan activities, editorialized: "It is an unavoidable responsibility that the political parties . . . carry as candidates only those who, because of their preparation, honesty and spirit of justice, will be a sufficient guarantee of the good operation of the municipalities. . . . Let us leave aside hereafter low politics. . . ."[145]

Apparently the journal's advice was not followed, for in July, 1938, after the second municipal election was held, it printed the following editorial:

Today, unfortunately and much to our chagrin, we find ourselves obligated to once again refer ourselves to this matter, for, far from heeding our desires and recommendations, there have not been a few but many cases in which, both in the constitution and installation of the new Municipalities, as in their short period of operation, there has been irrefutable evidence that an appreciable number of Regidores and Alcaldes proceed in the exercise of their faculties only and exclusively in accord with the interest of the political party or the combination of parties they represent, and thus neglect the true general

144. Gustavo Silva, *Nueva Era de las Municipalidades,* p. 179.
145. *Boletín Municipal de la Republica,* 5 (January, 1935), 31.

interests of the locality; . . . it is indispensable to do away with partisan politics.[146]

Despite this exhortation, party politics in Chile continued to prosper in succeeding decades. Though the jurisdiction of local governments was reduced further and their financial situation continued to be bleak, through party networks local authorities were able to extract resources from the rapidly expanding state bureaucracy. During the Radical years log-rolling politics at the center reenforced the pattern of center-local linkages which developed in the Parliamentary Republic. And, though Carlos Ibañez attempted to form a new political movement in his second presidency (1952–1958), and Jorge Alessandri (1958–1964) sought to impose neutral administration, it was not until the one-party administration of Eduardo Frei that log-rolling tactics diminished somewhat in importance. However, only with the military coup of 1973, which deposed President Salvador Allende, did the pattern of politics which emerged at the turn of the 20th century come to an abrupt halt, and the tradition of anti-partyism emerge with a vengeance.

Postscript

The air force missiles which, with deadly precision, sent the presidential palace up in flames, marked not only the demise of Salvador Allende's socialist experiment, but ushered in a radical attempt to reshape Chile's political traditions. Ironically, in the name of preserving institutions and practices deemed obsolete by the Marxist government, the military leaders proceeded to dismantle those same institutions in a more dramatic fashion than ever envisioned by the Popular Unity authorities. The generals argued that Chile's distinctive party system and democratic processes were responsible for social unrest and the rise of "foreign" Marxist influence. Only by transforming the foundations of a "weak" democracy with the inauguration of a new order exalting "national values" would the once apolitical military return to the barracks. As the governmental Junta proclaimed in its decree abolishing the Popular Unity parties, "on the new government rests the mission of exterpating Marxism from Chile, of rebuilding morally and materially to provide new institutional forms to permit the establishment of a modern democracy purged of the vices which favored the actions of its enemies."[147]

146. *Boletín Municipal de la Republica*, 8 (July, 1938), 10.
147. Junta de Gobierno, *100 Primeros Decretos Leyes dictados por la Junta de Gobierno de la Republica de Chile* (Santiago: Editorial Jurídica, 1974), p. 178. The Decree Law is number 77. For further discussion of the Junta's position see Arturo

In attacking the "vices" of Chilean democracy, the Junta took measures which went much further than anything adopted or envisioned by the government of Carlos Ibañez in the 1920s. Though Ibañez had also sought to destroy the party system, his measures pale by contrast with the wholesale arrests, torture and executions which followed the September 11, 1973 coup.[148] While Ibañez introduced important modifications in the nation's institutional framework, the Junta led by General Augusto Pinochet swept aside the basic elements of a constitutional tradition extending back to the early 19th century. Congress was closed, much to the chagrin of opposition congressional leaders who, earlier, had called on the military to protect the Constitution from the Allende government.[149] Electoral registers were destroyed, elections prohibited, in public as well as private organizations. The political parties of the left were abolished and their leaders detained and sent to concentration camps. Parties which had opposed the Allende government were declared in "recess" and prohibited from making any public declarations, conducting organizational activity or even selecting new officers.[150] The courts were preempted by military tribunals which meted out swift and harsh penalties to the defenders of the deposed constitutional regime.[151] Those who had sought to defend the legally constituted government, or who had simply hesitated to move against it, were called traitors. When challenges were brought in the courts suggesting that the Junta's decree-laws violated the same Constitution it had sought to preserve, the Junta merely issued a new decree-law proclaiming that all previous decree-laws which conflicted with constitutional precepts, whether intended or not, automatically modified the Constitution. The mere act of rising to overthrow a government accused of having violated the law, according to the Junta, gave it the right to issue not only new laws, but to transform the Constitution.[152]

Valenzuela and J. Samuel Valenzuela, "Visions of Chile," LARR, 10, no. 3 (Winter, 1975), 155–175.

148. Systematic violations of human rights in Chile have been amply documented by agencies such as Amnesty International, the International Commission of Jurists, the International Labor Organization, the Organization of American States, and the Human Rights Commission of the United Nations. Some of the reports of these agencies can be found in the Hearings before the Subcommittee to Investigate Problems Connected With Refugees and Escapees of the Committee on the Judiciary of the United States Senate held on July 23, 1974 and published by the U.S. Government Printing Office.

149. See Decree Law No. 27 in 100 Primeros Decretos, pp. 62–63.

150. See Decree Laws 77 and 78 in 100 Primeros Decretos, pp. 178–183.

151. On the military tribunals see the Hearings before the Subcommittee on Refugees of the U.S. Senate cited in note 148.

152. See Hector Rieles, "La Legitimidad de la Junta de Gobierno," in Chile, Junta de Gobierno, Algunos Fundamentos de la Intervención Militar en Chile (Santiago: Editora Nacional Gabriela Mistral, 1974), pp. 114–115 for this argument.

Chile's municipalities, with roots in Colonial times, were among the first institutions to feel the impact of these revolutionary transformations. In the aftermath of the coup hundreds of Popular Unity mayors and municipal councilors were arrested. Many were tortured and killed. Other local officials also lost their jobs and were forced to leave their communities. Only days after the coup, the Junta, through Decree Law No. 25 abolished all municipal councils and dismissed all mayors from their posts.[153] General Pinochet reappointed most of the National party mayors and a majority of the Christian Democratic mayors to serve at his pleasure. Mayors who had supported the Allende government were replaced by military officers, retired officers, and civilians of conservative political views. As table 8.9 shows, the rightist National party increased substantially its representation in mayoral ranks after the coup. The Christian Democrats, by contrast, lost about a fourth of their mayors in global terms. In fact many Christian Democratic mayors were also removed from office only to be succeeded by Christian Democrats more to the government's liking.[154] From one day to the next, the entire infrastructure of local

Table 8.9. Distribution of mayoralty posts by party before and after the September 11, 1973 coup.

Party	Before Sept. 11, 1973	After Sept. 11, 1973
Opposition to Popular Unity		
Christian Dem	91	70
National	48	79
Other	15	20
Total	154	169
Popular Unity		
Socialists	60	0
Communists	36	0
Radicals	20	0
Christian Left	4	0
Total	120	0
Other and Indep	12	81
Military	0	29
Grand total	286	286

Source: Figures for the period before Sept. 11, 1973 are drawn from lists published in *Revista Municipal*, no. 37 (December 1971), pp. 8–21. Figures for the period after Sept. 11, 1973 were obtained from unpublished lists available in the Confederación Nacional de Municipalidades in Santiago.

153. See *100 Primeros Decretos*, pp. 55–56.
154. By the end of 1974 several prominent Christian Democratic mayors were removed from office, including the mayors of Talcahuano and San Miguel as government

government was dismantled. The system of democratic local representation, as well as the complex brokerage networks which had evolved over the years as linkages between locality and center, disappeared.

Pending the adoption of a new municipal law by decree, Decree Law 25 specified that the mayor would exercise all of the attributes of the municipal council, thus, converting him in theory into the most powerful local figure. In practice, however, the powers of the mayor and the municipality were drastically curtailed.[155] Municipalities became merely another branch of the national bureaucracy. Like other agencies they were required to submit their budgets to the Office of Budgets of the Ministry of Finance for review, and to the Junta for final approval. All municipal revenues were sent to Santiago, only to have fewer funds return to municipal coffers than previously. All local government staff members became state employees serving in a "temporary" capacity until further notice. This, combined with a severe relative reduction in salaries for local employees created uncertainty and hardships unparalleled in recent memory. In one provincial capital alone, municipal workers joined the more than three hundred heads of families who migrated during the first year of the Junta to Argentina in search of work.

But, the real curb on the power of the municipality did not come from financial stringencies. The main difficulty came from the drastic

---

relations with the Christian Democrats deteriorated further. Officials at the Confederacion Nacional de Municipalidades told the author that only 20% of all mayors were Christian Democrats by December of 1974.

155. The following paragraphs are based on interviews conducted by the author in Chile in the months of November and December of 1974. The author returned to eight of the 14 municipalities where he had conducted field research in 1969. Interviews were conducted with mayors and municipal secretaries and with two ex-mayors who had served at least for two months under the Junta. Except for one, all were Christian Democrats. Attempts to locate former regidores or mayors from Popular Unity parties proved to be difficult. In most cases they had left the community. Three regidores interviewed in 1969 had apparently been killed. It was possible to speak to two Popular Unity government regidores. They had both been arrested and beaten. In one community of no more than 1,000 people, the author was able to ascertain that about 14 people had been killed and several families had escaped to avoid trouble. In at least two of the communities, Christian Democratic officials were in close touch with counterparts of the Popular Unity parties in an attempt to establish relations for a future return to party politics. In most communities local leaders argued that considerable friction existed still at the barrio level between partisans of the Allende government and of the opposition, but that at the level of local leadership the animosity was not as great as it was earlier. The author gained access to these local leaders by recalling earlier interviews conducted in 1969 or by referring to some of the party officials the author had spoken to in Santiago. Local leaders were anxious to talk about their problems, but were naturally promised anonimity. Information about the situation of municipalities was also obtained from top leaders of the National Confederation of Municipalities (both present and past) familiar with the municipal situation in other parts of the country.

curtailment of municipal autonomy. Not only had the elected council been dismissed, but the mayor, who inherited on paper the council's functions, found that his jurisdiction had been severely limited. True to its institutional traditions, the military sought to govern the country in the same way that they ran the military institution. Military officers were named as governors in each department and intendants in each province. The hierarchical line of authority was to be respected—with the mayor reporting only to his governor and the governor to his intendant. Mayors could no longer approach governmental agencies as representatives of local governments, but had to follow the rigid chain of command and bring their problems to the attention of the military superior. Mayors found themselves competing with other mayors for the favor of the governor and most complained that they got nowhere.

Matters were made worse by the fact that the governor was not only the superior—but that he had jurisdiction over the same territory. The situation was particularly serious in municipalities which doubled as the seats of the departments. In these departmental capitals, mayors found that the military governors continually interfered with their duties. One mayor, for example, complained bitterly that he had refused to grant a series of permits to local merchants, only to find that the same permits had been approved in the governor's headquarters on the other side of the Plaza. Another mayor complained that the governor had simply ignored the mayor's right to appoint the leaders of private and public community organizations. He found himself in a serious predicament when the governor appointed different individuals to head up several groups, including the local chess club, invalidating his own appointments. A third mayor had been removed from office after several months of service under the Junta simply because he argued continuously with the governor over jurisdictional questions. Rather than appointing another man to succeed him in office, General Pinochet simply appointed the governor to fill the mayor's role as well. Another mayor noted that he was lucky to have succeeded in working out a division of labor with the governor, a personal friend of the family. Though he mentioned several incidents in which his jurisdiction had been usurped, he noted that the governor had given him complete responsibility for several municipal projects and that he had appointed the leaders of the Junta's de Vecinos. However, he was quite worried because it seemed that the governor would soon be transferred to another position and he feared that he would be replaced by a younger officer who was very authoritarian. "He is a real fascist," he noted. "I will have no recourse but to resign my post.

In municipalities which did not double as departmental capitals, mayors had more prerogatives. Governors were typically preoccupied with the affairs of the departmental capital and did not interfere as much in the day to day affairs of the other departmental municipalities. Though one governor reserved for himself the right to appoint community leaders in other municipalities, this was not typical. Mayors in outlying communities, did, however, have to meet periodically with the governor to discuss regional planning and bring to his attention the problems of their communities. However, most of the mayors in these municipalities were also critical of the new arrangement. They noted that the governors were generally too preoccupied with the departmental capital to respond to the needs of their communities. Though the governor and provincial authorities promised to devote their attention to the problems of outlying areas, concrete action was rare. Like the provincial officials during the earlier constitutional regime, military governors and intendants were simply more sensitive to the pressures and needs coming from the larger cities in their areas of jurisdiction. In the absence of resources, the smaller communities were lowest on the order of priorities.

The mayor of Quille, the same man the author had interviewed in 1969, summarized the predicament of his community. Before, small communities had also been neglected, but through party contacts enterprising mayors could approach the government directly to obtain programs and projects. Whereas during both the Frei and Allende administrations he had journeyed two or three times a month to Santiago, during the year he had been in office under the Junta he had not made one trip on municipal business. All of his projects, including several already underway, had been frozen. The governor payed little attention to his needs. The role of mayor had become a bureaucratic nightmare. His office had been deluged with requests from government agencies including the Indentant, the Contraloría, the National Planning Office (ODEPLAN), the Bureau of the Budget, and the National Commission for Administrative Reform (CONARA), all asking for detailed information and statistics from the municipal office. The municipal secretary and the mayor were simply unable to keep up with the requests and unable to conduct the studies necessary to come up with the data. The secretary complained bitterly that if he did not respond properly, his municipality would not receive any funds; and yet he did not see how these studies, based on data that was impossible to obtain, could ever adequately measure the needs of the community.

When asked what had happened to the system of processing small favors which was so important to councilors and mayors before the coup, local officials in all of the towns visited noted that small favors were no longer being taken care of. Citizens were now approaching local military officers asking them to resolve their social security and other problems. However these officers simply had no mechanism for dealing directly with governmental agencies to enquire about individual demands. As one mayor put it, "officers are supposed to work through channels, and they simply don't want to pester their superiors with the insignificant problems of some poor widow." An ex-mayor, a Christian Democrat, who had served as mayor for two months after the coup, told the author that he still maintained a full-time secretary to help his former constituents with their tramites. Despite the fact that he had been arrested twice for "political activities" he continued to work through his Christian Democratic contacts in the party and in the bureaucracy in an attempt to service his people. His results were meager at best, but he felt that it was his responsibility to continue to do the best he could under difficult circumstances. "If I don't help, who will?" Since he extended his aide not only to Christian Democrats but to members of the outlawed Popular Unity parties, the former mayor was subjecting himself to considerable personal risk.

It would be a mistake to convey the impression that all of the local officials interviewed were negative about the future, even though they were uniformly concerned about their current predicament. Three mayors noted that they had confidence that the new municipal law being drafted in the government would put an end to the period of uncertainty and restore power and jurisdiction to the mayor and through him to the municipality. Research in Santiago into the progress of this legislation revealed, however, that optimism in this regard was not well founded.[156] The commission working on municipal matters was hopelessly bogged down, and though a majority of its members favored the concept of local autonomy, it was quite clear that the government was not prepared to move to change the system that was already in force.

Towards a New Municipal System: Attempts at Constitutional Reform. Shortly after the coup, the governmental Junta named a Constitutional Commission composed of well-known conservative constitutional experts to draft a new fundamental charter for the nation. The

156. Interviews were conducted with members of the commission and with several prominent experts in municipal affairs including former top leaders of the National Confederation of Municipalities and mayors and regidores of the Santiago area familiar with the municipal reform proposals. Interviews were also conducted at Contraloría and at the Comision Nacional de Reforma Administrativa. Though not all respondents insisted on anonimity, it would be improper to identify my sources at this time.

commission in turn appointed a subcommittee charged with designing a new set of administrative subdivisions to "modernize" the country and a new code of municipal regulations. A similar effort was undertaken by the Ministry of the Interior, charged with internal administration (and soon to lose its more significant jurisdiction over police and investigations). To avoid duplication, the Ministry of the Interior's committee coopted members from the Constitutional commission committee.

The committee on municipal reform was made up of technical staff members from the Ministry of the Interior, Contraloría, and the associations of municipal technicians, as well as university experts in municipal law and administration. At first the National Confederation of Municipalities was not represented, but after some pressure from municipal leaders of that organization, a Christian Democratic mayor was included as a member of the committee.

Inspired by the Spanish system of local administration, the members of the commission agreed that the concept of an elected council representing the community at large should be abolished. In its place, they proposed a body that would represent the principal economic groups of the community. It would include in addition to the professional directors of municipal agencies representatives from the business community. The exact representation would vary from community to community depending on the principal economic characteristics of the region. Labor leaders would also be included. The council would have a say in budgetary and planning matters, but otherwise would act as an advisory body to the mayor. The mayor, appointed by the president of the Republic, would serve as the "local authority" and would not be considered merely as another civil servant.

The guiding force behind the action of the committee was an effort to retain a certain degree of municipal autonomy, while at the same time insuring that party politics would not return to local administration. In a report submitted in February, 1974, the committee noted that "the excessive and unwarranted politization which characterized the current municipality, has been one of the most important factors in the distortion of its functions and, perhaps, the gravest obstacle to a coordinated process of development planning at all levels."[157]

Before the Ministry of the Interior committee could finish its work, however, the governing Junta set up a National Commission for Administrative Reform with the mandate to restructure the entire

157. Ministerio del Interior, Comisión de Reforma del Régimen Municipal, *Informe de la Comisión de Reforma del Régimen Municipal* (Santiago: mimeo, 1974), p. 2.

governmental system. All public as well as private groups studying reforms were required to submit their recommendations to this high level body. Members of the Commission on Municipalities of the Ministry of the Interior were simply brought over to CONARA to continue their work.

From the outset the new commission was hampered by vague guidelines given it by military leaders. Abstractions such as "patriotism," "national security," "efficiency," and "chilenidad" were very difficult to translate into municipal legislation. Several members of the commission complained that the military leaders seemed to be totally unsure of what they really wanted. It soon became clear, however, that many military officers in the top levels of the government were not prepared to support a proposal that would give any type of local autonomy to municipal governments. Though Junta members talked about local responsibility, they did not mean this to imply a departure from a hierarchical system of authority. Members of the municipal commission noted that Intendants as well as governors made it clear that they did not want any reduction in their authority.

By November, 1974, little progress had been made in adopting new municipal legislation. The Municipal Commission in CONARA was forced to report out a proposal that was substantially less favorable to municipalities than the earlier draft of the Ministry of the Interior. Reluctantly, the committee dropped the notion that the mayor be considered a "local authority" and agreed that he should simply be another employee of the government, subject to the same restrictions and privileges as other governmental officials. Even more significantly, the committee agreed to drop the provision which gave the municipal council decisional power. Instead, the council would merely be an advisory body to the mayor.[158] This change reflected not only pressure from governmental officials, but fear on the part of the committee that if changes were not made to make for a weaker local authority, other aspects of the reform measure might also be compromised. In particular, members of the committee were concerned that influential people in CONARA might seek to limit even further the jurisdiction and functions of local government. One member of the CONARA governing board, a former roommate of Pinochet's in the Military Academy and a top official in Contraloría, was known to favor a very short and cryptic municipal law. Members of the municipal committee lived in fear that he, or others like him, would

158. See CONARA Comisión Consultiva sobre Municipalidades, *Proyecto de Decreto Ley sobre Organización y Atribuciones de las Municipalidades* (Santiago: mimeo, 1974), Articles 9, 10, 19–22.

gain the attention of Junta members and convince them to follow their line of reasoning. Indeed, one of the most important members of the committee told the author that he lived in fear that from one day to the next he would pick up the Diario Oficial (Official Register) and find a municipal law different from the one he had worked on published as the law of the land. In the absence of regularized channels of authority committees were often bypassed in this way, leading to confusion and uncertainty at the highest levels of government. The same CONARA expert noted that the entire government had bogged down. Experts often disagreed with each other. "The tecnicos from the University of Chile can't stand those from the Universidad Católica. Lawyers don't see eye to eye with architects, who in turn can't accept the views of city planners. Everyone attempts to bypass his detractors by seeking special channels to the top. It is confusing and chaotic. We will never get anywhere under these circumstances."

In early 1975 the proposal of the Municipal Commission was supposed to go to a CONARA review commission in preparation for its submission to the Junta which would proclaim the matter law. Almost a year later municipal reform was still not a reality. Two years had transpired since the military took over the Chilean government and the same ad hoc system of internal administration prevailed. Even if a municipal law is approved, however, it is not likely to make much difference as far as local governments are concerned. They will still be run by an appointed mayor with little final authority. The hierarchical system which the military is so fond of precludes any return to representative government while the soldiers remain in power.

Two years after the overthrow of Chile's constitutional system, it is clear that the destruction of elected local governments, the Congress and the parties, essential ingredients in the brokerage system which had evolved over generations, had left an enormous void. The breakdown of Chilean democracy has been particularly harsh on the weak and disadvantaged sectors of society. Not only have they suffered from coercive policies which have denied individuals of human rights and deprived them of basic liberties, but they have lost those mechanisms which have served to articulate demands and distribute resources. The wealthy and the powerful have had little difficulty establishing lines of communications with the new authorities and have succeeded admirably in obtaining policies which are beneficial to their interests. But for the vast majority of the society the absence of institutions of representation and accountability has meant a loss of power and influence unparalleled in this century. Small communities are no longer able to mobilize political networks, in exchange for votes, in order to obtain minimal resources. Individuals are incapable of obtaining redress of grievances from the complex governmental bureaucracy because the loss of political intermediaries has meant the loss of influence and expertise. Municipalities are at the mercy of planners with dubious programs based on questionable data which will lack adequate input from the community in their formulation. The new hierarchical order designed to provide "responsible decentralization" is, except for a small fraction of the society, a one way street. The authorities can listen, but in general they have little impetus to respond.

A basic ingredient in the success of the military junta in instituting its drastic changes in Chilean society has been the liberal use of terror and repression. With the destruction of institutions structured over the years to represent the key sectors of society it has been easy to merely issue decrees to structure a new order. But such a strategy cannot last forever. The Junta has been more successful in dismantling the old than in creating something new. Its repression will undoubtedly make it much more difficult than in the period following the overthrow of Ibañez to restructure once again the traditional party system. But, in somewhat altered form, party networks similar to those which evolved in the parliamentary period are bound to reappear once again to fill the institutional void.

Appendix I. Sketch of Interior Government and Administration in Chile Before 1973

According to the 1925 constitution, the municipality was the lowest governmental body in the Chilean political system, charged with administering the affairs of the commune, a geographical area which may contain rural as well as urban areas.[1] *Regidores* (municipal councilors) were elected at large under a D'Hondt proportional representation system for a period of four years. Elections were held the first Sunday in April. Regidores elected the *alcalde* (mayor) from their own ranks, except in the municipalities of Santiago, Valparaiso and Viña del Mar, where mayors were appointed by the president. The Constitution of 1925 called for appointment of mayors in all cities of over 100,000, but this provision did not go into effect because Congress never officially recognized recent censuses for reapportionment purposes. Though the mayor was required to serve a full four-year term, electoral pacts divided up the mayoralty between several individuals or parties. The mayor could be removed from office only if a majority of regidores on the council voted to impeach him and the Court of Appeals concurred with that decision. Mayors appointed by the president served at his pleasure and could be removed at his discretion.

Municipal officials were not, however, the only officials with jurisdiction over local communities. The Chilean Constitution made a distinction between Interior Administration and Interior Government. The municipalities and the provincial assemblies were designated as the two organs of internal administration with jurisdiction over the commune and the province, respectively. Since provincial assemblies were never created by enabling legislation, the intendant was granted by law several of the functions specified in the Constitution as falling within the jurisdiction of the assemblies.

Agents appointed by the chief executive of the country constituted the organs of Interior Government. The intendant, appointed for a three-year term, served at the pleasure of the president as the chief officer of the province. He was charged with implementing government policy, maintaining public order and guaranteeing external security. The intendant in turn designated as governors individuals who were chosen for that post by the president, and was responsible

1. This section relies on the discussion in Alejandro Silva Bascuñan, *Tratado de derecho constitucional* (3 vols., Santiago: Editorial Jurídica de Chile, 1963), chs. 8, 9.

for the actions of these subalterns. The governors had jurisdiction over several communes brought together in a *departamento*. They were charged with appointing the subdelegates, whose areas of jurisdiction, the subdelegations, coincided with the communes. Subdelegates, finally, appointed inspectors responsible for local districts. The positions of subdelegate and inspectors carried no really significant functions and were largely patronage rewards. Only a fraction of the inspectors in fact were ever appointed. The higher status of municipal officials was illustrated by the fact that subdelegates may seek local office or hold the office jointly with a local office.

Some communes served as capitals, or *cabeceras,* of provinces or departments. In a commune such as Concepción, the provincial capital of the Province of Concepcion and the capital of the department of the same name, the intendant also served as governor and subdelegate. In the provincial capital a municipality was entitled to have nine regidores, in a departmental capital the number was seven, while in an ordinary municipality the council was composed of five members. The exceptions to this rule were the municipalities of Santiago with fifteen regidores, Valparaiso with twelve, and Viña del Mar with nine. Table I.1 summarizes the basic political and administrative divisions of the nation as of 1973.

The distinction between interior government and interior administration, or political and administrative functions, derives from the desire of the drafters of the Constitution of 1925 to make clear that the Chilean state is a unitary state. The municipality was to be purely an administrative unit because in a unitary state, as defined

Table I.1. Internal government and administration in Chile.

Internal administration		Internal government	
Unit	Administrator	Unit	Executive
Nation	President	Nation	President, Minister of the Interior
Province (25)	Provincial assembly[a]	Province	Intendant
		Department (93)	Governor
Commune (302)	Municipality (277)	Subdelegation	Subdelegate
		District (2,537)	Inspector[b]

[a] Provincial assemblies have not been created. Some of their functions have been granted to the intendants.
[b] Only a small fraction of inspectors have been appointed.
Source: A detailed listing of all political and administrative subdivisions with population and geographical surface of each unit is found in Chile, *División Político-Administrativa* (Santiago: Dirección de Estadísticas y Censos, 1966).

by the Constitution, policy decisions for the entire nation are to be made by the central government only. These purely legal distinctions were of course blurred in practice. The municipality was certainly political, in that many choices were made which involved matters of policy. Even more significantly, agents of the central government, dependent on the Ministry of the Interior as well as on other ministries and semi-autonomous public agencies, performed many "administrative" functions at the provincial and local levels.

Appendix II. Sampling Techniques and Interviewing Procedures

During the first three months of field research in Chile, from November 1968 to January 1969 I worked on the collection and analysis of data relating to Chilean local governments as a whole and reported in the first three Chapters of the book. I also spent a good deal of time studying the legal and financial base of Chilean municipalities. This task was facilitated by my participation in a special course designed for municipal administrators and technical personnel at the Urban Research Center (Centro Interdisciplinario de Desarollo Urbano-CIDU) at the Catholic University in Santiago. The seminar was run by Arturo Aylwin, chief counsel of the Contraloría General de la República and one of Chile's foremost experts on municipal law. I was also able to interview over a dozen municipal councilors, mayors and technical personnel from municipalities in the Santiago area.

This preliminary work led to the clear conclusion that it would be necessary to isolate several municipalities for more intensive study. The findings in chapter 1 of the book, showing that peripheral and marginal communities divided as much politically as their developed counterparts, suggested that the sample should consist primarily of such communities. It also became clear in the preliminary work done in Santiago, that the large municipalities of Santiago province were not the most appropriate ones for scrutinizing local politics and the possible linkages to the center, and that municipalities in provincial areas would be the most appropriate for study.

For some time I considered focusing on one or two municipalities in great depth. While such a strategy would have enabled me to describe in greater detail the politics of a local community, it would have detracted from the goal of drawing a more representative picture of Chilean local politics and of isolating significant variations between communities. Both strategies entailed advantages and limitations. Particularly since there was no other study of Chilean local politics to guide research, I decided to follow the second alternative. It promised to be the most fruitful one in coming to grips with some of the questions raised by my preliminary work with national statistics.

The choice of drawing a larger number of municipalities raised the problem of how the sample should be chosen. The selection at random of ten or twenty communities was not feasible, due to a lack of funds to travel back and forth in a country 2,600 miles in length. After some reflection I decided to concentrate the study in the Seventh Region, as defined by the Oficina de Planificación Nacional (Office of National Planning). This area, known as the Region del Bío-Bío, after a river which winds through its five provinces, is in many respects a microcosm of the country. It contains Chile's third largest city and fastest-growing industrial metropolis, Concepción. At the same time it has extensive rural areas, such as the rich agricultural land east of Chillán, and the eroded, desert-like, squalid wheat fields west of that city. Though there is no copper mining in the Bío-Bío area, coal mining is a major though depressed economic activity, primarily in the communes of Lota, Coronel, and the province of Arauco.

In addition, the area is relatively compact, facilitating travel from one extreme to the other by automobile.[1]

The five provinces (Ñuble, Concepción, Arauco, Bío-Bío and Malleco) contain a total of fifty-seven communes, most of which, following the national norm, are of small and intermediate size. Using a table of random numbers, fourteen (or twenty-five percent) of the municipalities were picked for the study. Since the purpose of the study was to focus on smaller municipalities, the six communes with a population of fifty thousand or more were eliminated before the sample was drawn. The fourteen communities thus selected were a good cross section of communes in the region. They ranged from the tiny, rural, poverty-stricken commune of Hueña to the capital of a province, to the mining community of Minas.[2] Nine were classified as rural by the Chilean census. The majority of communities ranged in size from ten thousand to twenty thousand inhabitants. Table 1 presents the distribution of municipalities of different sizes in the sample, the region of Bío-Bío, and the nation as a whole.

As table II.1 makes clear, the Bío-Bío region presents roughly similar distributions of communes of differing size as the nation does. The major discrepancies are found in categories I and III. The Bío-Bío area does not have any communes under five thousand inhabitants and has a greater proportion of communes in the ten-to-twenty-thousand category. The sample in turn is generally similar to the distribution of communities in the region, though the absence of larger communes increases the number of communes in the middle ranges.

1. The distance between the northern border of Ñuble and the southern border of Malleco is approximately 340 kilometers; the distance between the Andes and the sea is 210 kilometers.

2. Names are fictitious to protect the identity of respondents. This is particularly important since the coup.

236 · Political Brokers in Chile

Table II.2 shows the distribution of communes in the sample by province as compared to the distribution of all communes by province in the region. Ñuble is somewhat over-represented, while Arauco is under-represented.

For the purposes of this study it is important to provide some measure to assess the representativeness of the sample with respect to political indicators. To this end the distribution of the vote by party in the nation as a whole, in the region and in the sample was compared, utilizing data from the 1967 municipal elections. Table II.3 summarizes that information.

As Table II.3 shows, the Bío-Bío area has a distribution of electoral strength which is similar to that of the nation, except that in the region the Radicals tended to be stronger, whereas the Nationals were weaker. The Radical party in the Bío-Bío area made substantial inroads among the same elements—agricultural elites—which in the middle section of the country supported the traditional Conservative

Table II.1. Population in the nation, the region of Bío-Bío, and the sample.

Population type	Nation		Bío-Bío		Sample	
	N	percent	N	percent	N	percent
I 0–5,000	22	8.1	0	0	0	0
II 5,001–10,000	71	26.1	16	28.1	4	28.5
III 10,001–20,000	93	34.3	27	47.4	7	50.0
IV 20,001–30,000	33	12.2	6	10.5	2	14.3
V 30,001–50,000	16	5.9	2	3.5	1	7.1
VI 50,001–100,000	25	9.2	5	8.8	0	0
VII 100,001 and over	11	4.1	1	1.6	0	0
Total	271	99.9[a]	57	99.9[a]	14	99.9[a]

[a] Percentages do not add up to 100 because of rounding.

Table II.2. Distribution of communes by province in Bío-Bío and the sample.

Province	Total communes in sample		Total communes in province	
	N	percent	N	percent
Ñuble	5	35.7	18	30.0
Concepción	3	21.4	14	25.0
Arauco	1	7.1	6	10.0
Bío-Bío	2	14.3	8	12.0
Malleco	3	21.4	11	19.0
Total	14	99.9[a]	57	96.0[a]

[a] Percentages do not add up to 100 because of rounding.

and Liberal parties. The sample communities had a lower percentage of Communists and Socialists and a slightly higher percentage of Radicals and Nationals than the regional totals. These differences are mainly due to the fact that the sample excluded the communes of Lota and Coronel, large mining cities in which the Communists and Socialists dominated political life.

It should be noted at this point that while care was taken in selecting a relatively representative sample, it became evident during field research that ecological characteristics had little to do with political patterns in the communities studied. Important differences in political patterns would, however, be more evident in large cities such as Concepción, where, for example, interest groups and intermediary-level brokers played a more significant role.

Interviewing Local Officials

The preliminary interview schedule was prepared in Santiago, after consultation with researchers at the Instituto de Administración (INSORA) of the University of Chile. Particularly helpful were Jorge Tapia Videla, Rafael López, Francisco Salazar, Jose Daie and Gilberto Flores. Participants in the course on municipal administration were also helpful in clarifying some questions.

One of the main preoccupations which I had at the time concerned the possibility that local officials might refuse to answer clearly political questions or that the project might be unfeasible due to opposition from one or another political party. Particularly since the project Camelot scandal, many researchers, from foreign countries as well as native Chileans, voiced concern that interviews with local political leaders would not be possible in Chile.[3] This concern took on special poignancy when the socialist magazine *Punto Final* carried a story

Table II.3. Comparison of party vote in nation, Bío-Bío region and sample.

Party	Nation	Bío-Bío	Sample
Radical	16.6	20.4	23.2
Christian Democratic	35.6	33.8	32.4
Communist	14.8	15.5	10.9
Socialist	13.9	13.3	10.2
National	14.3	10.2	11.3

3. See Irving Louis Horowitz, ed., *The Rise and Fall of Project Camelot* (Cambridge, Mass.: MIT Press, 1967), for a discussion of this Defense Department study which was supposed to study the potential for revolution in Chile and other countries.

accusing a researcher in sociology from the University of Wisconsin of being a CIA agent. To prove its point it published sections of his questionnaire of "marginal populations" with specifically political questions. He was forced to cut his study short.

In order to avoid the possibility of running into these kinds of difficulties, the first draft of the questionnaire was structured with very few openly political questions. Most of the questions dealt with municipal problems, finances and administration. The hope was that by probing for explanations political content would be revealed. The questionnaire was pretested in February of 1969 in two towns in the province of Bío-Bío. For approximately two weeks, with the aid of J. Samuel Valenzuela, then a last-year student in sociology at the University of Concepción, the questionnaire was revised and improved in a field situation.

The pretest experience proved to be very valuable, for it demonstrated that the fears I had had that local officials might not want to address themselves to political questions were unfounded. While somewhat nervous in talking about municipal jurisprudence or administration, regidores, mayors and municipal secretaries had no reservations about expressing their views on party and municipal politics. The final questionnaire thus included a balance of questions dealing with municipal and political problems. It also incorporated many new questions which the interview process had suggested. Especially important in this regard were questions dealing with relationships between municipalities and the center which had been largely ignored in the earlier versions. The pretest period also revealed that it was extremely useful to try to interview all of the relevant political actors in a particular municipality. To have chosen a sample of regidores and interviewed them without necessarily interviewing their colleagues in the same municipality would have been a mistake. By interviewing all of the regidores, the mayor, the municipal secretary and some party officials, the whole of politics in the community could be grasped. Operation of the municipality and the reality of local politics, as opposed to the mere perceptions of the actors, could also be assessed, as the views, opinions and actions of different actors could be cross-checked and evaluated in the light of views, opinions and actions of other actors, either of the same or of opposite parties. In conducting interviews in the sample communities, then, an attempt was made to speak to all of the important local leaders as defined by the positional approach. That is, leaders occupying the positions of mayor, regidor and municipal secretary in each of the municipalities were interviewed.[4]

4. On many occasions the author interviewed other individuals in the various municipalities. Sometimes long periods of time went by without a formal interview.

Upon arrival in a particular municipality the first thing I did was to go to the municipal building and present my card to the municipal secretary. I said that I was very interested in the problems of Chilean municipalities, and that I wanted to conduct interviews with all of the elected officials. Often the municipal secretaries told me that there was no need to conduct such interviews, since they knew what was really going on and the regidores knew very little. I asked the municipal secretary to evaluate the current municipality and to inform me of projects and programs which the municipality was carrying out. I also asked him to allow me to examine the municipal budget, the municipal minutes and the municipal correspondence for the year 1968. Except for one case, municipal secretaries did not hesitate to show me these documents and took pride in the fact that I was interested in their work. Examination of a sample of the minutes was very useful in determining who took the initiative in municipal sessions, who was active in municipal affairs, what conflicts seemed to exist, what issues were predominant, and what projects were being undertaken. Examination of the correspondence revealed to some extent what types of contacts the municipality had with other agencies and officials. This preliminary work, which took anywhere from a couple of hours to a day-and-a-half, depending on the amount of material, proved to be very valuable in later interviews, as I was often able to probe beyond the first answer to the structured question.

Interviewing the regidores and mayors in the Chilean summer and fall of 1969 proved to be very difficult. Though occasionally I was able to interview officials in the municipal building only a few hours after I arrived, most of the time it was necessary to go and find them in their homes, or farms or places of work, often several miles away on poor roads. My standard procedure was to try to get the interviewee to consent to an interview right away, so that I would not have to wait around for hours. Thus regidores were interviewed everywhere — on a log in a field, in a home, on a bench in the plaza, in the car, in a bar, in a store, etc. Several were interviewed after eleven o'clock at night (though on several occasions I arrived at distant farms late at night, introduced myself and made an appointment for the following morning, and if not invited to stay overnight, slept on the ground or in the car).

Thus, using an unstructured interview, the author spoke to party leaders, priests, merchants, national government officials stationed in the area, ordinary townspeople, *campesinos*, etc. Though only regidores and mayors were asked to list the most prestigious people in the town, this "participant observation" revealed that the local elected leaders and the heads of local parties were clearly the most important people in the community from a political standpoint. If landowners and other high status notables were important at one time, in Chile today their influence is no longer as significant.

The interviews lasted between two and four hours, with the average about two-and-a-half hours. Invariably after the interview I was invited by my host to have a drink or to have a meal. This postinterview period was often more illuminating than the interview itself, as officials set aside their inhibitions and reservations and spoke freely about the municipality and their colleagues.[5]

I was fortunate that in no instance was I refused an interview, though in a couple of cases I had to insist by coming back several times and following the regidor around. The Socialist and Communist regidores were among the most helpful and open, and by and large the most dedicated, local officials interviewed. Several Radical school teachers, on the other hand, were the most hostile interviewees, tremendously afraid that they might reveal ignorance of municipal matters. Several regidores were unavailable for interviewing because they were out of town; one regidor had died, and two were too sick to be interviewed. In no case was less than a majority of the councilors interviewed, and fortunately all of the mayors were interviewed, bringing the total number of municipal officials interviewed to seventy-four.

This portion of the study lasted approximately three months, during which time I was able to observe at the grass roots level the electoral campaign for the 1969 congress. It was a very enjoyable but tiring experience. I drove a total of 3,880 miles. Often the roads were in poor condition, which meant that I had to clean the air filter on the rented Volkswagen squareback daily. Five flat tires and a broken shock absorber also slowed down the project. A further difficulty was presented by the fact that many communities had no lodging facilities, so that it was necessary to sleep in the car or, where possible, in a rural police station. The availability of a good hotel and restaurant in Los Angeles, which is located in the center of the Bío-Bío region, meant that occasionally I could relax in a good bed and have a full meal. However, on many occasions my interviewees provided me with lodging and treated me to marvelous Chilean country dinners. I am very indebted to them for their cooperation in the study and for their warm hospitality.

Returning to eight of the municipalities where I had done field research in 1969 in December of 1974 was, by contrast, a shocking experience. Several of the regidores who I had interviewed had been

5. My Chilean background and my familiarity with *chilenismos* certainly contributed to the success of these interviews. A North American scholar would probably have had great difficulty with sentences such as "Hay que pechare no ma pu iñor," which in correct Spanish would be "Hay que pechar no mas pues señor." The verb *pechar* is a Chileanism derived from *pecho*, or chest, and means to employ much effort to accomplish a particular goal.

killed. Others were in jail or in concentration camps — or were simply missing. Municipal secretaries on occasion simply refused to inform me about what had happened to former local officials. Interviews were conducted with mayors and local officials sympathetic to the Junta, as well as with several former mayors and regidores of the Christian Democratic party. I was able to talk to a few regidores who had been members of the Popular Unity coalition — but these interviews had to be conducted with great discretion. Though a difficult experience, it was possible to get a good picture of the situation of Chilean municipalities under the military Junta, and the impact of the military's changes on the brokerage system described in this book.

Appendix III. Questionnaire of Mayors and Municipal Councilors

1. Cuáles diría Ud. que son los tres problemas principales de la municipalidad?
   1.
   2.
   3.
   4. otro
   5. no sabe
   6. no contesta
2. Cuáles diría Ud. que son los tres problemas principales de los habitantes de la comuna de _____?
   1.
   2.
   3.
   4. otro
   5. no sabe
   6. no contesta
3. Qué proyectos importantes está desarrollando o desarrollará la municipalidad?
   1.
   2.
   3.
   4.
   5. no sabe
   6. no contesta
4. Qué cosas tienden a desprestigiar la municipalidad?
   1.
   2.
   3.
   4.
   5. no sabe
   6. no contesta
5. Algunos técnicos de Santiago piensan que el *Consejo Municipal* no desempeña una labor significativa. Qué importancia le da Ud. al *Consejo Municipal?*
6. a. Entre el Consejo Municipal y el alcalde encuentra Ud. que existe
   1. mucha tensión
   2. algo de tensión
   3. nada de tensión
   4. otro
   5. no sabe
   6. no contesta
   b. Por qué?

7. a. En las votaciones del consejo, los regidores votan generalmente por partido o según su propio criterio?
   1. votan por partido
   2. por criterio propio
   3. no sabe
   4. no contesta
   5. otra
  b. Generalmente los acuerdos se toman por unanimidad, o casi siempre hay votos en contra?
   1. por unanimidad
   2. votaciones en contra
   3. otro
   4. no sabe
   5. no contesta
8. Quién toma generalmente la iniciativa in la presentación de nuevos proyectos?
9. a. De qué partido es Ud.?
   1. Radical
   2. Demócrata Cristiano
   3. Comunista
   4. Socialista
   5. PADENA
   6. Nacional
   7. Otro _____
   8. Ninguno
  b. Cuál fue la mayoría que elijió al alcalde al constituirse esta municipalidad?
  c. Ha habido cambios en esta mayoría? Cuáles?
10. a. En general cree Ud. que es más fácil trabajar en la localidad con algunos partidos que con otros?
   1. sí
   2. no, con todos igual de fácil
   3. no, con todos igual de difícil
   4. no sabe
   5. no contesta
   SI SÍ:
  b. Diría Ud. que depende más del individuo que del partido?
  c. Con qué partidos es más fácil trabajar en esta localidad?
   1. Radical
   2. Demócrata Cristiano
   3. Comunista
   4. Socialista
   5. PADENA
   6. Nacional
11. a. Hay clubes o asociasiones que se interesan activamente por el funcionamiento de la municipalidad?
   1. sí
   2. no
   3. no sabe
   4. no contesta

SI SÍ:

b. Cuáles son?

c. Cómo participan en las decisiones? (Por ejemplo, escriben cartas, vienen a sesiones, etc.)

12. En las sesiones del Consejo Municipal, cuánto tiempo se toma en discusiones políticas e ideológicas que no tienen relación directa con los asuntos de la municipalidad?

1. más de un 50%
2. de 20 a 50%
3. menos de 20%
4. nada
5. no sabe
6. no contesta

13. a. Los organismos del gobierno nacional, según algunos, le dejan pocas atribuciones a la municipalidad. Está Ud.

1. muy de acuerdo
2. algo de acuerdo
3. en desacuerdo
4. no sabe
5. no contesta
    con esta aseveración?

b. Por qué?

14. a. Algunos técnicos han dicho que la municipalidad debiera pasar a ser administrada por el gobierno nacional. Está Ud.

1. muy de acuerdo
2. algo de acuerdo
3. en desacuerdo
4. no sabe
5. no contesta
    con esta aseveración?

b. Por qué?

15. a. Cree Ud. que la ideología de partido es a nivel local

1. más importante que a nivel nacional?
2. igual de importante que a nivel nacional?
3. menos importante que a nivel nacional?
4. no sabe
5. no contesta

b. Por qué?

16. a. Piensa Ud. que la gente en esta región vota más bien por el hombre o por el partido?

1. por el hombre
2. por el partido
3. no sabe
4. no contesta

b. SI "POR EL HOMBRE":
    Encuentra Ud. que hay alguna diferencia, al respecto, entre elecciones municipales y parlamentarias?

17. Con qué partido fuera del suyo simpatiza Ud. más? (Supongamos que el día de mañana dejara de existir su partido. A cúal otro se asociaría Ud. con más facilidad?)

18. Nos podría decir quiénes son los parlamentarios que actualmente representan esta región?
19. Está Ud. en contacto con parlamentarios?
   1. sí
   2. no
   3. no sabe
   4. no contesta
20. EN CASO QUE SÍ:
   a. Con quiénes tiene más contacto?
   b. Cuántas veces diría Ud. que los ve en un año?
   c. Los ve Ud. más bien durante las campañas electorales?
21. a. Diría Ud. que esta municipalidad ha recibido en sus gestiones ante el gobierno
   1. mucha ayuda
   2. algo de ayuda
   3. nada de ayuda
   4. no sabe
   5. no contesta
      de parte de los parlamentarios?
   b. Nos podría clarificar por qué piensa así?
22. a. En esta municipalidad se recurre más a la ayuda de los parlamentarios de gobierno?
   1. sí
   2. no
   3. otra
   4. no sabe
   5. no contesta
   6. ninguno hace nada
      SI NO:
   b. A qué partido se recurre más?
23. Ha viajado Ud. a Santiago o a la capital de la provincia por asuntos municipales?
   a. Santiago
   1. sí
   2. no
      Cuántas veces el año pasado?
   b. Capital de provincia
   1. sí
   2. no
      Cuántes veces el año pasado?
24. SI HA IDO A SANTIAGO:
Podría Ud. describir su viaje a Santiago?
   a. Qué hizo primero el llegar a la capital? (Con quién se puso en contacto primero?)
   b. Con cuáles ministerios se entrevistó?
   c. En general cómo lo recibieron?
   d. Cómo lo ayudaron los parlamentarios?
   e. Quién más le dió ayuda especial?
   f. Cuánto tiempo estuvo en la capital por asuntos municipales?

25. Algunos expertos han dicho que el alcalde tiene gastos de representación y de libre disposición demasiado altos. Está Ud.
    1. muy de acuerdo
    2. algo de acuerdo
    3. en desacuerdo
    4. no sabe
    5. no contesta
26. SI CONTESTA EN 1 o 2:
    Por lo general, en qué utiliza el alcalde estos fondos?
27. a. Se considera Ud. político o administrador?
    1. político
    2. administrador
    3. ninguno o otro
    4. no sabe
    5. no contesta
    6. ambos
    b. Por qué?
28. Cree Ud. que en esta localidad los conflictos entre individuos son de tipo personal o se deben a que militan en distintos partidos?
    1. son personales
    2. son partidistas
    3. otra _____
    4. no sabe
    5. no contesta
    Por qué?
29. a. Ha establecido esta municipalidad un plan de desarrollo comunal?
    1. sí
    2. no
    3. no sabe
    4. no contesta
    EN CASO QUE SÍ:
    b. Cuáles son las metas que se propone?
30. En general en la asignación de gastos del presupuesto municipal, hay entre los regidores
    1. mucho desacuerdo
    2. algo de desacuerdo
    3. poco desacuerdo
    4. nada de desacuerdo
    5. no sabe
    6. no contesta
31. De los cinco factores que vamos a nombrar, cuáles cree Ud. que son más efectivos para conseguir votos en una elección municipal o parlamentaria? (MOSTRAR TARJETA NO. 1)
    1. propaganda en la prensa y la radio
    2. afiches y letreros pintados en la calle
    3. trabajo personal e influencia de los miembros del comando
    4. discursos del candidato
    5. presencia personal del candidato
    6. otra _____
32. a. Al finalizar su actual período de regidor, va a continuar Ud. en la vida pública?

1. sí
2. no
3. quizás
4. no sabe
5. no contesta
   SI NO:
   b. Por qué?
33. a. En general, diría Ud. que la relación entre las municipalidades chilenas y los diversos ministerios es
1. buena
2. regular
3. mala
4. no contesta
5. otra _____
6. no sabe
   b. Por qué diría Ud. que son buenas/malas?
34. Cree Ud. que los ministerios toman iniciativa para ayudar a los municipios o toda la iniciativa viene de parte de las municipalidades?
1. de los ministerios
2. de las municipalidades
3. ambos
4. no sabe
5. no contesta
35. a. Cree Ud. que hay muchos regidores que llegan a ser diputados, o sea, piensa Ud. que el cargo de regidor es un escaño importante en la carrera política?
1. sí
2. no
3. otra _____
4. no sabe
5. no contesta
   b. Por qué?
36. Tratándose de asuntos comunales, diría Ud. que los partidos políticos tienen divergencias
1. muy importantes
2. relativamente importantes
3. poco importantes
4. otra _____
5. no sabe
6. no contesta
37. Podría hacernos el favor de ubicar a su colectividad en este continuo de derecha a izquierda? (MOSTRAR TARJETA NO. 2)
   I_____D
38. Cuáles cree Ud. que son los tres problemas más graves que aborda el país actualmente?
1.
2.
3.
4. otro _____
5. no sabe
6. no contesta

39. Por qué cree Ud. que nuestro país es subdesarrollado?

40. a. En general diría Ud. que el sistema de gobierno en Chile funciona
    1. bien
    2. regularmente
    3. mal
    4. otra _____
    5. no sabe
    6. no contesta
       b. Por qué?

41. Asistió Ud. a la conferencia de la CONAM en Osorno?
    1. sí
    2. no
    3. no contesta

42. En general qué impresión tiene Ud. de la CONAM?

43. Cree Ud. que su municipalidad ha obtenido
    1. mucho
    2. algo
    3. nada
       de provecho de la participación en CONAM?
    4. no sabe
    5. no contesta

44. Encuentra Ud. que hay
    1. mucho
    2. algo
    3. nada
       de resentimiento en provincias y en las municipalidades por el centralismo chileno?
    4. no sabe
    5. no contesta

45. Como Ud. bien sabe, casi todos los miembros de la mesa directiva y del comité ejecutivo de la CONAM son del Gran Santiago. Qué impresión le causa ésto a Ud.?

46. Qué piensa Ud. de las reformas a la constitución que se han debatido en el senado recientemente?
    1. sabe
    2. sabe algo
    3. no sabe

47. Algunas personas piensan que si un individuo tiene capacidad y esfuerzo personal puede conseguir una *buena* posición social y económica. Cree Ud. que quienes dicen ésto tienen
    1. mucha razón
    2. algo de razón
    3. nada de razón
    4. no sabe
    5. no contesta
    6. otra _____

48. En la última campaña electoral para regidores a qué problemáticas se refirieron especialmente los candidatos? (Asuntos locales, nacionales, etc.)

49. Algunos dicen que la propaganda electoral no influye mucho en los

resultados de la elección, ya que ésta está bien decidida por la labor e influencia de los colaboradores de los candidatos. Está Ud.

1. muy de acuerdo
2. algo de acuerdo
3. en desacuerdo
   con esta aseveración?
4. otra _____
5. no sabe
6. no contesta

50. Quién cree Ud. que piensa la gente que tiene más prestigio en una localidad cualquiera? (MOSTRAR TARJETA NO. 3)

   Indique en orden descendiente de importancia:
1. el alcalde
2. el médico
3. el cura
4. los regidores
5. los propietarios de tierra
6. los jefes de sindicatos
7. el gobernador (delegado o subdelegado)
8. los jefes de partido
9. otro _____

DE 51 A 56 PARA ALCALDES SOLAMENTE

51. Ha tenido contacto con el departamento de municipalidades del Ministerio del Interior. Qué opinión tiene Ud. de ese departamento?

52. a. Han venido inspectores y examinadores de la Contraloría a la municipalidad?
1. sí
2. no
3. no sabe
   SI SÍ:
   b. Entienden los problemas municipales? Qué opinión tiene de ellos?

53. a. Qué opinión tiene del programa del Ministerio de la Vivienda?
   b. Cuál ha sido la frecuencia de contactos con ese ministerio?
   c. Tienen las municipalidades una colaboración efectiva en el desarrollo de programas de ese ministerio en la localidad?

54. a. En general qué opinión tiene de los otros ministerios?
   b. Con cuáles ha tenido mejores relaciones y con cuáles peores?

55. a. Cómo son sus relaciones con el intendente de la provincia?
1. buenas
2. regulares
3. malas
4. no hay relaciones
5. no sabe
6. no contesta
   b. Con qué frecuencia ve al intendente?
   c. Ayuda el intendente en gestiones con el gobierno central?

56. Diría Ud. que el intendente ayuda más que los parlamentarios?
1. sí
2. no
3. no sabe
4. no contesta

57. Diría Ud. que si un regidor recibe a un político importante en su casa ello contribuiría a darle
   1. mucho prestigio
   2. algo de prestigio
   3. nada de prestigio
   4. otra _____
   5. no sabe
   6. no contesta

58. a. En general, diría Ud. que cuando la gente tiene un problema, se dirige a la municipalidad para hablar con cualquiera o se pone en contacto con uno de los regidores fuera del edificio municipal?
   1. municipalidad en general
   2. uno de los regidores
   3. las dos cosas
   4. otra _____
   5. no sabe
   6. no contesta
   b. Por lo general qué problemas le trae la gente?
   c. Le trae la gente problemas personales también? Cuáles?

59. Qué importancia le daría Ud. a los siguientes factores en su decisión inicial de incorporarse al partido _____? (MOSTRAR TARJETA NO. 4)
   Evalue si el factor ha tenido mucha importancia, regular importancia, poca importancia, o nada de importancia:
   1. la influencia de los miembros de su familia
   2. la impresión de que el partido sabía cómo se conseguía el bienestar para todos
   3. la atracción de la ideología o filosofía del partido
   4. la influencia de buenos amigos
   5. el contacto personal con regidores o dirigentes locales del partido
   6. su conformidad con el programa del partido
   7. el contacto personal con parlamentarios del partido
   8. la impresión de que el partido representaba mejor que ninguno a su clase social
   9. otra (especifique) _____

60. Diría Ud. que la gente de la localidad tiene en las decisiones municipales
   1. mucha influencia
   2. algo de influencia
   3. nada de influencia
   4. otra _____
   5. no sabe
   6. no contesta

61. a. Diría Ud. que en general hay un predominio de gente de un mismo partido en cada uno de los clubes y asosiaciones de esta comuna? Por ejemplo, hay más radicales en un club deportivo mientras que en otro hay más Demócratas Cristianos?
   1. sí
   2. no
   3. no sabe
   4. no contesta
   SI SÍ:
   b. Me puede dar algunos ejemplos?

62. a. Los ediles son elegidos por el pueblo para servirlo desde el municipio. Los funcionarios son profesionales de carrera que se especializan en los aspectos técnicos de la municipalidad. Percibe Ud. cierta tensión entre ellos?
  1. sí
  2. no
  3. no sabe
  4. no contesta
  SI SÍ:
  b. Por qué?
63. a. En la práctica, cree Ud. que el secretario municipal tiene sobre las decisiones municipales
  1. mucha influencia
  2. algo de influencia
  3. nada de influencia
  4. no sabe
  5. no contesta
  SI CONTESTA EN 1 o 2:
  b. Por qué?
64. Dónde nació Ud.?
65. En qué año?
66. a. Cuántos años vive en la comuna?
  b. Cuántos años vive en la provincia?
67. a. Cuántos años ha servido como regidor?
  b. Cuántos años ha servido como alcalde?
68. Ha cursado Ud. estudios?
  1. primarios
  2. secundarios
  3. técnicos
  4. universitarios (Qué estudió?)
  5. título universitario
69. Cuál es su ocupación? (Si es agricultor, cuántas hectareas tiene?)
70. a. Ha sido candidato a otro cargo político?
  1. sí
  2. no
  SI SÍ:
  b. Cuál?
71. Cuál fue la ocupación de su padre?
72. Cuántos años ha estado Ud. en el partido?
73. a. Perteneció Ud. a otro partido antes?
  1. sí
  2. no
  SI SÍ:
  b. Cuál?
74. A qué partido pertenecía su padre?
75. A qué asociaciones de la comunidad pertenece Ud.?
76. Qué otros cargos públicos ha ocupado?
77. a. Qué diarios y revistas lee Ud.?
  b. Cuántas veces a la semana?
78. En los últimos 6 meses cuántos libros ha leído?
79. a. Lee Ud. publicaciones de su partido?
  b. Cuáles?

80. Podría indicarnos en la siguiente tarjeta, en qué categoría de ingreso se ubicaría Ud.? (MOSTRAR TARJETA NO. 5)
    1. menos de E° 1.000
    2. de 1.000 a 2.000
    3. de 2.000 a 3.000
    4. de 3.000 a 4.000
    5. de 4.000 a 5.000
    6. de 5.000 a 7.000
    7. más de 7.000

Appendix IV. Sources and Procedures for a Comparative Study of Elites in the Chilean Presidential and Parliamentary Republics

This appendix provides information on the sampling procedure and sources used in compiling data for table 8.3, "Constituency Service of a Sample of Deputies from the Presidential and the Parliamentary Republics." In addition to material on recruitment patterns, data were collected on social background characteristics in the different periods for a larger comparative study now in progress.

The sampling technique used involved taking every kth case from a list of all of the deputies for each Chamber of Deputies arranged in alphabetical order. (The presidential chambers were combined, and the combined list was arranged in alphabetical order.) For this study every fifth case was taken, producing, consequently, a sample of approximately twenty percent of the original population. So as to insure that the sample would be a probability sample (that is, that each case have the same probability of being selected), the first case from the first five cases was selected randomly. It must be noted that in systematic sampling of this type, once the first case is selected, the chances of the other cases are altered. In other words, if the first case drawn is number 4, every fifth case thereafter would mean that cases 9, 14, 19, 24, etc. will be drawn, and the cases between these numbers have no chance of being included. Since all possible cases do not have the same chance of being included, the results of a systematic sample may be very deceptive if the cases in the list are arranged in some cyclical order. Thus, for example, a sample of houses in a community built according to a systematic plan may consistently miss corner houses, which are usually larger and more expensive than those within the block.[1]

A systematic sample is, however, adequate for this study, since an alphabetical listing of Chilean deputies does not place them in any type of cyclical order. It is conceivable that this type of systematic sample would not be useful for a study of elites in certain "developing" countries. If within a nation the spelling of individuals' last names can be used to identify them as members of a certain group or residents of a certain region, then systematic sampling of this variety would be very misleading. A large number of cases from a single

1. Claire Selltiz, et al., *Research Methods in Social Relations* (rev. ed., New York: Holt, Rinehart and Winston, 1964), p. 523.

region or caste might cluster in one area of the alphabet and be distorted by the sample drawn.[2] In the Chilean study it was feared that some of the important families might have several representatives in a given Chamber of Deputies, and thus cluster in the same area of the alphabet. For the chambers from which the samples were drawn for this paper, such a possibility did not present itself. In a few cases the same family had two deputies in a given congress, but it was felt that while this might alter slightly the sample, the alteration would be of no consequence.

The sample was drawn by using the volume *Monografía de la Cámara de Diputados: 1811–1945*,[3] published by the Cámara de Diputados. This work contains an alphabetical listing of all the members of each Chamber. The listings in this volume were checked against those published in the excellent work of Luis Valencia Avaría, *Anales de la República*, which lists the deputies according to constituency. This cross-checking proved to be valuable because the *Monografía* included in its lists of the presidential chambers some members who had been elected not as deputies but as substitutes, or *suplentes*. Since *suplentes* did not serve in Congress unless the deputy vacated his seat, they did not belong in the sample. Fortunately, Valencia Avaría's work includes lists of *suplentes* and it was possible to correct the errors.

Since complete information on all deputies for each Congress was not obtained, it was not possible to verify the validity of the sampling procedure by contrasting the sample with a characteristic of the population, with one exception. Data for the 1912–1915 Chamber gave complete information on the party affiliation of each individual in the sample. Since information was available on the party distribution of the entire chamber for this particular congress, it was possible to compare the percentages which each party had of the total, both in the whole population as well as in the sample. Table IV.1 compares the two sets of percentages and gives an indication of the extent of error to be found in the sampling procedure.

The background information for Chilean deputies was provided by four kinds of sources: biographical encyclopedias and dictionaries, government publications, party publications, and magazine articles.

By far the most valuable source of information was that provided by

2. An example of the problems of a systematic sample of this variety might be found in India. The name Singh is almost invariably a Sikh name. A large number of Singhs in an alphabetical listing would lead to an under-representation of Sikhs in the sample. Since Sikhs are mainly from the Punjab, that region would also be under-represented.

3. Chile, Cámara de Diputados, *Monografía de la Cámara de Diputados* (Santiago: Publicaciones de la Cámara de Diputados, n.d.).

various biographical encyclopedias and dictionaries. Particularly useful was the splendid five-volume dictionary by Virgilio Figueroa.[4] Figueroa had an intimate knowledge of Chilean society and history and was thus able to list large numbers of individuals, each arranged by family. Thus, in this well-indexed work, it was possible to ascertain the background of many members of important Chilean families. It is reasonable to assume that if an individual does not appear in Figueroa, he was probably not considered to be a member of the higher class in the small and restricted Chilean society. The older three-volume work by Pedro Pablo Figueroa was also valuable in checking on individuals from the 1876–1881 chambers.[5] The *Diccionario Personal de Chile*,[6] published in 1920, gave some valuable information on deputies of the 1912–1915 and 1918–1921 congresses. In addition, the *Chilean Who's Who*[7] and the *Diccionario Biográfico de Chile*,[8] both of which were published in 1937, aided in the gathering of information. Though the overwhelming majority of the deputies did not appear in these works, it was possible in several cases to trace information such as party affiliation and occupation by looking up children of the deputies in question. The Latin American practice of using the last names of both parents was particularly valuable in this endeavor. By finding out the name of the wife of the deputy, which was often cited in Figueroa, one could accurately identify

Table IV.1. Percentage of party members in Chamber compared to sample, 1912.

Party	Number in chamber	Percent	Number in sample	Percent
Conservatives	25	21.2	5	21.9
Nationals	14	11.9	1	4.3
Democrats	4	3.4	1	4.3
Radicals	25	21.2	7	30.4
Liberal Democrats	25	21.2	4	17.9
Liberals	22	18.4	5	21.9
Total	118	100.0	23	100.0

4. Virgilio Figueroa, *Diccionario histórico, bibliográfico y biográfico de Chile* (5 vols., Santiago: Balcells and Co., 1920–28).

5. Pedro Pablo Figueroa, *Diccionario biográfico de Chile* (3 vols., Santiago: n.p., 1897).

6. Carlos Pinto Duran, ed., *Diccionario personal de Chile* (Santiago: Imprenta Claret, 1921).

7. *Chilean Who's Who* (*Quien es Quien en Chile*) (Santiago: n.p., 1937).

8. *Diccionario biográfico de Chile* (Santiago: n.p., 1937–38).

children of the couple, whose biographical sketches contained at times information on the father. The *Diccionario Biográfico de Chile,* which began publication with the volume noted above, has continued to appear regularly ever since, and would be an indispensable source of information for a larger study of political elites, encompassing more contemporary congresses.

Among the government publications the most valuable was Luis Valencia Avaría's already mentioned work, *Anales de la República.* This work, commissioned by the Chilean Congress, contains a complete listing of all Chilean congressmen from the first congress to the Congress of 1949–1953. Though it provides no biographical information as such, it lists the constituencies from which each deputy and senator were elected. It also lists the holders of all important congressional offices, membership on congressional committees, and holders of ministerial posts. For all these positions the two-volume work gives the date of appointment and the data of retirement. Clearly this work is invaluable to any study of Chilean political elites.

Another useful source of biographical material was the *Album Político,*[9] published in 1915, and containing sketches of all of the congressmen in the 1912–1915 term. Apparently this work was initiated by a private individual with official sanction from the Congress. One only wishes that this type of initiative could have produced similar volumes for other years. Finally, another very useful source of information was a small, quasi-official volume containing a list of all Chileans who up until 1899 had received law degrees.[10] The book included the date on which each degree was conferred. It contains two listings, one in alphabetical order and the other in chronological order, enabling the researcher to ascertain quickly who got the degree in similar years.

The proceedings of three party congresses, the Liberal Congresses of 1907 and 1912 and the Conservative Congress of 1918, provided some useful historical material on the period in question. However, these proceedings also aided in party identification of a few individuals for whom this information was lacking. By scanning the lists of delegates in attendance it was possible to locate a few of the unknowns. (Unfortunately, the above party congresses were the only ones available.)

The final source of information was magazines of the period. *Revista Chilena,*[11] *Pacífico Magazine*[12] and *Política Ilustrada*[13] were

9. Alejandro Valderrama, *Album Político* (Santiago: n.p., 1915).
10. *Abogados Recibidos en Chile* (Santiago: Imprenta Nacional, 1899).
11. *Revista Chilena,* 1915–18.
12. *Pacífico Magazine,* 1907–9.
13. *La Política Ilustrada,* 1911–12.

scanned for several years of the parliamentary period for biographical information and general articles on politics. Only *Política Ilustrada* was a useful source of biographical data. The weekly issues of this magazine were examined for the only years available, 1911–1912.

Bibliography

Sources on Chilean Politics

Books

Abogados Recibidos en Chile. Santiago: Imprenta Nacional, 1899.

Alemparte, Julio. *El Cabildo en Chile colonial*, 2nd ed. Santiago: Editorial Andrés Bello, 1966.

Alfonso, José A. *El parlamentarismo i la reforma política en Chile*. Santiago: Cabeza i Cia, Impresores, 1909.

Amunátegui Solar, Domingo. *La democracía en Chile: Teatro político 1810–1910*. Santiago: Universidad de Chile, 1946.

Amunátegui, Gabriel. *Partidos políticos*. Santiago: Editorial Jurídica de Chile, 1952.

Andrade Geywitz, Carlos. *Elementos de derecho constitutional chileno*. Santiago: Editorial Jurídica de Chile, 1963.

Aravena, Eugenia F., and Calderón, Ivan J. *Organización y atribuciones del servicio de gobierno interior del estado*. Concepción: Escuela Tipográfica Salesiana, 1956.

Barría Serán, Jorge. *Trayectoria y estructura del movimiento sindical chileno, 1946–62*. Santiago: Instituto de Organización y Administración, Universidad de Chile, 1963.

Barría Soto, Francisco. *El Partido Radical, su historia y sus obras*. Santiago: Editorial Universitaria, 1957.

Bello Codesido, Emilio. *Recuerdos políticos*. Santiago: Editorial Nascimiento, 1954.

Bernaschina González, Mario. *Cartilla electoral*. Santiago: Editorial Jurídica de Chile, 1958.

Cabero, Alberto. *Chile y los chilenos*. Santiago: Editorial Lyceum, 1948.

Cademártori, José. *La economía chilena*. Santiago: Editorial Universitaria, 1968.

Campos Harriet, Fernando. *Historia constitucional de Chile: Las instituciones políticas y sociales*, 4th ed. Santiago: Editorial Jurídica de Chile, 1969.

Castro A., Jorge Luis. *El sistema electoral chileno*. Santiago: Editorial Nascimiento, 1941.

Chilean Who's Who (Quién es Quién en Chile). Santiago: n.p., 1937.

Cifuentes, Abdón. *Memorias*. 2 vols. Santiago: Editorial Nascimiento, 1936.

Cortés, Lia and Fuentes, Jordi. *Diccionario político de Chile*. Santiago: Editorial Orbe, 1968.

Cruz Coke, Ricardo. *Geografía electoral de Chile*. Santiago: Editorial del Pacífico, S.A., 1958.

Daugherty, Charles H. *Chile: Election Factbook*. Washington, D.C.: Institute for Comparative Study of Political Systems, 1963.

DESAL. *Tenencia de la tierra y campesinado en Chile*. Buenos Aires: Ediciones Troquel, 1968.

Diccionario bibliográfico de Chile. Santiago: Empresa Periodística Chile, 1937–38.

Donoso, Ricardo. *Alessandri, agitador y demoledor*. Mexico City: Fondo de Cultura Económica, 1953.

———. *Desarrollo político y social de Chile*. Santiago: Imprenta Universitaria, 1943.

———. *Las ideas políticas en Chile*. Mexico City: Fondo de Cultura Económica, 1946.

Durán, Florencio. *El Partido Radical*. Santiago: Editorial Nascimiento, 1958.

Edwards Vives, Alberto. *La fronda aristocrática*. Santiago: Editorial del Pacífico, 1952.

———, and Frei, Eduardo. *Historia de los partidos chilenos*. Santiago: Editorial del Pacífico, 1949.

Encina, Francisco. *Historia de Chile*, vols. 9–20. Santiago: Editorial Nascimiento, 1942.

———. *Nuestra inferioridad económica*. Colección América Nuestra. Santiago: Editorial Universitaria, S. A., 1955.

Espinosa, J. Bañados. *Balmaceda, su gobierno y la revolución de 1891*. 2 vols. Paris: n.p., 1894.

Facultad de Derecho de la Universidad de Chile. *La constitución de 1925 y la Facultad de Ciencias jurídicas y sociales*. Santiago: Editorial Jurídica de Chile, 1951.

Fichter, Joseph H. *Cambio social en Chile: Un estudio de actitudes*. Santiago: Editorial Universitaria Católica, 1962.

Figueroa, Virgilio. *Diccionario Histórico bibliográfico y biográfico de Chile*. 5 vols. Santiago: Balcells and Co., 1920–28.

Galdames, Luis. *A History of Chile*. Trans. and ed. Issac J. Cox. Chapel Hill: University of North Carolina, 1941.

Gil, Federico. *Chile: Election Factbook*. Washington, D.C.: Institute for the Comparative Study of Political Systems, 1965.

———, and Parrish, Charles J. *The Chilean Presidential Election of September 4, 1964*. Washington, D.C.: Institute for the Comparative Study of Political Systems, 1965.

———. *The Political System of Chile*. Boston: Houghton Mifflin Company, 1966.

Girard, Alain, and Samuel, Raúl. *Situación y perspectivas de Chile en septiembre de 1957: Una investigación de opinión pública en Santiago*. Santiago: Editorial Universitaria, 1958.

Gross, Leonard. *The Last Best Hope: Eduardo Frei and Chilean Democracy*. New York: Random House, 1967.

Guilisati, Sergio. *Partidos políticos chilenos*. Santiago: Editorial Nascimiento, 1964.

Halperin, Ernst. *Nationalism and Communism in Chile*. Cambridge, Mass.: MIT Press, 1965.

Heise Gonzalez, Julio. *150 años de evolución institutional*. Santiago: Editorial Andres Bello, 1960.

Hamuy, Eduardo. *Chile: El proceso de democratización fundamental*. Santiago: Centro de Estudios Socio-Económicos, 1967. Cuaderno 4.

Herrick, Bruce H. *Urban Migration and Economic Development in Chile*. Cambridge, Mass.: MIT Press, 1965.

INSORA. *Recursos humanos de la administración pública chilena: Informe complementario.* Santiago: n.p., 1965.

Jobet, Julio César. *Ensayo crítico del desarrollo económico-social de Chile.* Santiago: Editorial Universitaria, 1955.

———. *Recabarren: Los origines del movimiento obrero y del socialismo Chileno.* Santiago: n.p., 1955.

Kaufman, Robert. *The Chilean Political Right and Agrarian Reform.* Washington, D.C., ICOPS, 1967.

Landsberger, Henry A., and Cantrot M., Fernando. *Iglesia, intelectuales y campesinos.* Santiago: Editorial del Pacífico, 1967.

Lopez, Rafael. *Algunos aspectos de la participación política en Chile.* Santiago: INSORA, 1969.

Mamalakis, Markos, and Reynolds, Clark W. *Essays on the Chilean Economy.* Homewood, Ill.: Richard D. Irwin, 1964.

Mattelart, Armand. *Atlas social de las comunas de Chile.* Santiago: Editorial del Pacífico, 1965.

Morodó, Raúl. *Política y partidos en Chile: Las elecciones de 1965.* Madrid: Tauris Ediciones, S. A., 1968.

Morris, James D. *Elites, Intellectuals, and Consensus: A Study of the Social Question and the Industrial Relations System in Chile.* Ithaca, N.Y.: Cornell University Press, 1966.

Palma, Luis. *Historia del Partido Radical.* Santiago: Andrés Bello, 1967.

Parrish, Charles, von Lazar, Arpad, and Tapia, Jorge. *Chile Election Factbook.* Washington, D.C.: Institute for the Comparative Study of Political Systems, 1967.

Partido Conservador. *Convención del Partido Conservador.* Santiago: Imprenta Cervantes, 1918.

———. *Convención nacional, 1947, celebrada en Santiago el 27, 28, y 29 de Junio: Notas para la historia política del Partido Conservador.* Santiago: Imprenta Chile, 1947.

Partido Liberal. *Convención del Partido Liberal.* Santiago: Imprenta Litografía Encuadernación Barcelona, 1907.

———. *La reforma electoral ante el Senado.* Santiago: Imprenta Universitaria, 1912.

Petras, James. *Chilean Christian Democracy: Politics and Social Forces.* Berkeley: Institute of International Studies, University of California, 1967.

———. *Politics and Social Forces in Chilean Development.* Berkeley: University of California Press, 1969.

Pike, Fredrick. *Chile and the United States.* South Bend: Notre Dame University Press, 1963.

Pinto, Durán, Carlos, ed. *Diccionario personal de Chile.* Santiago: Imprenta Claret, 1921.

Pinto Santa Cruz, Aníbal. *Chile: Un caso de desarrollo frustrado.* Santiago: Editorial Universitaria, S. A., 1959.

Poblete, Renato. *La iglesia en Chile.* Madrid: FERES, 1961.

Ramírez Necochea, Hernán. *La Guerra Civil de 1891: Antecedentes económicos.* Santiago: n.p., 1951.

———. *Origen y formación del Partido Comunista de Chile.* Santiago: Editorial Austral, 1965.

Rivas Vicuña, Manuel. *Historia política y parlamentaria de Chile.* 3 vols. Santiago: Editorial Nascimiento, 1964.

Rodriguez Bravo, Joaquín. *Balmaceda y el conflicto entre el congreso y el ejecutivo.* 2 vols. Santiago: n.p., 1921 and 1926.

Sanfuentes, Marcial. *El Partido Conservador.* Santiago: Editorial Universitaria, 1967.

Silva Bascuñan, Alejandro. *Tratado de derecho constitucional.* 3 vols. Santiago: Editorial Jurídica de Chile, 1963.

Silva Cimma, Enrique. *Derecho administrativo chileno y comparado.* 2 vols. Santiago: Editorial Jurídica, 1961.

Silvert, K. H. *Chile: Yesterday and Today.* New York: Holt, Rinehart and Winston, 1965.

Stevenson, John R. *The Chilean Popular Front.* Philadelphia: University of Pennsylvania Press, 1942.

Urzúa, German. *El Partido Radical: Su evolución política.* Santiago: Escuela de Ciencias Políticas y Administrativas, 1961.

_____. *Los partidos políticos chilenos.* Santiago: Editorial Jurídica, 1968.

Valderrama, Alejandro. *Albúm político.* Santiago: n.p., 1915.

Valencia Avaría, Luis, ed. *Anales de la República.* 2 vols. Santiago: Imprenta Universitaria, 1951.

Valenzuela, Arturo. *The Breakdown of Democracy in Chile.* Baltimore: Johns Hopkins University Press, forthcoming, 1977.

Valenzuela, Arturo, and J. Samuel Valenzuela, eds. *Chile: Politics and Society.* New Brunswick, N.J.: Transaction Inc., 1976.

Articles and Periodicals

Agor, Weston H. "The Senate in the Chilean Political System." *Legislatures in Developmental Perspective.* Ed. Allan Kornberg and Lloyd D. Musolf. Durham, N.C.: Duke University Press, 1970.

Barría Cerán, José. "Chile: La cuestión política y social en 1920–26." *Anales de la Universidad de Chile,* 117, no. 116 (1959), 56–73.

Blakemore, Harold. "The Chilean Revolution of 1891 and Its Historiography." *Hispanic American Historical Review,* 45 (August, 1965), 393–421.

Bray, Donald W. "Chile: The Dark Side of Stability." *Studies on the Left,* 4, no. 4 (Fall, 1964), 85–96.

Briones, Guillermo. "La estructura social y la participación política: Un estudio de sociología electoral en Santiago, Chile." *Revista Interamericana de Ciencias Sociales* (October, 1961), 376–404.

Cope, Orville G. "The 1964 Presidential Election in Chile: The Politics of Change and Access." *Inter-American Economic Affairs,* 19, no. 4 (Spring, 1966), 3–29.

Dillon Soares, Gláucio Ary, and Hamblin, Robert L. "Socio-economic Variables and Voting for the Radical Left: Chile, 1952." *American Political Science Review,* 61 (December, 1967), 1033–65.

Edwards, V., Alberto, and Phillipi, Julio. "La reforma del sistema tributario fiscal." *Revista Chilena,* año 2 (August, 1918), 5–18.

_____. "Nuestro régimen tributario en los últimos 40 años." *Revista Chilena,* año 1 (April, 1917), 337–56.

König, Abraham. "Necesidad de reformar el sistema de elección presidencial." *Revista Chilena de Historia y Geografía,* 50 (2nd semester, 1924), 29–34.

Maza, José. "El cambio de nuestro sistema de sufragio." *Revista Chilena*, año 2 (June, 1918), 115-27, 218-34.
Philippi, Julio. "La nuestra ley de contribuciones." *Revista de Gobierno Local*, 1 (June, 1916), 9-10.
Pike, Fredrick. "Aspects of Class Relations in Chile." *Hispanic American Historical Review*, 43 (February, 1963), 14-33.
Portes, Alejandro. "Leftist Radicalism in Chile: A Test of Three Hypotheses." *Comparative Politics*, 2 (January, 1970), 254-57.
Reinsch, Paul S. "Parliamentary Government in Chile." *American Political Science Review*, 3 (November, 1909), 507-38.
Rivas Vicuña, Manuel. "La clausura del debate." *Revista Chilena*, año 2, no. 4 (June, 1918), 64-82.
Sigmund, Paul E. "Christian Democracy in Chile." *Journal of International Affairs*, 20 (1966), 332-42.
Sunkel, Osvaldo. "Change and Frustration in Chile." *Obstacles to Change in Latin America*. Ed. Claudio Veliz. New York: Oxford University Press, 1965.
Zeitlin, Maurice. "Determinantes sociales de la democracia política en Chile." *Revista Latinoamericana de Sociología*, 2 (July, 1966), 223-36.

Unpublished Materials and Newspapers

El Colono. Angol, Chile. May 1890 to May 1891.
Guadagni, Alieto. "La estructura ocupacional y el desarrollo económico de Chile." Documento de Trabajo, Instituto Torcuato di Tella, 2a edición. Buenos Aires, 1967. Mimeograph.
Lopez Pintor, Rafael. *La participación política en Chile*. Santiago, 1968.
El Mercurio. September 30, 1968 to September 30, 1969.
Powell, Sandra. "Social Structure and Electoral Choice in Chile, 1952-1964." Ph.D. dissertation, Northwestern University, 1966.
Valenzuela, Arturo. "The Chilean Political System and the Armed Forces." Masters Thesis, Columbia University, 1967.

Sources on Chilean Municipalities

Books

Aylwin, Arturo, et al. *Analisis crítico del régimen municipal y proposiciones para una nueva legislación*. Santiago: Editorial Jurídica, 1971.
Bastías, Lionel. *Responsibilidad en el régimen municipal*. Santiago: Editorial Jurídica, 1966.
Bell Escalona, Eduardo. *Derecho municipal al día*. Valparaíso: by the author, n.d.
Bernaschina, Mario Gonzales. *Derecho municipal chileno*. 3 vols. Santiago: Editorial Jurídica, 1952-54.
Cheetham, Rosemond, et al. *Pobladores: del legalismo a la justicia popular*. 2 vols. Santiago: CIDU, 1972.
Cleaves, Peter S. *Developmental Processes in Chilean Local Government*. Politics of Modernization Series, no. 8. Berkeley: Institute of International Studies, University of California, 1969.

Correa Bravo, Agustín. *Comentarios sobre la ley de municipalidades de 1891.* Santiago: Imprenta Cervantes, 1903.

_____. *Comentario y concordancia de la Ley de Organización y atribuciones de las municipalidades,* 3a ed. Santiago: Librería Tornero, 1914.

Gustavo Silva, Jorge, ed. *La nueva era de las municipalidades en Chile: Recopilación histórica de la vida comunal del país que abarca desde los primeros cabildos en la epoca colonial hasta nuestros días, y que se completa con una información gráfica y monográfica de las municipalidades de la República.* Santiago: Boyle y Pellegrini, Ltda., 1931.

Junta de Reforma Municipal. *El libro de la reforma municipal.* Santiago: Imprenta Barcelona, 1913.

Maza G., Joselín. *Apuntes para un estudio sobre la organización local en Chile.* Santiago: Imprenta Claret, 1917.

Mesa Torres, Luis Alberto, ed. *1er Congreso de Gobierno Local: Celebrado en Santiago en los días 13, 14, 15 de septiembre de 1914.* Santiago: Imprenta Universitaria, 1918.

_____. *2o Congreso de Gobierno Local: Celebrado en Valparaíso los días 23, 24, 25 de febrero de 1919.* 2 vols. Santiago: Imprenta Universitaria, 1920.

Ochagavía Hurtado, Silvestre. *Dos causas de la ineficiencia de nuestro sistema comunal.* Santiago: Imprenta Cervantes, 1920.

Orrego Luco, Luis. *El gobierno local y la decentralización.* Santiago: n.p., 1890.

Partido Comunista de Chile. *Labor de los regidores comunistas en mayoría FRAP.* Municipalidad de Nogales, 1960–62. Santiago: 1962.

Pascal, Andres. *Relaciones de poder en una comunidad rural.* Santiago: Icare, 1969.

Valdebenito, Alfonso. *Evolucion jurídica del régimen municipal en Chile (1541–1971).* Santiago: Editorial Jurídica, 1973.

Articles

Alfaro O., Aníbal. "Cuadro ilustrativo y comparativo de las municipalidades de la República." *Boletín Municipal de la República,* 3 (June, 1933), 58–65.

Alzamora, Patricio K. "Pueden los gobiernos municipales planificar el desarrollo de sus comunas." *Planificación,* 3 (June, 1966), 83–92.

Arancibia, Manuel. "Estudio sobre la Ley Municipal de 22 de deciembre de 1891." *Revista Forence Chilena* (July/August, 1892), 142–67.

Barahona Sotamayor, Manuel. "Jurisprudencia Judicial sobre la Ley de Municipalidades 1924–37." *Boletín del Seminario de Derecho Público,* 9 (1937), 56–68.

Boletín Municipal de la República. Enero de 1933 a abril de 1939.

Contreras Yañez, Ramón. "Elección de futuras municipalidades." *Boletín Municipal de la República,* 5 (January, 1935), 31–32.

Edwards V., Alberto. "Datos y observaciones sobre las finanzas municipalidades de Chile." *Revista de Gobierno Local,* 2 (May, 1917).

Francis, Michael, and Lanning, Eldon. "Chile's 1967 Municipal Elections." *Inter-American Economic Affairs,* 21 (Autumn, 1967), 23–36.

Larraín Torres, Domingo. "Intervención de los residentes extranjeros en el gobierno comunal." *1er Congreso de Gobierno Local.* Ed. Luis Alberto Mesa Torres. Santiago: Imprenta Universitaria, 1918.

Lopez R., Jorge. "La crisis municipal Chilena en [sic] enfoque bajo el concepto de eficiencia." *Boletín Informativo PLANDES*, 23 (1967), 44–50.
———. "Problemas administrativos y financieros de la municipalidad Chilena." *Boletín Informativo PLANDES*, 23 (September/October, 1967), 18–19.
McDonald, Ronald H. "Apportionment and Party Politics in Santiago, Chile." *Midwest Journal of Political Science*, 13 (August, 1969), 455–70.
Marín Vicuña, Santiago. "La división comunal de la República: Finanzas municipalidades." *Revista de Gobierno Local*, 4 (November, 1919), 2189–2201.
Pacífico Magazine. 1907 to 1909.
Philippi, Julio. "El Avalúo de la Propriedad Territorial." *2o Congreso de Gobierno Local*. Ed. Luis Alberto Mesa Torres. Santiago: Imprenta Universitaria, 1920.
———, and Salvá, Vergara. "Observaciones para la reforma del sistema tributario municipal." *Revista de Gobierno Local*, 5 (November, 1920), 626–27.
La Política Ilustrada. 1911 a 1912.
Revista Chilena. 1917 a 1918.
Revista de Gobierno Local. Julio de 1916 a diciembre de 1921.
Revista de las Municipalidades de la República. Mayo de 1939 a 1945.
Revista Municipal. Febrero de 1955 a octubre de 1968.
Reyes, Jorge. "Las limitaciones y perspectivas de la acción municipal en Chile." *Boletín Informativo PLANDES*, 23 (September/October, 1967), 33–36.
Ross, Agustín. "Reforma del sistema municipal." *Revista Chilena*, año 2 (April, 1918), 153–65.
Silva, Jorge. "El municipio y la economía nacional." *2o Congreso de Gobierno Local*. Ed. Luis Alberto Mesa Torres. Santiago: Imprenta Universitaria, 1920.
Sociedad Chilena de Planificación y Desarrollo (PLANDES). *Boletín Informativo PLANDES*, 23 (September/October, 1967).
Subercaseaux, Carlos. "Anotaciones sobre las principales causas del malestar económico de algunas municipalidades de la región Salitrera." *1er Congreso de Gobierno Local*. Ed. Luis Alberto Mesa Torres. Santiago: Imprenta Universitaria, 1918.
Ugarte B., Rogelio. "Ante el problema de la conformación definitiva de nuestros gobiernos comunales." *Boletín Municipal de la República*, 3 (March, 1933), 40–44.
Velasco, Fanor. "La autonomía municipal." *Revista Forence Chilena*, (September/October, 1897), 556–65.
Vicuña, Augusto. "La autonomía comunal ante la reforma municipal." *Revista de Derecho y Jurisprudencia*, 6 (February/March, 1908), 135–46.
Vigil, Hector. "Como disminuyeron las rentas municipales en Chile." *Revista de Gobierno Local*, 45 (October, 1920), 542–50.

Unpublished Materials

Alid Neilson, Jens and Klenner Merxner, Arno. "Decentralización y desconcentración en la administración pública Chilena." Memoria de Prueba, Universidad de Chile, 1968.

Barahona Sotomayor, Manuel. "Ley orgánica de municipalidades." Memoria de Prueba, Universidad de Chile, 1940.

Chalmers, Douglas A., and Riddle, Donald H. "Urban Leadership in Latin America: Report of the Eagleton Institute of Politics to USAID." Mimeograph.

Cruz Fabres, Jorge. "Organización municipal." Memoria de Prueba, no publicada. University de Chile, 1967.

DESAL. *Antecedentes y criterios para una reforma del gobierno municipal.* 2 vols. Santiago, 1967. Mimeograph.

Giadach Ghani, Rodolfo. "Hacia una política de desarrollo urbano en el gran Santiago." Memoria de Prueba, no publicada. Universidad de Chile, 1968.

Guerra, Hector Arnaldo. "La facultad de los alcaldes para ordenar el pago de multas." Memoria de Prueba. Universidad de Chile, 1918.

Irarrázaval L., José Miguel, 2o. "El municipio autónomo." Memoria de Prueba. Universidad de Chile, 1902.

Manríquez Riviera, Horacio. "Contribuciones municipales." Memoria de Prueba. Universidad de Chile, 1901.

Moya Figueroa, Luis. "Estudio comparativo de la Ley de Municipalidades de diciembre de 1891." Memoria de Prueba. University de Chile, 1901.

Ramirez, Diógenes; Salazar, Francisco; and Zunino, Hugo. *El sistema de gobierno local de Chile.* Santiago, n.d. Mimeograph.

Peña López, Rolando. "Apuntes para un estudio sobre el actual régimen municipal Chileno." Memoria de Prueba. Universidad de Chile, 1927.

Salas Zepeda, Edmundo. "Las municipalidades como fiscalizadoras y recaudadoras de ingresos públicos." Memoria de Prueba. Universidad de Chile, 1963.

Smith, Giles Wayland. "The Christian Democratic Party in Chile: A Study of Political Organization with Primary Emphasis on the Local Level." Ph.D. dissertation, Syracuse University, 1968.

Valenzuela Silva, Elsa Ivonne and Salazar Muñoz, Francisco Gastón. "Administración descentralizada: Posibilidades de acción a nivel comunal." Memoria de Prueba, Universidad de Chile, 1967.

Public Documents

Chile. Cámara de Diputados. *Boletín de las sesiones extraordinarias en 1892.* Santiago: Imprenta Nacional, 1892.
_____. *Boletín de las sesiones estraordinarias en 1906.* 2 vols. Santiago: Imprenta Nacional, 1906.
_____. *Boletín de las sesiones ordinarias en 1889.* Santiago: Imprenta Nacional, 1889.
_____. *Boletín de las sesiones ordinarias en 1890.* Santiago: Imprenta Nacional, 1890.
_____. *Monográfia de la Cámara de Diputados.* Santiago: Publicaciones de la Cámara de Diputados, n.d.

Chile. Cámara de Senadores. *Boletín de las sesiones ordinarias en 1890.* Santiago: Imprenta Nacional, 1890.

Chile. *Constitución política de la República de Chile (Conforme a la Edición oficial).* Santiago: Editorial Nascimiento, 1969.

Chile. Contraloría General de la República. *Boletín de la Contraloría Gen-*

eral de la República, 37 (January/December, 1964) and 41 (March, 1969).
_____. *Circulares y boletines de jurisprudencia municipal.* Santiago: Contraloría General de la República, 1964–69, passim.
_____. *Memoria de la Contraloría General correspondiente al año 1968 y balance general de la Hacienda pública al 31 de diciembre de 1968.* Santiago: Sociedad Impresora Camilo Henriquez, 1969.
Chile. *Diario oficial*, September 14, 1955.
Chile. Dirección General de Estadísticas. *Finanzas, bancos, y cajas sociales.* Santiago: Dirrección General de Estadísticas, años 1937, 1941, 1951, y 1966.
_____. *Censo de población de la República de Chile: Levantado al 15 de diciembre de 1920.* Santiago: Sociedad Imprenta y Litografía Universo, 1925.
Chile. Dirección de Estadística y Censos. *División político-administrativa del país y modificaciones introducidas.* Santiago, 1966. Mimeograph.
_____. *Entidades de población, XX Censo de Población.* Santiago: Dirección de Estadísticas y Censos, 1960.
_____. *Finanzas, bancos, cajas sociales: Año 1966.* Santiago: Dirección de Estadísticas y Censos, 1966.
Chile. Dirección del Registro Electoral. "Nómina de cuidadanos elegidos regidores." Mimeograph.
_____. *Elecciones generales de diputados de 1965.* Mimeograph.
_____. *Elecciones generales de municipalidades 1967.* Mimeograph.
Chile. *Ley de Presupuesto del Ministerio de Hacienda: Para el año 1968.* Santiago, 1968.
Chile. *Ley de Presupuesto del Ministerio de Obras Públicas y Transportes: Para el año 1969.* Santiago, 1969.
Chile. Ministerio de Hacienda, Dirección de Presupuestos. *Manual de la organización del gobierno de Chile.* Santiago: Ministerio de Hacienda, 1960.
Chile. Ministerio de la Vivienda y Urbanismo. Decreto No. 289. Santiago, April 2, 1969. Mimeograph.
_____. Dirección de Planificación del Desarrollo Urbano. *Boletín informativo*, 12 (March, 1969). Mimeograph.
_____. Dirección de Planificación del Desarrollo Urbano. *Manuel sobre el Presupuesto Municipal.* Santiago: Ministerio de Vivienda y Urbanismo, 1967.
Chile. Ministerio del Interior. *Memoria del Departamento de Municipalidades correspondientes al Período comprendido entre el 16 de mayo de 1928 y el 31 de diciembre de 1929.* Santiago: Departamento de Municipalidades, 1930.
Chile. Oficina Central de Estadísticas. *Censo electoral, elecciones ordinarias de senadores, diputados y municipales.* Santiago: Sociedad Imprenta y Litografía Universo, 1916.
_____. *Sinopsis estadística y geográfica de la República de Chile en 1891.* Santiago: Imprenta Mejía, 1898.
Chile. Oficina de Planificación Nacional. *Informe sobre la actividad económica en 1967 y cuentas nacionales de Chile 1960–67.* [Santiago.] Mimeograph.
_____. *Kardex de estadísticas regionales.* Santiago, 1968. Mimeograph.

_____. *Región del Bío-Bío: Evaluación de los Años 1966-67*. Concepción, 1968. Mimeograph.
Chile. Senado. Oficina de Informaciones. *Boletín de Información General*, 48 (April 10, 1969).
_____. Oficina de Informaciones. *Boletín Estadístico*, 31 (December, 1968).

Index